PROGRAMMING, PROBLEM SOLVING, AND ABSTRACTION WITH C

Revised Edition

Alistair Moffat

Department of Computing and Information Systems
The University of Melbourne, Australia

Pearson Originals is an imprint of Pearson Australia, a division of Pearson Australia Group Pty Ltd. It has been established to provide academics throughout Australia and New Zealand with fast and efficient access to the printing, warehousing and distribution services of Australia's leading educational publisher, ensuring a smooth supply channel to your campus bookseller.

For more information about the **Pearson Originals** service, contact the Editorial Department, Pearson Australia, Unit 4, Level 3, 14 Aquatic Drive, Frenchs Forest, New South Wales, 2086. Telephone: 02 9454 2200.

Managing Editor: Jill Gillies
Solutions Consultant: Claire Sadler
Senior Project Manager: Lisa D'Cruz
Production Controller: Julie McArthur

ISBN 9781486010974

Pearson Australia
Unit 4, Level 3,14 Aquatic Drive
Frenchs Forest NSW 2086
www.pearson.com.au

Contents

Preface to the Revised Edition

When I commenced this project in 2002, I was motivated by twenty years of teaching programming to first-year university students, watching their reactions to and behavior with a range of texts and programming languages. My observations at that time led to the following specification:

- *Length*: To be palatable to undergraduate students, and accessible when referred to, a programming text must be succinct. Books of 500+ pages are daunting because of their sheer size, and the underlying message tends to get lost among the trees. I set myself a length target of 250 pages, and have achieved what I wanted within that limit. For the most part I have avoided terseness; but of necessity some C features have been glossed over. I don't think that matters in a first programming subject.

- *Value for money*: Students are (quite rightly) sceptical of $100 books, and will often commence the semester without owning it. Then, if they do buy one, they sell it again at the end of the semester, in order to recoup their money. I sought to write a book that students would not question as a purchase, nor consider for later sale. With the cooperation of the publishers, and use of the "Pearson Original" format, this aim has also been met.

- *Readability*: More than anything else, I wanted to write a book that students would willingly read, and with which they would engage as active learners. The prose is intended to be informative rather than turgid, and the key points in each section have been highlighted, to allow students to quickly remind themselves of important concepts.

- *Practicality*: I didn't want to write a reference manual, containing page upon page of function descriptions and formatting options. Students learning programming for the first time instead need to be introduced to a compact core of widely-applicable techniques, and be shown a pool of examples exploring those techniques in action. The book I have ended up with contains over 100 examples, each a working C program.

- *Context*: I wanted to do more than describe the syntax of a particular language. I also wanted to establish a context, by discussing the programming process itself, instead of presenting programs as static objects. I have also not shirked from expressing my personal opinions where appropriate – students should be encouraged to actively question the facts they are being told, to better cement their own understanding.

- *Excitement:* Last, but certainly not least, I wanted a book that would enthuse students, and let them see some of the excitement in computing. Few programs can match the elegance of quick sort, for example.

Those thoughts led to the first edition, finalized in late 2002, and published in early 2003. Now it is nearly 2013, and another decade has gone by. I have used this book every year since then in my classes, and slowly built up a list of "I wish I hadn't done it that way" issues. Those "I wishes" are all addressed in this revised edition. Most of the changes are modest, and I think I have remained true to the original goals. (One of the more interesting changes is that I have removed all mention of floppy disks!)

How to use this book

In terms of possible courses, this book is intended to be used in two slightly different ways. Students who are majoring in non-computing disciplines require C programming skills as an adjunct rather than a primary focus. Chapters 1 to 8 present the core facilities available in almost all programming languages. Chapter 9 then rounds out that treatment with a discussion of problem solving techniques, including some larger programs, to serve as models. There are also six case studies in the first nine chapters, intended to provide a basis on which the exercises at the ends of the chapters can be tackled. For a service course, use Chapters 1 to 9, and leave the more able students to read the remainder of the book on their own.

Chapters 10 to 13 delve deeper into the facilities that make C the useful tool that it is, and consider dynamic structures, files, and searching and sorting algorithms. They also include two more case studies. These four chapters should be included in a course for computer science majors, either in the initial programming subject, or, as we do at the University of Melbourne, as a key component of their second subject.

In terms of presentation, I teach programming as a dynamic activity, and hope that you will consider doing the same. More than anything else, programmers learn by programming, in the same way that artists learn by drawing and painting. Art students also learn by observing an expert in action, and then mimicking the same techniques in their own work. They benefit by seeing the first lines drawn on a canvas, the way the paint is layered, and the manner in which the parts are balanced against each other to make a cohesive whole.

The wide availability of computers in lecture theaters has allowed the introduction of similarly dynamic lessons in computing classes. By always having the computer available, I have enormous flexibility to show the practical impact of whatever topic is being taught in that lecture. So my lectures consist of a mosaic of prepared slides; pre-scripted programming examples using the computer; and a healthy dose of unscripted exploratory programming. With the live demonstrations I am able to let the students see me work with the computer exactly as I am asking them to, including making mistakes, recognizing and fixing syntax errors, puzzling over logic flaws, and halting infinite loops.

The idea is to show the students not just the end result of a programming exercise as an abstract object, but to also show them, with a running commentary, how that result is achieved. That the presentation includes the occasional dead end, judicious backtracking and redesign, and sometimes quite puzzling behavior, is all grist for the mill. The students engage and, for example, have at times chorused out loud at my (sometimes deliberate, sometimes inadvertent) introduction of errors. The web also helps with this style of teaching – the programs that are generated in class can be made accessible in their final form, so students are free to participate, rather than frantically copy.

Running a lecture in this way requires a non-trivial amount of confidence, both to be able to get it right, and to deal with the consequences of sometimes getting it wrong. More than once I have admitted that I need to go and read a manual before coming back to them in the next class with an explanation of some obscure behavior that we have uncovered. But the benefits of taking these risks are considerable: "what will happen if..." is a recurring theme in my lectures, and whether it is a rhetorical question from me, or an actual interjection from a student, we always go to the computer and find out.

Supervised laboratory classes should accompany the lecture presentations. Students learn the most when trying it for themselves, but need to be able to ask questions while they do. Having students work on programming projects is also helpful. The exercises at the end of each chapter include broader non-programming questions, for use in discussion-based tutorial classes.

Software and teaching support

All of the program fragments in this book exist and are available for your use, as are sample answers to many of the exercises. If you are planning to make use of this book in an educational environment, please contact me (`ammoffat@unimelb.edu.au`) identifying your institution, and the subject you are teaching. I will gladly reply with a complete set of programs, and a guide as to which page of the book each is from. A set of PDF lecture slides to match the book is also available on request. For obvious reasons, I do not plan to make these resources publicly available via a web page, so you do have to ask. An errata page listing known defects in the book appears at `http://www.csse.unimelb.edu.au/~alistair/ppsaa/errata2.pdf`.

Acknowledgements

I learned programming in the first half of the 1970s as a secondary school student in Wellington, New Zealand, and will always be grateful to my two maths teachers, Bob Garden and Ron Ritz, for their vision and enthusiasm. Our programming involved a dialect of Fortran, and was carried out with a bent paper clip; special preprinted cards that you popped chads out of; and a bike ride to the local bank branch to drop the completed programs into a courier bag for transmission to their "Electronic Data Processing Center". Each compile/execute cycle took about three days, so we quickly learned to be accurate.

My interest in computing was deepened during my University study, and I thank all of the Computer Science staff that worked at the University of Canterbury in New Zealand during the period 1977–1979. Worth special mention is Tadao Takaoka: in his own inimitable way, it was he who interested me in algorithms, and who served as a role model for the academic life that I have pursued for thirty years.

Since then, it has primarily been academic colleagues at the University of Canterbury and at the University of Melbourne that have influenced me, by sharing their knowledge and skills. I first taught introductory programming in 1982, and have done so every year since then. The people that I have worked with on those subjects, or on other academic projects, have all left a mark on this book. In roughly chronological order, they include: Rod Harries, Robert Biddle, Tim C. Bell, Ian Witten, Ed Morris, Rodney Topor, Justin Zobel, Liz Sonenberg, Lee Naish, Harald Søndergaard, Roy Johnston, Peter Stuckey, Tim A.H. Bell, Bernie Pope, Peter Hawkins, Martin Sulzmann, Owen de Kretser, Michael Kirley, Lars Kulik, and Alan Blair. Many students have pointed out errors or assisted in various ways, and will continue to do so into the future; I thank them all.

Finally, there is family, and I gratefully acknowledge the long-ago input of my parents, Duncan and Hilda Moffat; and the more recent encouragement supplied by my wife Thau Mee, and our own children, Anne and Kate.

Alistair Moffat,
Melbourne, Australia
`http://www.csse.unimelb.edu.au/~alistair`
November 28, 2012

Chapter 1

Computers and Programs

Physicists study energy – how it is created, how it is stored, how it is measured, and how it is transformed from one representation to another. Chemists study matter in the same way. In Computer Science we study *information*. We are interested in understanding how it is created, how it is stored, how it is measured, how it is used, and what limits there are on our ability to exploit it.

Like physicists and chemists, in computing we make use of special notations and tools. In terms of tools, physicists use laser interferometers, radio telescopes, and high-energy synchrotrons; chemists use mass spectrometers, gas chromatographs, and wet labs; and in Computer Science our tool is the computer. This conflict between the name of the discipline and the tool used in the discipline is somewhat confusing, and in this sense the title "Computer Science" is a little unfortunate. In some parts of the world, Computer Science is known as *Informatics*, a rather more descriptive name; in other regions, Informatics is a more nuanced discipline, and includes the application of computing techniques and methodologies to extracting and presenting useful information out of large volumes of scientific and other data.

> Computer Science is the study of information – how it is represented, manipulated, and transformed.

Engineering disciplines take the knowledge developed by science and apply it on an industrial scale to develop goods and services that benefit the community. Chemical Engineers design and build safe and reliable plants for converting matter from one form to another that is more useful, desirable, or valuable. Electrical Engineers design and build safe and reliable processes for converting energy from one form to another that is more useful, desirable, or valuable. Similarly, *Software Engineers* design and build safe and reliable mechanisms for converting information into forms that are more useful, desirable, or valuable.

> Software Engineers design and implement large-scale software systems, and do so in a manner that is both socially responsible, and maximizes the likelihood of a successful outcome.

Society places a professional obligation on engineers to act ethically and responsibly, and to manage the design and construction processes in a way that maximizes

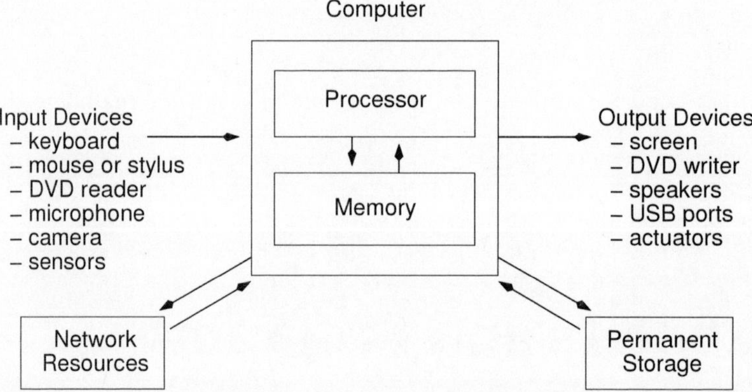

Figure 1.1: Typical schematic layout of a computer. Input devices allow the processor to obtain information from its environment, and output devices allow it to communicate with or alter its environment.

the likelihood of a successful outcome within the contracted time frame, and minimizes the likelihood of the investors losing their investment capital. Risk management is a key concept in all engineering projects; and because of the scale of the systems being built, it is almost inevitable that engineers work in teams.

1.1 Computers and computation

Everyone knows what a computer is – a screen, or monitor; a keyboard or touch-screen; and often other peripherals like mouse, camera, microphone, and speakers. Most computers also have some form of on-board permanent storage such as disk or semiconductor memory; ports for mounting external memory devices such as DVD drives and flash memory; and a network connection, often via a wireless network. Your smart phone certainly meets this definition of a computer, as does your digital camera; your flat screen tv set is probably a computer; and there are also likely to be several computers inside your car. Computers really are everywhere.

Inside every computer is a set of complex and quite remarkable electronic devices. The main logical components are the processor unit, and the memory. The *memory* stores information while it is being directly manipulated. When you are typing an email to a friend, for example, each of the keys you strike on the keyboard sends an electrical signal through to the mailer program you are using, and a character is stored in the memory. The other main electronic component is the *central processing unit* (CPU), which executes instructions, also stored in memory. The possible instructions are all relatively straightforward, and of the form "add the number at this memory location to the number you already know about", or "store this number to that memory location", or "if the result of the arithmetic you just completed is zero, skip the next step". Figure 1.1 shows the standard schematic layout of a computer, and lists a range of input and output devices.

While the set of possible instructions is limited, the computer makes up by being extremely fast in executing them, and unbelievably accurate. A typical small computer has the capacity to easily add a hundred million multi-digit numbers together in just one second. To get an idea of what this means, try calculating $345{,}648+856{,}984$ by hand. How long did it take? For a human to reliably do arithmetic like this in a second would be pretty good. But even if you could do one sum like this in a second, it would still take more than three years – working every minute of every hour of every day at the same rate – to add up a hundred million such numbers. And you would probably make a mistake within the first hour without even realizing it.

To put another slant on this incredible performance, think about the modern long-distance airplane. It travels at about 1,000 kilometers per hour, or around 200 times faster than we can walk. So it represents a technology that augments a human ability (our legs) by a factor of around 200. The computer augments our calculation ability by a factor of a hundred million or more – and as a technology, is still only 60 years old. If a plane was a hundred million times faster than walking, you could get from Australia to New York in around a tenth of a second. You just spent far longer reading a sentence describing the journey than it would take for the journey itself. Wow!

A computer has a limited repertoire of operations, but carries them out extremely quickly and with astounding reliability.

1.2 Programs and programming

The previous section discussed the *hardware* of a computer system. To be useful, a computer also requires *software*, or *apps* as they are increasingly known as. Word- and image-processing tools, spreadsheet tools, web browsing tools, and email systems all came with our computers and smart devices when we purchased them, and for many people that is all that they need. These tools are how we, as computer users, manipulate the information we have stored on our computer. There is a myriad of other software that we are only vaguely conscious of, that controls the hardware, and helps us use it – this is called *system software*, or the *operating system*.

There are several important operating systems in use in the world. Microsoft's Windows system is one, the Unix system is another, and the Macintosh MacOS (a Unix derivative) is a third. To be an effective user of a computer, you must be familiar with the operating system on that machine. It provides facilities for managing collections of files, for executing programs, and for both sharing the resources and simultaneously ensuring that users cannot access other users' files. In short, it provides the "friendly" interface that we now take for granted.

How is software created? The use of notation in the various science and engineering disciplines was mentioned above. To a chemist, the notation H_2SO_4 means a particular chemical compound (sulphuric acid); and to a physicist the notation $\frac{1}{2}mv^2$ refers to the kinetic energy of a moving object. In computing, one of the special notations used is a *program* – a precise written definition of some set of rules for transforming or otherwise manipulating information. Because natural languages such as English are notoriously imprecise[1], to be sure that the program is unambiguous, we

[1] Think about the simple phrase "Just put it in the oven", said by person A to person B. Is it an instruction to B telling them to put the thing into the oven? Or is A saying that they have recently placed the thing into the oven?

use an artificial notation called a *programming language*, in which the meaning, or *semantics*, of each statement is absolutely clear.

> A program is a description of a set of rules for manipulating information, written in a programming language in which the meaning of each statement is unambiguously specified.

We still have to use some kind of language to specify the details of the programming language, and there is another kind of notation for that. In the end we have to resort to natural language somewhere in the chain of description, but by being careful, the imprecision inherent in natural language can be controlled.

Hundreds, perhaps even thousands, of programming languages have been developed. They are all different, with particular idiosyncrasies, weaknesses, and strengths. Just as a carpenter has many different kinds of saw, from a humble key-hole saw right up to a high-powered bench-top one, so too a software engineer needs different programming languages for different tasks. Some programming languages are suited to small-scale prototyping, "quickly knock something together" programming. Others are suited to applications involving real-time systems, where the inputs come from temperature and pressure sensors, and the outputs involve adjustments to values controlling a furnace or nuclear reactor where speed of response is critical. Still others have been developed to meet the needs of the telecommunications industry, where the packets of data that represent mobile phone calls must be efficiently routed between the correct pair of base stations.

Despite this enormous variance, programming languages also share many common features, and can be categorized into four broad classes:

- Procedural, or imperative, languages. Well-known members of this class include Basic, Fortran, Pascal, PL/1, Algol, and C. In a procedural language the computation that is to be performed is described blow-by-blow in the order in which it is to be carried out.

- Object-oriented languages. Smalltalk, Java, and C++ are all object oriented languages. They share many of the features of procedural languages, but add facilities for describing generic operations on data types.

- Functional languages. Lisp, Scheme, Haskell, ML, and Erlang are all functional languages. In a functional language, computations are described almost exclusively in terms of functions that calculate values based on their arguments.

- Logic-based languages. Prolog is a famous language in this class, but there are many others. In a logic-based programming language, facts and rules are stated, and the system then uses an inference engine based upon a formal logic or constraint satisfaction to derive a set of results consistent with the stipulated facts and rules.

Fortran is usually regarded as being the first programming language, with Lisp developed shortly thereafter. Since those early days there has been a steady stream of language developments, as we learn more about both the fundamental nature of computation, and about the engineering techniques necessary to the development of large software systems.

The intended audience of this book – you – is engineers and scientists whose professional study requirements include a substantial component of computer science or software engineering. Fifty years ago everyone studying science subjects needed to know how to carry out calculation using a slide rule. Then, in the 1970s, the pocket calculator made the slide rule redundant, and engineering students were easily identified by the expensive "scientific" calculators clipped to their belts. The really up-market ones were programmable – up to 100 or so steps could be coded temporarily in their internal memory, or stored more permanently on a small magnetic card – and repeated calculations could be automated if tables of values were required. At that time computers were large, awkward, and ridiculously expensive. They were regarded as items of major capital infrastructure that were bought on a whole-of-University (and in some cases, whole-of-country) basis. And they were inaccessible to most professionals.

The computer has now all but completely replaced the calculator. The unbelievable improvements made in electronics fabrication techniques over the last fifty years mean that almost all undergraduate engineering and science students have access to a computer that is four or more orders of magnitude more powerful, and three orders of magnitude cheaper, than the central University computers used by engineering students in the late 1970s. We have come a long way.

> A desktop computer today has more power than a million-dollar computer of thirty-five years ago.

But some things are the same. Engineers and scientists outside the discipline of computing still need to calculate answers, and to prepare tables of values. And while there are many software packages that are designed for particular engineering application areas – stresses in beams, circuit layout, mathematical integration – a professional in these non-computing technical disciplines must also be able to implement their own calculations.

Engineers and scientists within the computing disciplines need an even greater knowledge of programming and computers – they must understand a wide range of fundamental information-transformation techniques, and be able to write programs that encapsulate them.

Which is why you are reading this book. One question you might be asking yourself is "why use C?". C is a member of the procedural family of languages, and was developed initially by Brian Kernighan and Dennis Ritchie, two researchers at Bell Labs in the United States. Their original book *The C Programming Language*, published in 1978, is rightly regarded as a computing classic, and for many programmers "K&R", as it is affectionately known, has a status somewhere between a dictionary and a Bible.

C has a number of advantages compared to other possible languages. First, it is now almost universally available. There is a wide range of high-quality implementations available, many of them free; and compilers for most computer architectures have been developed. Programs are portable when written in C.

Second, it is robust. Over the last thirty-five years C has evolved into a stable and mature language that is controlled by a formal standard, and guided by a wealth of practical experience. You can find information about the standard at `http://www.open-std.org/jtc1/sc22/wg14/`, and purchase a copy of the current version, ISO/IEC 9899:2011 at `http://www.ansi.org`. (The previous version is ISO/IEC 9899:1999, and before that the ANSI C standard was published in 1989, and made an ISO standard in 1990.)

Third, it is appropriate to a wide range of applications. For example, much of the Unix operating system is written in C, and so are a wide range of programming and other software tools. Commercial software houses use it for product development, and hobbyists use it for their personal computing. And because its lineage stretches back to Fortran, a wide range of software – old, but perhaps still useful – can be rewritten in C and used if necessary, with a minimum of translation effort.

Finally, as a procedural language, there is a close mapping between constructs in the language and the facilities in the hardware it executes on. Because of this close correspondence, a great deal of general-purpose programming work is carried out using C and related languages – programs are likely to be efficient when written in C. Advances both in programming language technology and in hardware have reduced this link in recent years, but there is still a sense in which C is close to the raw machine.

There are better languages for particular applications – just as a carpenter has many saws at their disposal. But if you are going to use only one saw, it needs to be a general-purpose one, a jack of all trades. And that is the role filled by C.

> C is a robust, standardized, portable, and widely available language suitable for a broad range of computing, engineering, and scientific calculations.

1.3 A first C program

Having convinced you that C is a useful tool in your future career, it is time to look at a C program:

```
/* A first C program. Just writes a message, then exits.
   Alistair Moffat, ammoffat@unimelb.edu.au, July 2002.
*/
#include <stdio.h>

int
main(int argc, char *argv[]) {
    printf("Hello world!\n");
    return 0;
}
```

The program in the box doesn't do much, nevertheless, it is always a useful task to get this program working on any new computer system you encounter, and to also write the equivalent program in any new language you must master.

There are several points to note. First, the text between the `/*` and `*/` pair is discarded by the C system, and is purely for the benefit of any human readers – it is a *comment*. Comments can be placed at almost any point of a program, and once the `/*` is read, all further text is discarded until a `*/` combination is encountered. Unfortunately, comments cannot appear within other comments – there is no sense of nesting. Later C standards also allow a form of comment where any text that follows a `//` pair in a line is disregarded, but this is not legal in ANSI (C90) C programs.

Programs typically commence with a comment that records the author of the program, a history of any modifications to the program and a set of associated dates, and a summary of the operation of the program. For brevity the programs shown in this book contain relatively terse commenting, and you should be more expansive in the software that you write.

Second, most of the rest of the program is a kind of standard recipe that is used without discussion for the next few chapters – the `#include` line and `int main` lines are going to appear exactly the same way in every program, as are the `return` statement and final closing brace.

In fact, the only interesting part in this program is the `printf` line, which says that the sequence of characters – or *string* – `Hello world!` is to be written to the output. The next box shows a possible interaction with this program on a computer running the Unix operating system, assuming that the program's lines have been typed into a file called `helloworld.c` using a program known as an *editor*. The word `mac:` is the prompt from the computer's operating system, and indicates that user input is expected. The commands beside each prompt (`ls`, which lists the files in the current directory, and `gcc`, which compiles the program) were typed by an imaginary user; the other lines resulted from the execution of those commands.

```
mac: ls
helloworld.c
mac: gcc -Wall -ansi -o helloworld helloworld.c
mac: ls
helloworld helloworld.c
mac: ./helloworld
Hello world!
mac:
```

The `gcc` command *compiles* the C source code in file `helloworld.c` using the C compiler distributed by the Free Software Foundation[2], and creates an executable file called `helloworld` that contains machine-language instructions corresponding to the C source program. On a Windows system the executable would have a `.exe` filename extension, but in the Unix and MacOS contexts it is conventional to create executables that have no extension. All of the examples in this book presume a Unix/MacOS environment, as shown in the example. The last command executes the compiled program, and the "Hello world!" output message appears.

Figure 1.2 shows a second C program, and an execution of it. This one reads a set of numbers, and calculates and prints their sum. It is presented to give you a feel for what a more substantial program looks like, and you are not expected to have

[2]See `http://www.gnu.org`.

```
/* A second C program -- reads and adds a set of values.
*/
#include <stdio.h>

int
main(int argc, char *argv[]) {
    int sum;   /* the running sum */
    int next; /* the next value to be added */

    sum = 0;

    /* get the numbers one by one */
    while (scanf("%d", &next) == 1) {
        sum = sum+next;
    }

    /* and print their sum */
    printf("The sum of the numbers is %d\n", sum);
    return 0;
}
```

```
mac: gcc -Wall -ansi -o addnumbers addnumbers.c
mac: ./addnumbers
345648
856984
212345
634534
The sum of the numbers is 2049511
mac:
```

Figure 1.2: A program that reads numbers, and calculates and prints their sum. The lower box shows an example compilation and execution of the program.

yet mastered the intricacies of how it was put together (so please don't panic!). But with a bit of luck, by reading the code – and the comments – you can identify the basic building blocks: some variable declarations; a `while` loop that gets the input numbers one by one into variable `next`, and adds them onto a running total `sum` that is at first set to the value zero; and a `printf` that prints out the value of `sum`.

Most programs, including the one in Figure 1.2, contain these components:

- Comments, which help human readers understand the program;
- Declarations, which tell the compiler what *variables* are being used in the program, and what their *types* are;
- Assignment statements, which cause arithmetic to be carried out, and the values of variables to be modified;
- Control structures, which direct the flow of execution, perhaps depending upon the values of the variables; and

- I/O statements, which get values into the program (the program *input*), and then back out again (the program *output*).

Look at Figure 1.2, and see if you can decide which of these categories each statement falls into. The next few chapters discuss these various types of statements one by one, and give dozens more examples of their use.

> The principal features in most programs are comments, declarations, assignment statements, control structures, and I/O statements.

Because different operating systems require different interactions, from now on examples usually show only the C source code for programs (or fragments of programs) and their output, without giving details of the compilation process or the file names involved.

1.4 The task of programming

How do we go about the task of writing programs? An analogy that might help is that learning programming is like learning how to ride a bike. One can study physics and know of angular momentum, but the ability to balance is quite independent of that knowledge, and only comes after (for most people) scraped knees and tears of frustration. Similarly, it is possible to study the properties of a programming language in the abstract, but successfully conceiving and implementing a working program requires more than purely abstract skills. The moment of truth as they learn to "balance" is a watershed point for most students learning programming.

The single most important thing is to practice – exactly the same requirement as when learning to ride a bike. You can't develop the necessary skills if you never get around to writing small programs, on your own, or working with a friend. And you can memorize this entire book, but unless you have spent time in front of a computer making mistakes, you won't have the practical skills necessary to complement your academic knowledge.

The basic steps in writing a program are always:

- Think about the problem, and decide how you, as a human "computer", would tackle it.

- Write down your proposed solution as a sequence of steps using a natural language such as English.

- For each step, decide how it should be solved, breaking it down into smaller sub-steps.

- When the steps are straightforward enough, convert each into instructions in the programming language.

- Use an editor to create a file containing your program. Start with a simple skeleton, inserting as few lines as possible, and including only a small fraction of the eventual functionality.

- Use the compiler to check the *syntax* of what you have typed, and to convert your instructions into the very simple repetitive commands that the computer actually executes.
- Once it is syntactically correct, test your partial program on a range of data.
- To fix errors, go back as far as necessary in the process.
- Then add the next step, or unit of functionality, and start the testing process again.

In general, the more time spent at the beginning of this process, the less time will need to be spent at the end. Carpenters don't saw much wood on the first day of a house construction project – they spend that day making plans, knowing that in the end the time invested will be more than repaid. When they do start sawing, they know exactly what piece they are cutting, where it is going to go, and what order they are going to install the various functional components of the house – framework, electrical, plumbing, exterior wall cladding, interior wall linings, painting, and so on. A good programmer does the same.

Note also that you can test a partial program and make sure that the parts that have been implemented so far carry out the desired tasks, even when not all of the functionality has been incorporated. We don't write programs as monolithic wholes, and then start testing when they are too big to manage – that is as silly as supposing that when eating pizza you should stuff three slices into your mouth before starting to chew and swallow. Little kids at birthday parties do that with lollies, but always choke in the end. Adults know to get each mouthful dealt with before embarking on the next. The same "bite, chew, swallow" routine is just as important when constructing a program. The following "hacker's motto" neatly summarizes this process:

> A day of debugging can save an hour of planning.

Another useful motto to remember is this next "KISS" one. It says that the best programs are the ones that carry out the desired transformation, from input to output, in a simple and straightforward way, without being cluttered by excessive functionality or dubious features:

> Keep it simple, stupid.

1.5 Be careful

We end this first chapter with a stern warning about computers, and their propensity to fail. Yes, they are enormously reliable and accurate, often running for months or years without hardware failure. But they do eventually fail, and if the user has been naive, that failure can be heart-breaking. For a home computer, the value of the hardware may be ten times the value of the software and data. You spent perhaps $1000 on the computer, and have purchased a few hundred dollars worth of games. In this case, the actual hardware of the computer is easily replaceable when it reaches the end of its life, and there is relatively little to worry about.

But if you have used that computer as an authoring or storage device – for example, because you are working on a programming assignment, or writing a book, or managing the accounts for a small business, or storing your holiday photos – what is stored quickly becomes more valuable than the hardware it is stored on. It would not be unusual for a home computer used in this way to contain data that is worth ten times the cost of the hardware. If this is the case, you need to be careful – losing $10,000 worth of data is very upsetting. For a business computer, in a small or medium-sized enterprise, the value of the data could be ten times the value of the programs that manipulate it, and one hundred times the value of the hardware. That $1,000 computer may well be storing $100,000 worth of work orders, invoices, and overdue accounts.

So it makes sense to be careful with your data. For you, your "data" might only be your programming work, plus some snapshots from your phone, plus some music. But even so, keeping backups should be regarded as fundamental good discipline. Somehow, the hardware always knows when you have become lazy with your backup routine, and fails at the worst possible instant. Losing a week of work because of hardware failure is stupid. Losing a month of work because of hardware failure is unforgivable. And the truth is, losing more than a couple of hours of work is completely avoidable.

What does this mean? Unless you have a permanent high-speed internet connection, the best way to manage backups of media files (photos and videos that you have created) is to either regularly burn DVDs of files that have been added to your computer, or copy them on to a removable thumb drive. Keep a careful record (in a file or even a notebook) of what files you copied and when, and use more than one thumb drive. Indeed, best practice would be to alternate between at least two thumb drives, and keep one of them somewhere other than on the desk beside your computer. And if you are authoring documents, such as programs and essays, every hour or two of editing time on your home computer, you should similarly make a copy of the files onto backup media; or copy them over your internet link into a cloud-based storage service. Then, the inevitable day your computer refuses to boot, and just says "Hard Disk Error", you will be enormously glad that you have reasonably up-to-date versions of your files available.

As a second level of security, once a month or so you should make a complete copy of all your files (everything you have created, not just the ones you have been working on recently) onto removable disk drive, carefully label and write-protect it, and store it right away from your computer, in your locker at school, or at a friend's house. This kind of *off-site backup* doesn't have to be quite as regular as the routine copying of files off the computer, but is no less important – a fire in your house is traumatic enough without losing a year's worth of assignment work, even when you have carefully carried out the first level of the backup regime.

Keep up this routine whenever you are working on the computer actually creating information. It is easy enough to buy a fresh copy of some game program, or a music track you can't live without. But no amount of money could, for example, resurrect the photos you took in Nepal, climbing mountains; or the effort spent writing a book such as this one.

> Time spent working on a computer is a resource far more precious than the hardware itself. To minimize the impact of hardware failure, you should adopt a regular backup routine.

If you are using a shared computer in a professional installation, then the backups should be done centrally for you, and off-site storage arranged as part of a proper disaster recovery plan. But you can still take some responsibility – why not periodically make a copy of your files, and load them onto your home machine? Just in case the backup regime at the central computer isn't being done regularly? Gnashing your teeth, and calling for the resignation of the system programmer who didn't check that the backups were working properly cannot absolve you from the responsibility of being careful with your own files. If you always act as if the worst is about to happen, you will be better prepared for the inescapable moment when the worst does happen.

Exercises

1.1 Ask an older friend or relative about the first computer they ever bought. Try to pin down the year, the price, and some of the physical characteristics of their machine – disk space, memory space, and processor speed. Then look at some newspaper or magazine advertisements, and find the same values for a modern computer.

Once you have some "then" and "now" figures, calculate the annual compound growth rate on performance that they represent. If you want to make an accurate assessment, you probably need to allow for inflation too, but ignoring it won't affect your answer by much.

1.2 Find out how to use the editor on your computer to create a file, and type in the "Hello World" program. Compile and execute it.

1.3 Study the program in Figure 1.2. Without trying to write any detailed C instructions, discuss with a friend what would need to be added if the average (mean) of the input numbers was to be printed as well as their sum.

What do you think the original program does if no numbers are typed?

What should the extended program do if no numbers are typed?

1.4 Suppose that you get paid $18 per hour to do some work using a computer – perhaps writing a book, or doing some programming. Suppose that you spend three hours a day working on that task, five days a week.

After one year of effort, what is the value of the data stored in the computer? And after three years? How does that compare with the cost of a computer?

Chapter 2

Numbers In, Numbers Out

This chapter introduces the three elemental components of any C program: reading numbers from the input; doing some calculation on them; and then printing numbers back to the output. But first you need to know about the rules for forming identifiers (Section 2.1), and about constants and variables (Section 2.2).

2.1 Identifiers

An *identifier* is a name used in a C program to represent a value. The rules for forming valid identifiers are relatively simple:

- They must begin with a letter or underscore ("_") character;
- They can then use any combination of letters, digits, and underscore; and
- They may not contain any other characters.

For example, all of `date` and `temperature` and `mean` and `big_long_name` and `nitems` and `__funny` are valid identifiers.

These ones are not: `fast-food`, because it contains a hyphen "-" character (and as the hyphen represents subtraction, the C systems interprets it as being `fast` take-away `food`); `76trombones`, because it starts with a digit; and `#_of_words`, because it contains a hash ("#") character.

You are also free to use identifiers like `ghadft76dfM` and `f5g6h7j8k9` in your programs. Using names like these does not affect the execution of your program in any way, and the C system doesn't care what names you use. On the other hand, use of non-mnemonic strings makes it harder for human readers to browse your program – and it is reasonably likely that the next human who has to try and understand your work will be you, in a week, a month, or a year. So it pays to use appropriate variable names.

> Use meaningful identifiers, so that names reflect the quantities being manipulated.

The exception to this advice is where an identifier is used extensively over a short section of your program, in which case it is usual to have names like `i` and `j`.

There is a set of words that cannot be used as identifiers, because they have special significance in the C system. These include words like `int` and `while`, both of which have already been used in Figure 1.2. Several more such *reserved words* will be encountered in the next few chapters.

> Reserved words have special meanings in C, and may not be used as identifiers.

2.2 Constants and variables

Some numbers used in programs are *constants* – fixed values that do not (and should not) change during the course of execution. C offers a useful facility for assigning symbolic names to these: the `#define`. To define a symbolic constant, pick a suitable identifier, and make sure that the "#" is the first non-blank character in each line:

```
#define SEC_PER_MIN 60
#define MIN_PER_HOUR 60
#define EXAM_PERCENTAGE 60
#define PROJECT_PERCENTAGE (100 - EXAM_PERCENTAGE)
#define KM_PER_MILE 1.609
```

Note that you should *not* put a semi-colon at the end of these lines. Note also how in this example there are several different constants that all have the same value. If a different symbolic name is used for each logically distinct quantity, even when they are numerically the same, it is much easier to correctly modify the program. For example, if the `EXAM_PERCENTAGE` was to be changed from 60 to 70, and symbolic constants were not being used, there is a very real possibility that in hunting through your program looking for occurrences of 60 to be changed you will end up with some hours containing 70 minutes, or some minutes containing 70 seconds. Note also that constants can depend upon the value of other constants: `PROJECT_PERCENTAGE` is definitely constant, but with a value that is not explicitly given. A change of `EXAM_PERCENTAGE` to 70 automatically changes `PROJECT_PERCENTAGE` too.

There is no rule that says that symbolic constants should be all-uppercase letters, and any identifiers can be used. Nevertheless, use of uppercase constants is a widely followed custom, and is the style adopted in this book.

It is also both permissible and sensible to use constants for any fixed *character strings* used in your program:

```
#define ERROR_MSG "Values must be greater than zero"
```

Strings are dealt with in more detail in Section 7.8 on page 116.

> Use symbolic constants for all fixed values manipulated in your programs, to improve readability, and to facilitate subsequent modifications.

One extreme view is that the only permissible raw constants in your programs should be zero and one, and then only when they are being used as the additive and multiplicative identities respectively. You might not want to take it quite this far, but if you directly code any fixed value into your program, pause for a minute and consciously decide whether or not in a years time it will look like a "magic number", and if so, give it a symbolic name.

The other values manipulated in a program are *variables*. In mathematics, variables are used to represent unknown, but fixed, quantities. In a program, variables represent values that change. Consider, for example, the statement `sum=sum+next` in Figure 1.2 on page 8. Writing the similar $s = s + n$ in mathematics as an assertion implies that n must be zero, and that s can be any value. In Figure 1.2, the statement `sum=sum+next` is a directive that means: "take the current value stored in the variable called `sum`, add to it the current value stored in the variable `next`, and then store the result back into `sum`". At the end of that sequence, variable `sum` has an altered value (presuming `next` is non-zero); and `sum` changes again if the statement is repeated. That is, at any point while the program is executing, `sum` has a value that is determined as an exact function of the sequence of numbers entered by the program's user.

Combinations of variables and constants are calculated as *expressions*, and their values are preserved into the same or other variables using *assignment statements*. Here are some more assignment statements that make use of the constants that were defined earlier. Each assignment presumes that the various right-hand-side variables have been given suitable values:

```
nitems = nitems+1;
miles = km/KM_PER_MILE;
tot_seconds = (hours*MIN_PER_HOUR + mins)*SEC_PER_MIN +
              secs;
final_mark = (exam_mark*EXAM_PERCENTAGE +
              project_mark*PROJECT_PERCENTAGE)/100;
```

Note the use of a semi-colon to terminate each of the calculations. This is how C knows where one statement ends and the next begins. Note also that none of the white-space layout – achieved through the judicious insertion of blank, newline, and tab characters – is significant in C. Long statements should be broken over several lines in a neat and tidy manner. Observe how helpful it is to use sensible identifiers – well-written program text can be read almost as if it were prose.

Semi-colons are used to terminate statements.

Each variable used in a program must be assigned a *type* in a preliminary statement called a *declaration*. In Figure 1.2 on page 8, `sum` and `next` are both declared to be integer-valued variables by the initial line `int sum,next`. Similarly, all of `km`, `miles`, `tot_seconds` (and so on) need to have been declared prior to the assignment statements given in the previous example. But it is probably not sensible to declare `km` and `miles` to be of type `int`, as they might not be integer-valued. A range of other types are described shortly, including one suitable for `km` and `miles`.

Each variable in a program has a type associated with it.

One common misconception is that declaring a variable also gives it an initial value. This is not the case. The declaration indicates to the compiler that the variable exists, but does not give it any particular value. That must be done by an assignment statement, which is why `sum` is explicitly set to zero in the program in Figure 1.2 on page 8. C does permit one small shorthand to reduce the need for duplicate handling, and variable declarations and an initial assignment can be combined in a single statement if desired:

```
int sum=0;
```

This statement both declares the integer variable `sum`, and sets it to zero.

> Variables must be assigned values before they can be used in expressions.

If a variable is used without an initial value being assigned, the results are unpredictable. If you are *un*lucky, the system assigns zero or some other initial value, and your program works. If you are *lucky*, your program fails, and you are forced to investigate why. This second path is definitely the more desirable one – it is better to find out early that a program is erroneous, than to use it for many years, then one day transfer it to a different computer and have it mysteriously fail.

The type of a variable determines how its value is represented in the computer, and how operations on that variable are carried out.

Integer variables store exact values, but only within a somewhat limited range. On the majority of current computers the allowable range of integers is from $-2^{31} = -2{,}147{,}483{,}648$ to $+2^{31} - 1 = +2{,}147{,}483{,}647$, values determined by the use of 32 bits of memory for each `int` variable. Computations that result in integer values outside this range result in incorrect answers, with no warning whatsoever. This unfortunate fact is demonstrated by the next program fragment:

```
int big, bp1, bt2, bp1t2;
big   = 2147483647;
bp1   = big+1;
bt2   = big*2;
bp1t2 = bp1*2;
printf("big=%d, bp1=%d, bt2=%d, bp1t2=%d\n",
    big, bp1, bt2, bp1t2);
```

In this program, a number of assignment statements are executed in the order they are written, and then each of the "`%d`" fields in the `printf` statement is replaced by the next corresponding value in the list of variables that follows. (The `printf` statement is considered in more detail shortly.) When executed on a standard 32-bit computer, the program fragment produces this output line:

```
big=2147483647, bp1=-2147483648, bt2=-2, bp1t2=0
```

Wow! To the novice user, this behavior is little short of bizarre. Even to an expert, someone who understands the underlying representation, these results are hard to anticipate. Section 13.2 on page 230 explains what is actually happening in these examples, if you really want to know. Integer overflow is clearly something to be watched out for.

> Beware. Integer overflow and underflow in C programs results in incorrect values propagating through the remainder of any computation without warning message being produced.

The alternative is to declare numeric variables to be of type `double`. These numbers are stored in the computer in two parts: an integer exponent; and a fractional mantissa. The exponent can be both negative and positive, and in a range from approximately minus one thousand through to plus one thousand, meaning that a very wide range of values can be accommodated. But the mantissa part of a `double` has only a fixed amount of precision – typically, a number of bits (binary digits) corresponding to 14 or 15 decimal digits – so the numbers stored are usually approximations of the true underlying value. Some values are still stored exactly – positive and negative integer values of up to 14 or 15 digits, for example, which is more than can be held in an `int` – but fractional numbers as simple as 0.1 have trailing digits in their binary representation truncated, and are stored approximately. This limitation is illustrated by the next program fragment. Again, only the relevant part of the program is shown:

```
double x, y, z;
x = 0.1;
y = x+x+x+x+x+x+x+x+x+x;
z = y - 1.0;
printf("x=%23.20f\ny=%23.20f\nz=%23.20f\n", x, y, z);
```

```
x= 0.10000000000000000555
y= 0.99999999999999988898
z=-0.00000000000000011102
```

Because the numbers are of type `double`, the `printf` statement in this fragment makes use of a "`%f`" descriptor, asking for each value to be printed using 23 character positions in total, and showing 20 decimal places. The output makes it clear that with `double` values we must not presume that $10 \times 0.1 = 1.0$, since the final value `x` printed is not zero. Even the initial value of `x` is only accurate to 16 decimal digits on this computer.

> Beware. Floating point numbers are approximations. Rounding errors affect the accuracy of numbers computed.

Here is some more simple arithmetic:

$$1.23 \times 10^{16} + 4.56789 - 1.23 \times 10^{16}$$

Clearly, the answer *should* be 4.56789. But if this arithmetic is implemented and executed (with the "`e`" in the constant meaning "times 10 to the power of" in C):

```
double x, y, z;
x = 1.23e16;
y = x + 4.56789;
z = y - x;
printf("x=%25.7f\ny=%25.7f\nz=%25.7f\n", x, y, z);
```

the output is:

```
x=12300000000000000.0000000
y=12300000000000004.0000000
z=                4.0000000
```

and it is clear that it is not possible to add small values to large numbers and expect accurate answers. You need to remember that fact when you are planning programs. Floating point arithmetic is risky, especially if the large values in question are later reduced to small values by further operations. Accumulated rounding errors have the potential to make any answer that you compute meaningless.

> Variables of type `double` store approximate values over a much larger range than do `int` variables.

If reduced numeric precision can be tolerated, C offers a third numeric data type: the `float`. Variables of type `float` require less memory in the computer than do those of type `double`, but unless they are being used in very large arrays (Chapter 7), the difference in cost is small, and it makes more sense to declare `doubles`.

Constants also have types. All of the following are numeric constants:

```
1              -22
345            0
3.14159        10000.
-.12345        1e10
-2.72e+0       1.0e-6
156e+52        -2.78e-17
```

The "`e`" that appears in some of the numbers is an *exponent part*, and represents a scale factor as a power of ten. For example, `2.4e5` represents the number $2.4 \times 10^5 = 240{,}000$, and `1e-6` represents $1.0 \times 10^{-6} = 0.000001$ (and not 1^{-6}).

Any numeric value that contains neither a decimal point nor an exponent part is inferred to be of type `int`. Numeric values that contain either a decimal point or an exponent are of type `double`. It is also possible to explicitly declare numeric constants in several other ways, including as octal and hexadecimal integers. These options are beyond the scope of this book.

Use of inappropriate constants can create problems. For example, to implement the physics calculation $e = \frac{1}{2}mv^2$ to work out the kinetic energy e of a mass m moving at velocity v, it is tempting to write:

```
double energy, mass, velocity;
/* BEWARE -- incorrect code */
energy = (1/2)*mass*velocity*velocity;
```

The problem is that in this form both `1` and `2` are integers, so the first operation carried out is an integer division, and an initial result of integer zero obtained. Only when the multiplication by `mass` is considered is the integer value in the first subexpression converted to a `double`. By then it is too late – zero as an `int` converts to zero as a `double`, and the damage has been done. The fix is simple once the mistake is noticed – the factor `(1/2)` can be replaced by `0.5`, for example. But until the mistake is identified, the program is erroneous. Notice also that the C compiler is completely silent about the potential problem here. You have to be aware of this kind of thing as you write the program. The next section considers expressions, and type conversions during the evaluation of expressions, in more detail.

> Be sure that you use constants of types that match the variables they are being combined with.

Character constants can also be created. Single quotes are used to delineate them: `'a'`, `'8'`, `' '`, and so on. Because the backslash character and quote character have special meanings, they are *escaped* to make character constants: `'\\'` and `'\''` respectively. Other special characters are newline, `'\n'`; and tab, `'\t'`. The corresponding variables are declared as `char`, and are read with a "`%c`" format descriptor.

2.3 Operators and expressions

The programs you have already seen in this chapter show some of the numeric operations possible in C. Table 2.1 lists all of the arithmetic operators, and gives examples of their use.

The multiplicative operators "`*`", "`/`", and "`%`", have a higher *precedence* than the additive operators "`+`" and "`-`". Operators of equal precedence are evaluated in left-to-right order. For example, `2+3*4` evaluates to `14`; and `15-6-2` evaluates to `7`; and `15%4*16%9` evaluates to `3`. Evaluation order can always be adjusted through the insertion of parentheses: `(2+3)*4` is `20`, and `(15%4)*(16%9)` is `21`.

As already noted, division when both operands are of type `int` results in an integer quotient being calculated and then being used in the next part of the computation: `1/2*2` is `0`, and `1/2*2.0` is `0.0`. The next code fragment shows another example:

```
int n_pass, class_size;
double pass_percent;
/* BEWARE -- incorrect code */
pass_percent = n_pass/class_size*100;
```

One solution is to force, via the rules themselves, the desired result:

```
pass_percent = 100.0*n_pass/class_size;
```

Another is to use an explicit *cast* operation, which forces a type conversion:

```
pass_percent = (double)n_pass/class_size*100;
```

Casting is a *unary* (one operand) operation in the same way that the "`-`" in `x=-y` is a unary operator. Any type can be used in a cast, with some conversions being more sensible than others.

Suppose instead that an integral pass percentage is required, rounded off to the nearest integer. Even more care is required:

```
int n_pass, class_size, pass_percent;
pass_percent = (int)(0.5 + 100.0*n_pass/class_size);
```

In particular, note that an explicit cast to `int` is by itself not enough after doing the `double` arithmetic, since the defined `double` to `int` conversion process discards any fractional part, and the requirement was to get a rounded-off integral pass rate. To get the right rounding, the addition of `0.5` is necessary before the cast is executed.

> Each expression and subexpression within that expression has a type. Operations are performed according to the types of the two operands to that subexpression, not according to the overall type of the final expression.

If the second operand to either the `/` or `%` division-type operators is zero, a run-time error might occur, followed by program termination; or incorrect values might generated, but the program continues executing; or the special value `inf` (infinity) might be propagated through any further calculations involving that quantity. Another special value supported by some C systems is `nan`, standing for "not a number", which is the result returned when, for example, the square root of a negative number is requested. Neither of these two values can be used as constants in your program.

A simple program fragment can be used to determine how your computer and C system behave when presented with dubious expressions:

Operator	Operation	Examples	Results
*	multiplication	5.0*3.0	15.0
		5*3.0	15.0
		5*3	15
/	division	19.0/4.0	4.75
		19.0/4	4.75
		19/4	4
%	remainder after division	19.0%4.0	illegal
		19.0%4	illegal
		19%4	3
+	addition	7.5+3.0	10.5
		7.5+3	10.5
		7+3	10
-	negation	-3	-3
		-5*-3	15
-	subtraction	7.0-13.2	-6.2
		7-13.2	-6.2
		7-13	-6

Table 2.1: Operations on numeric values. When both operands to the binary operators are of type `int`, the result is always of type `int`. If either or both of the operands are of type `float` or `double`, the result is of type `double`. The modulus operator "`%`" can only be applied if both arguments are of type `int`. If both operands to a division are of type `int`, the result is the truncated integer quotient.

```
    printf("17.0/0 = %.3f\n", 17.0/0);
    printf("1.0/(17.0/0) = %.3f\n", 1.0/(17.0/0));
    printf("sqrt(-1.0) = %.3f\n", sqrt(-1.0));
    printf("1.0/sqrt(-1.0) = %.3f\n", 1.0/sqrt(-1.0));
    printf("17/0 = %d\n", 17/0);
```

When executed on one computer, the output was:

```
17.0/0 = inf
1.0/(17.0/0) = 0.000
sqrt(-1.0) = nan
1.0/sqrt(-1.0) = nan
Floating exception (core dumped)
```

Note how, in this example, the second division `1/inf` results in the calculation of zero; while `1/nan` continues to be `nan`. It also remains `nan` when squared or multiplied by `inf`. If your program is terminated, you may see the rather unhelpful error message "Floating exception (core dumped)". The reference to "core dumped" is a link back to the early days of computers, when the internal memory in which programs and data were stored was composed of small magnetic donuts threaded with wires – core memory. When a program fails like this, a file called `core` may be written. You should delete `core` files if you notice them in your directory.

When executed on a second computer, the final divison resulted in a bizarre number being generated, rather than an execution error. Beware.

2.4 Numbers in

To be useful, a program must be capable of operating on a range of data, not just the fixed numbers compiled into it. It needs to be able to *read* numbers typed on the keyboard. In C, the easiest way to read is through the use of the standard function `scanf`. The general form of `scanf` requires a control string and a list of variables:

`scanf (` *control string* `,` *list of variable addresses* `)`

where each component of the control string matches one of the variables, and indicates how the data should be stored into that variable. Here are two examples:

```
    int n_pass, class_size, pass_percent;
    double mass, velocity, force;
    scanf("%d%d", &n_pass, &class_size);
    scanf("%lf%lf%lf", &mass, &velocity, &force);
```

In the first, two `int` variables are to be read, and so the control string is `"%d%d"`, with each "`%d`" a *format descriptor* indicating that one integer is required. In the second, three `double` values are read, each controlled by a "`%lf`" format descriptor. Had these variables been of type `float`, format descriptors "`%f`" (for "float", rather than "long float") would be required. Similarly, "`%c`" is used to read one character into a variable of type `char`.

For `scanf` to operate correctly, the names of the variables must be prefixed by an ampersand character "`&`". This indicates the use of the *address* of the variable rather than its value; why addresses must be passed is discussed in Section 6.7 on page 93, and for the moment we will simply use the ampersands as part of a standard recipe.

In detail, what happens is that characters in the input buffer – from the keyboard, unless Unix input redirection is used – are examined one by one. As each character is read, it is added to a lengthening value of the type specified in the corresponding format descriptor. That format descriptor – and corresponding variable – is finished when an character that cannot be incorporated is encountered; that character is then the first one used for the next format descriptor, even if the next format descriptor is in a different `scanf` statement. These rules mean that leading whitespace is skipped over for "`%d`" and "`%lf`" descriptors, but not for "`%c`" descriptors. As another step in `scanf` processing, any additional characters in the control string are also matched, with a blank matching any/all whitespace characters, and so on. For example, the control string "`%d.%d#%c`" processes the input characters "`5.67###z`" (using "#" to show where the space characters are) into the `int` values 5 and 67, and the `char` value `'z'`.

If the control string format descriptors cannot be satisfied by the sequence of characters in the input stream, the `scanf` halts at that point, and the remaining variables are not assigned values. For example, if "`%d%d%d`" is given the input "`##123##45.6#89`" (where "#" is again used to show spaces) the first integer variable is assigned the value `123`, the second is assigned the value `45`, and the third is left unchanged – the period character terminates the second integer, but cannot be used as a component of the third.

These rules are reasonably complex. So an important piece of advice is this: *always* print out the values of variables after they have been read, so that there is at least some chance that any discrepancies (or outright errors) are detected. Another point worth noting is that `scanf` returns as a value the number of objects that were successfully read. So it can also be used as:

```
num = scanf("%d %lf %c", &n, &z, &c);
printf("There were %d values successfully read\n", num);
```

There is more that you need to know about `scanf` before you can be a proficient C programmer, but the minimalist treatment in this section is enough to get you operational. Section 4.5 on page 56 returns to `scanf` and explains more of its functionality.

The function `scanf` is used to read numeric values from the keyboard into program variables. Values read should always be echoed back to the output, to provide validation of the input process.

2.5 Numbers out

The examples in this chapter have already made use of the function `printf`. The general structure is:

`printf(` *control string* `,` *list of expressions* `)`

In simplest form, output is to the terminal screen or equivalent, a device that is character and line oriented, and often with a default of 80 characters wide.

As for `scanf`, the format descriptors must match the variables: "`%d`" for `int`-valued expressions; "`%f`" for `float`- and `double`-valued expressions, or "`%e`" if exponential form is required, for example, `6.67e-11`; "`%c`" for `char`-valued expressions; and "`%s`" for strings. Note that – confusingly – "`%lf`" is used only when reading `double` variables, and they are written using either "`%f`" or "`%e`".

More control can be exerted by modifying the format descriptor using a field width: "`%3d`" indicates that at least three character positions should be used, with more consumed if necessary; and "`%10d`" indicates that at least ten character positions should be used. In both cases, leading blank characters are inserted if the value being printed requires fewer digits than the number specified as the field width.

With doubles and floats, both the total width in characters and the number of character positions after the decimal point can be controlled: "`%5f`" indicates that at least five positions should be used; and "`%8.2f`" indicates that eight positions in total should be used, with the decimal point placed in the third-from-right position, and two characters after it.

If the character width value is negative, the output string is left justified within a field of the (positive) width. This is particularly useful in conjunction with the "`%s`" format descriptor used to format character strings – for example, "`%-20s`" formats a string at the left of a field of total width (at least) twenty characters.

When a line is to be terminated and a new line commenced, a "`\n`" character is written into the format control string.

> The function `printf` is used to create and structure program output.

The example in Figure 2.1 shows a range of formats, with hash characters used so that you can see where the blank characters are. Trace through the details, to be sure that you understand how each of the lines was generated.

One of the surprising things in Figure 2.1 is that `char` variables can be used in arithmetic. In fact, the type `char` is a numeric type, and the constant `'a'` equates to the integer 97 by virtue of the character ordering used in almost all computers. Moreover, the lowercase letters form a contiguous sequence, as do the uppercase letters starting at `'A'` equal to 65. Exercise 4.4 on page 60 explores the properties of this "American Standard Code for Information Interchange" (ASCII) in more detail.

2.6 Assignment statements

You have now seen nearly all of the parts needed to write simple programs that read numbers, do calculations, and print out answers. The only bit missing is a proper introduction of the *assignment statement*:

variable = *expression*

There have been several examples of assignment statements in the previous parts of this chapter, and there is nothing more that needs to be said about it at this stage, except to reiterate that the value of the expression on the right-hand-side is calculated,

```
#define MARY "Mary, Mary, quite contrary"

int
main(int argc, char *argv[]) {
    int n=12345;
    double x=3.14159;
    char c='a';
    printf("%d  %3d  %6d  %-6d\n", n, n, n, n);
    printf("%f  %.4f  %6.2f  %-6.2f\n", x, x, x, x);
    printf("%c  %d  %c\n", c, c, c+3);
    printf("%s\n%50s\n%-50s\n", MARY, MARY, MARY);
    return 0;
}
```

```
12345##12345###12345##12345#
3.141590##3.1416####3.14##3.14##
a##97##d
Mary,#Mary,#quite#contrary
########################Mary,#Mary,#quite#contrary
Mary,#Mary,#quite#contrary########################
```

Figure 2.1: Use of different format descriptors in `printf` statements. The symbol "#" is used in place of blanks.

and then that value is stored into the specified variable. It makes no difference if the left-hand-side variable is used in the right-hand-side expression – it just contributes to the final value that is calculated, exactly the same as any other constant or variable.

One convenient shorthand that it worth coming to terms with is the ability to omit repeated variable names, a mechanism that allows the assignment `sum=sum+next` to be abbreviated as `sum+=next`. This form, with an operator prior to the "=", can be used for any binary operator: `n/=2` divides `n` by two, and `m+=1` adds one to `m`. The latter of these has its own special shorthand: `m++` adds one to variable `m`. Similarly, `r--` subtracts one from `r`. These *postincrement* and *postdecrement* forms of the assignment statement are used sparingly in this book, but are common in C programs and you need to be aware of them. There are also *preincrement* and *predecrement* operators described in Table 13.1 on page 230 that are not used in any of the programs in this book.

The assignment statement allows the value of a variable to be changed.

One slight surprise arises with assignment statements: if the expression is of a different type to the variable to which it is being assigned, an automatic cast takes place. This process is shown in the next program fragment:

```
int n; double z; char c;
n = 42; z = 42; c = 42;
printf("n=%3d,  z=%12.8f,  c=%c\n", n, z, c);
n = 100.9; z = 100.9; c = 100.9;
printf("n=%3d,  z=%12.8f,  c=%c\n", n, z, c);
n = 'a'; z = 'a'; c = 'a';
printf("n=%3d,  z=%12.8f,  c=%c\n", n, z, c);
```

```
n= 42,  z= 42.00000000,  c=*
n=100,  z=100.90000000,  c=d
n= 97,  z= 97.00000000,  c=a
```

Note how `char`, `int`, and `double` values can all be assigned to each other, without any warning message being generated by the compiler. Note also that the values printed by the "`%c`" format specifier interpret values as codes in the ASCII character set, hence the asterisk (code 42) and "`d`" (code 100) values in the final column of the output. The fundamental message to take away from this example is that you – the programmer – need to take care to get the types right.

2.7 Case study: Volume of a sphere

Using the assignment statement, and the other C skills described in this chapter, you are now able to write a range of straightforward programs. You could also do exactly the same type of computation very easily with a calculator or spreadsheet, but be patient – you will soon see calculations that can't be done with a spreadsheet.

To confirm that you have learned these skills, try the following exercise before reading on. Don't forget to include the standard boiler-plate code at the top and bottom of your program. You can copy that from Figure 1.2 on page 8.

> Write a program that reads in the radius of a sphere, in meters, and calculates and outputs the volume of that sphere, in cubic meters. The volume of a sphere of radius r is given by $\frac{4}{3}\pi r^3$.

Figure 2.2 provides a solution to this exercise. Note the various parts: a comment at the top, followed by boiler-plate code; then declarations for two variables of type `double` (their values cannot be assumed to be integral); a `printf` statement to print a prompt, so that the user of the program knows when input is expected; a `scanf` statement to read in a value; an assignment statement to compute the desired output value; and a `printf` to do the writing.

The constant π has been given a symbolic name in Figure 2.2. In fact, as will be seen in Section 5.3 on page 70, a set of commonly used numeric values, including π, are already defined in many C installations, to greater accuracy than is shown here. Section 5.3 shows how to access these predefined values.

Finally, note that the program prints the input value too, as was recommended earlier. Doing so makes it more likely that you detect any errors in the `scanf` that might cause an incorrect value to be read and processed. Whether a `scanf` terminates prematurely is only partly in your hands – the person using your program also shares

```
/* Calculate the volume of a sphere given its radius.
*/
#include <stdio.h>

#define PI 3.14159

int
main(int argc, char *argv[]) {
    double radius, volume;
    printf("Enter sphere radius: ");
    scanf("%lf", &radius);
    volume = (4.0*PI*radius*radius*radius)/3.0;
    printf("When radius is %.2f meters, ", radius);
    printf("volume is %.2f cubic meters\n", volume);
    return 0;
}
```

```
Enter sphere radius: 4
When radius is 4.00 meters, volume is 268.08 cubic meters
```

Figure 2.2: Calculating the volume of a sphere. The lower box shows an execution of the program in the upper box.

that responsibility, and you should not rely on them – but you can at least show what value ended up being used in your program.

> Programs should always be written presuming that the user will either deliberately or accidentally abuse them.

The program shown in Figure 2.2 is typical of programs in the simple "calculate the output from the inputs" category discussed in this chapter. A wide range of functional relationships can be evaluated using the same basic template.

Exercises

2.1 For each of the following, decide whether or not it is a valid C identifier:

```
_hello             km_per_hour
Hello37            speed!
constant-value     sensible$name
subject#1          _num_incorrect_
n                  big_long_name_many_letters
M                  12oclock
```

2.2 Trace the following program fragment, and determine the final values of each of the variables.

```
    int a, b, c, d, e, f, g;
    a = 6;
    b = a + 3*4;
    c = b - b%4;
    d = b/3;
    e = a+b / 2;
    f = (a+b/2+c)/3;
    g = a-b+c-d+e-f;
```

2.3 Given the following declarations,

```
double r, area, perimeter, elapsed_hours;
int start_hour, start_min, start_sec,
    finish_hour, finish_min, finish_sec;
```

write assignment statements that calculate:

a. The area of a square of edge length `r`.

b. The perimeter of a square of edge length `r`.

c. The area of a circle of radius `r`.

d. The perimeter of a circle of radius `r`.

e. The time in elapsed hours between the start time (three variables) and the finishing time (three variables) of some event, assuming that the two times are within the same day.

2.4 Write a simple program that has `#include <limits.h>` added at the top, and then print out the values of the following constants: `INT_MAX`, `INT_MIN`, `FLT_MIN`, `FLT_MAX`, `DBL_MIN`, and `DBL_MAX`.

Do the values on your system agree with the values given in this chapter?

2.5 Try the calculation $1.23 \times 10^{16} + 4.56789 - 1.23 \times 10^{16}$ on a range of computers and calculators (including a spreadsheet program).

Which device is the most accurate?

2.6 Which of the following output lines (with hash characters representing blanks in the output) could *not* have been generated by the `printf` statement on the first line? (Note that the combination "`\"`" represents a single double-quote character.)

```
printf("n = %3d, x = %8.4f, m = \"%-15s\"\n", n, x, m);

n#=#123,#x#=#123.4567,#m#=#"hello,#hello###"
n#=#1234,#x#=#1234.567,#m#=#"hello##########"
n#=#-123,#x#=#-1234.5670,#m#=#"hello##########"
n#=#-123,#x#=#-1234.5670,#m#=#"##########hello"
n#=###1,#x#=####3.1472,#m#=#"hello,#hello,#hello"
n#=#1,#x#=#3.1472,#m#=#"##########hello"
n#=###1,#x#=####3.1472,#m#=#"hello"
```

2.7 Study this program fragment:

```
int num, n; double z; char c;
num = -1; n = 99; z = 9.99; c = '9';
num = scanf("%d %lf %c", &n, &z, &c);
printf("num = %d", num);
printf(", n = %d, z = %f, c = %c\n", n, z, c);
```

For each of these five input lines, determine what the program generates:

```
12 4.6 Z
4.6 12 Z
12 4.6 4.6
   12 4.6       Z
1234x56.6Y
```

If you are unsure, you might wish to compile and execute the program.

2.8 To convert from degrees Fahrenheit to degrees Celsius, you must first subtract 32, then multiply by $5/9$.

Write a program that undertakes this conversion. Confirm that 212° Fahrenheit maps to 100° Celsius, and that 82° Fahrenheit maps to a little under 28° Celsius.

Chapter 3

Making Choices

This chapter is about making decisions – choosing between alternative paths. We do this all the time in our daily lives: if it is raining we take an umbrella, and if it is sunny we do not; if it is dark we turn on a lamp, and if it is light we do not; and if we dial a wrong number, we apologize and then dial again more carefully.

In programs we need to make the same kind of conditional choices – if the number read using a `scanf` is negative, we might need to print an error message; if the `scanf` doesn't read enough values, we might want to repeat it; and so on. In C there are two mechanisms for performing this kind of *selection*, and they are discussed in detail in this chapter. But first, Section 3.1 introduces a new kind of expression, one that is regarded as being either true or false.

3.1 Logical expressions

Table 3.1 lists the standard relational and logical operators available in C. The first group in the table is the *relational operators*, which are used exactly as you would imagine: to compare two numeric values. Like the arithmetic operations listed in Table 2.1 on page 20, if either of the two operands is a `float` or a `double`, the other is cast to match before the comparison is undertaken. This makes sense: the expression "`1<1.1`", should be true, which would not happen if the `double` was converted to an `int` rather than vice versa. Note also – and this is critical – the use of "`==`" in the equality test rather than "`=`". Every C programmer has made the mistake of using an "`=`" when they really meant "`==`". The difference can be disastrous.

The table talks about "true" and "false" as if they are values. In fact, in C there are no explicit constants true and false the way there are in some other languages, and the result type of all of the operators in Table 3.1 is `int`. The rule in C is that the integer value zero is always taken to mean "false" in places where a logical expression is required; and that all non-zero values (including negative ones) are taken to mean "true". Conversely, when logical values are being generated, if a subexpression is false, the value 0 is produced from that subexpression; and if the subexpression is true, the value 1 is produced. This rather idiosyncratic interpretation means that it is possible to write statements like `num_neg+=(n<0)`, for example, which adds one to variable `num_neg` if variable `n` is negative.

Operator	Operation	True when...
<	less than	first operand is less than second
<=	less than or equal	first operand is not greater than second
>	greater than	first operand is greater than second
>=	greater than or equal	first operand is not less than second
==	equal to	first operand is equal to the second
!=	not equal to	first operand is not equal to the second
&&	and	both operands are true
||	or	either operand is true
!	not	the operand is false

Table 3.1: Relational and logical operators. As with the arithmetic operators in Table 2.1 on page 20, if either operand is of type `float` or `double`, the other is converted to the same type before the operation is applied. But here the result is always of type `int`. Note very carefully the use of "==" for equality testing, not "=", which indicates assignment.

Operands		Operation		
*e*1	*e*2	*e*1 && *e*2	*e*1 || *e*2	! *e*1
0	0	0	0	1
0	NZ	0	1	1
NZ	0	0	1	0
NZ	NZ	1	1	0

Table 3.2: Details of logical operators. Both operands are of type `int`, and are cast if they are not. For the purposes of these operators non-zero (NZ) values are treated as "true", and zero values as "false".

The three logical combining operators – "and", "or", and "not" – that are listed in Table 3.1 and defined in Table 3.2 may also be familiar. But there is one subtle difference to be aware of – in English, when we say something like "would you like coffee or tea?", we don't expect the answer to be "both". But in C, a logical "or" expression is true when either of the subexpressions is true, and is also true when *both* of the subexpressions are true.

Given these relational and logical operators, can you work out the circumstances under which each of the following integer-valued expressions is 1 (true)?

```
5<x
5<x && x<=10
5<x && x<=10 || 15<x && x<=20
month==4 || month==6 || month==9 || month==11
year%4==0 && (year%100!=0 || year%400==0)
```

These two useful identities are also worth noting:

`!(e1 && e2)` which has the same truth value as `(!e1 || !e2)`, and
`!(e1 || e2)` which has the same truth value as `(!e1 && !e2)`.

<table>
<tr><th>Operators</th><th>Operation class</th><th>Precedence</th></tr>
<tr><td>++, --</td><td>postincrement, postdecrement</td><td>Highest</td></tr>
<tr><td>!, -, (type)</td><td>unary not, unary negation, type casting</td><td></td></tr>
<tr><td>*, /, %</td><td>multiplication</td><td></td></tr>
<tr><td>+, -</td><td>addition</td><td></td></tr>
<tr><td><, >, <=, >=</td><td>comparison</td><td></td></tr>
<tr><td>==, !=</td><td>equality</td><td></td></tr>
<tr><td>&&</td><td>and</td><td></td></tr>
<tr><td>||</td><td>or</td><td></td></tr>
<tr><td>=, +=, *=, etc</td><td>assignment</td><td>Lowest</td></tr>
</table>

Table 3.3: Precedence hierarchy for the arithmetic, relational, and logical operators that have been introduced so far. The three unary operators not, negation, and cast, all have equal precedence. Assignment is also an operator, but unlike the other operators listed, is evaluated from right to left when precedence is equal.

These rules are known as *De Morgan's Laws*, after the mathematician who first demonstrated their use.

Relational and logical expressions generate `int` values that can be interpreted and used as if they correspond to true and false.

Having extended the set of operations, it is time to look at precedence again. Table 3.3 lists all of the operators that have been discussed so far, in decreasing precedence order. Using the table, for example, it is possible (but not exactly easy) to work out the value of:

```
- 1 + 2 * 3 && 4 - 5 || 6 <= 7 % 8 != ! 9 / 10 > 11
```

The answer here is 1. Whether or not a programmer should be rewarded – in any way at all – for writing such an awful expression is an entirely different story. There is no doubt that the best policy is to over parenthesize, especially when mixing arithmetic, relational, and logical operators in the same expression.

Including redundant parentheses costs nothing. Omitting necessary parentheses can cost everything.

A final point to be noted from Table 3.3 is that assignment is an operator, like any other. The *value* of an assignment statement is the value that is assigned, and the actual assignment is a *side effect* that happens while the expression is being evaluated. Assignment is also one of the few operations in C that is evaluated from right to left. Hence, expressions like "`n=m=p=q=0`" make perfect sense. That one is interpreted as "`n=(m=(p=(q=0)))`", and all four variables are assigned zero. More complex expressions are also possible: "`n+=n++`" is legal, but an absurd thing to write. If you write this kind of expression in your program, you will probably get exactly what you deserve.

The C system is free to determine the order in which the various components of an expression are evaluated. For example, in the expression $a*b+c*d$, the system is permitted to evaluate $a*b$ first and then $c*d$, or to do it in the other order. All that the precedence rules require is that the two multiplications take place before the addition. This flexibility means that if any of the subexpressions a, b, c, or d have side effects – as is automatically the case when any of them involve assignment operators – then the semantics are unclear. You should avoid such confusion in your programs by not trying to be too clever: remember to keep it simple, stupid.

> Beware of the side effects caused by assignment operators inside expressions. Use them cautiously and sparingly.

There are two operators for which the ANSI C standard does stipulate the evaluation order: in the expression "a `&&` b" (logical and) you are guaranteed that b will be evaluated *only* if a is found to be non-zero; and in the expression "a `||` b" (logical or) you are guaranteed that b will be evaluated *only* if a is found to be zero. That is, these two logical operators are evaluated in a strict ordering, and the second component is evaluated only if its value determines the whole expression. Hence, it is safe to write things like "`x!=0&&y/x>5`": by the time "`y/x>5`" is evaluated, you are guaranteed that "`x!=0`", so a "divide by zero" error cannot arise during computation of "`y/x>5`".

> The evaluation of the logical operators "`&&`" and "`||`" is performed in a lazy left-to-right manner. The second operand is evaluated only if it determines the value of the expression.

3.2 Selection

Now for the `if` statement. The most general form looks like this:

```
if ( guard )
    statement1
else
    statement2
```

There is a second version that omits the `else` part and looks like this:

```
if ( guard )
    statement1
```

Either or both of *statement*1 and *statement*2 can be empty statements (no statement at all), single statements, or compound statements bracketed by "`{`" and "`}`" pairs. The examples given shortly show what is meant by this.

When an `if` statement is executed, the value of the logical expression used as the *guard* is calculated. If the expression is true (non-zero), then *statement*1 is executed. If the expression is false, and an `else` part is given, then *statement*2 is executed. Figure 3.1 shows this flow of control.

The best way to grasp the power of this statement is to look at the examples shown in Figure 3.2. Although the two alternative branches on an `if` statement each

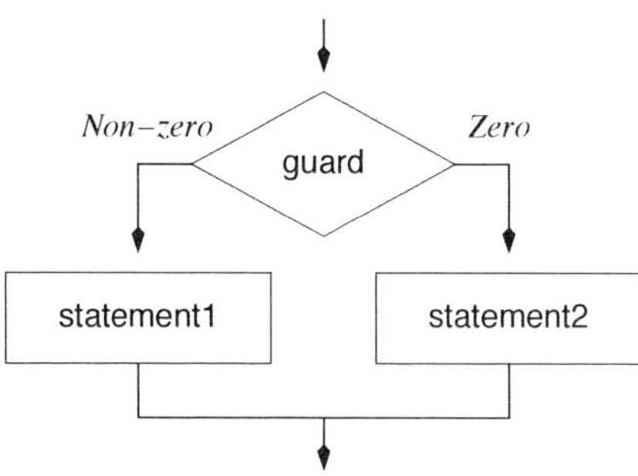

Figure 3.1: Execution flow through a `if` statement when an `else` part is given.

nominally contain just a single statement, a group of several statements can also be controlled if they are enclosed in a "`{`" and "`}`" pair to form a *compound statement*. If just one statement is being controlled, as is the case in the first example in Figure 3.2, the braces are not needed. Strictly speaking, they are not needed in the last example either, because the comments are not statements. But it doesn't hurt to have them there, and it is far easier to always put the braces in than it is to decide whether or not they are required; and potentially less confusing to a reader of the program.

> The `if` statement allows alternative execution paths to be followed, based upon the values of variables during execution. Multiple statements can be controlled if braces are used to create a compound statement.

The second example in Figure 3.2 shows how the `if` can be combined with `scanf` to verify that data is being read correctly. The call to function `exit` passing the argument `EXIT_FAILURE` is a directive to "quit executing the program, there has been a serious error". If execution is to be terminated without signaling an error, the call `exit(EXIT_SUCCESS)` should be used instead. Both `EXIT_FAILURE` and `EXIT_SUCCESS` are defined symbolically in the file `stdlib.h`. In many operating systems, the argument passed to the `exit` function is available after the termination of the program, and can be used as a diagnostic as to why the program terminated.

> The function `exit` can be used at any point to terminate program execution. Return of a non-zero exit value signals an "abnormal" termination.

The final example in Figure 3.2 shows a cascading `if` statement, in which more than two outcomes are available. Nothing special needs to be done to obtain this functionality, and any number of "`else if`" groups can be strung together. The last `else` clause catches the remaining cases not dealt with by any of the guards, and each time the overall construct is executed, exactly one of the alternatives is selected.

3.3 Pitfalls to watch for

There are a number of pitfalls associated with the use of `if` statements, usually in connection with the guard. Figure 3.3 shows the most common of these problems.

```
if (n < 0)
    num_neg += 1;
```

```
if (scanf("%d%d%d", &n, &m, &r) != 3) {
    printf("scanf failed to read three items\n");
    exit(EXIT_FAILURE);
}
```

```
if (year%4==0 && (year%100!=0 || year%400==0)) {
    /* need to allow for leap years */
    length_of_year = 366;
    length_of_feb = 29;
} else {
    /* not a leap year */
    length_of_year = 365;
    length_of_feb = 28;
}
```

```
if (month==2) {
    length_of_month = length_of_feb;
} else if (month==4 || month==6 ||
           month==9 || month==11) {
    /* thirty days hath september, april, june,
       and november */
    length_of_month = 30;
} else {
    /* all the rest have 31, except february... */
    length_of_month = 31;
}
```

Figure 3.2: Examples of the use of the `if` statement. Statements between a "{" and "}" pair are a compound statement, and treated as a single statement.

At face value, when the number zero is entered the program should print a message that more students can be accepted. But when the program is executed (the lower box in Figure 3.3), the other message is printed, and it is clear that the `if` statement took the first of the two alternative paths. Why? Well, you were warned about this earlier – look carefully at the guard in the `if`, and count the number of "=" characters. Two are required for an equality test, and when there is only one, it is an assignment statement. So that guard says "assign the value `MAX_CLASS_SIZE` to the variable `class_size`, and then, if the value that was assigned is non-zero, execute the first branch of the `if` statement".

Some – unfortunately, not all – C compilers allow you to check for this kind of problem. The `gcc` compiler used while preparing this book does not naturally give such warnings (see the first compilation line in the lower box of Figure 3.3), but can be instructed to look for potential problems via the use of the "`all`" option to the "`-W`" compiler warnings-level flag (the second compilation line), which asks for all warning messages to be listed. The `-ansi` flag similarly asks that the `gcc` compiler

```
#define MAX_CLASS_SIZE 50

    int class_size;
    printf("Enter class size: ");
    scanf("%d", &class_size);
    if (class_size = MAX_CLASS_SIZE) {
        printf("Class is now full\n");
    } else {
        printf("More students can be accepted\n");
    }
```

```
mac: gcc -o equalinif equalinif.c
mac: ./equalinif
Enter class size: 0
Class is now full
mac: gcc -Wall -ansi -o equalinif equalinif.c
equalinif.c: In function `main':
equalinif.c:11: warning: suggest parentheses around
    assignment used as truth value
```

Figure 3.3: A flawed `if` statement. The program always prints "Class is now full", even if a `class_size` of 0 is entered. The reason why is revealed in the second compilation line shown in the lower box, when all warning messages are requested using "`-Wall`". Now the compiler draws attention to the assignment statement inside the guard of the `if` statement, and suggests that it might be problematic, despite that fact that the program is technically correct as it stands.

```
    int x=3, y=4, z=6;
    if (x>2)
        if (y>6)
            z = 7;
    else
        z = 8;
    printf("After the if statement z=%d\n", z);
```

Figure 3.4: Another flawed `if` statement.

not accept any constructs that are not part of the ANSI standard definition of C. There is no reason at all why you shouldn't *always* use these warning and diagnostic facilities if they are available.

What about the program fragment in Figure 3.4? What is the final value of `z`? Should be 6, right? The first guard is true, but the second guard is false, right? So `z` remains unchanged, right? Wrong! The rule is that an `else` part attaches to the most recent unmatched `if` that is available to it, irrespective of program layout. So the `else` in this fragment belongs to the second `if`, and when the second guard is false, the statement `z=8` is executed.

Like the previous pitfall, the program in Figure 3.4 is correct according to the rules of C, and when compiled using the default `gcc` options, no warning message is generated. But when `-Wall` is used:

```
mac: gcc -Wall -ansi -o danglingelse danglingelse.c
danglingelse.c: In function 'main':
danglingelse.c:10: warning: suggest explicit braces to
    avoid ambiguous 'else'
```

This issue is known as the *dangling else* question, and the C rule is the one usually adopted in programming languages in which it arises. If you always put the braces in, as was recommended a few paragraphs ago, you will never encounter a dangling else in your programs.

> If your C compiler provides for additional warning and diagnostic facilities, you should gratefully accept the assistance.

One last example draws out another mistake that it is easy to make: what is the final value of `z` in this program fragment?

```
    int x=3, y=4, z=6;
    if (x < y < z)
        z = z+1;
    if (z > y > x)
        z = z+2;
    printf("After the two if statements z=%d\n", z);
```

The obvious answer is 9, but by now you are probably (and rightly) suspicious of the obvious answer. In fact, the program prints 7. To understand why, insert the implicit precedence-derived parentheses, which make the second guard `(z>y)>x`. Then remember that `(z>y)` will be either zero or one. When the first version of this book was written, using `-Wall` didn't help find this type of problem – the compiler was silent even when you asked to be warned of possibly erroneous constructs. But the `gcc` compiler is under constant development, and it now recognizes this potential problem and issues a warning message that "comparisons like $x \leq y \leq z$ do not have their mathematical meaning". Take the hint, and always use `-Wall`.

3.4 Case study: Calculating taxes

You now have enough C knowledge to tackle a non-trivial program. See if you can implement a solution to this calculation:

> The 2012/13 Australian tax rates stipulate that annual income between \$18,200 and \$37,000 is taxed at 19.0 cents in the dollar; income between \$37,000 and \$80,000 at 32.5 cents in the dollar; and income between \$80,000 and \$180,000 at 37.0 cents in the dollar. Any further income is taxed at 45.0 cents in the dollar. In addition, a Medicare levy of 1.5 cents in the dollar is applied to all income. For a given gross income, what net income is received?

```
/* Calculate Australian tax and Medicare levy, 2012 scales.
*/
#include <stdio.h>
#include <stdlib.h>

#define RATE0   0.000
#define RATE1   0.190
#define RATE2   0.325
#define RATE3   0.370
#define RATE4   0.450
#define RATEM   0.015

#define THRESH1  18200.00
#define THRESH2  37000.00
#define THRESH3  80000.00
#define THRESH4 180000.00

#define BASE0 0.00
#define BASE1 (BASE0 + RATE0*THRESH1)
#define BASE2 (BASE1 + RATE1*(THRESH2-THRESH1))
#define BASE3 (BASE2 + RATE2*(THRESH3-THRESH2))
#define BASE4 (BASE3 + RATE3*(THRESH4-THRESH3))

int
main(int argc, char *argv[]) {
    double gross, tax, medicare, net;
    printf("Enter gross salary: $");
    if (scanf("%lf", &gross) != 1) {
        printf("No value was entered\n");
        exit(EXIT_FAILURE);
    }
    if (gross <= THRESH1) {
        tax = BASE0 + gross*RATE0;
    } else if (gross <= THRESH2) {
        tax = BASE1 + (gross-THRESH1)*RATE1;
    } else if (gross <= THRESH3) {
        tax = BASE2 + (gross-THRESH2)*RATE2;
    } else if (gross <= THRESH4) {
        tax = BASE3 + (gross-THRESH3)*RATE3;
    } else {
        tax = BASE4 + (gross-THRESH4)*RATE4;
    }
    medicare = RATEM*gross;
    net = gross - tax - medicare;
    printf("gross income        $%9.2f\n", gross);
    printf("less tax            $%9.2f\n", -tax);
    printf("less medicare       $%9.2f\n", -medicare);
    printf("net income          $%9.2f\n", net);
    return 0;
}
```

Figure 3.5: A program to calculate net income as a function of gross income.

Figure 3.5 shows how the task can be tackled using a cascading `if` statement. Note how the use of symbolic constants avoids much of the complexity inherent to this computation – in a sense, the program is controlled by two tables, one of threshold amounts, and another of corresponding tax rates. Changes to the thresholds or tax rates can thus be made relatively easily, and even if the number of steps in the tax scale changes, it is clear how the program should be altered. On the other hand, the program is also repetitive in its computation, and there is scope for errors to creep in because of that. Chapter 7 introduces techniques that allow a more elegant implementation of this kind of task. Until then, the program in Figure 3.5 is pretty much the best we can do for this problem.

Here is what happens when it is executed:

```
mac: ./taxation
Enter gross salary: $98765.43
gross income         $ 98765.43
less tax             $-24490.21
less medicare        $ -1481.48
net income           $ 72793.73
```

Neat and tidy output is important if the eventual users of a program are to place their confidence in a program, and you should never forget that the only part of your program seen by most users is the interface though which input values are read and output values are reported.

> If the interface to a program is untidy or awkward to use, users will assume that the program itself is of poor quality.

3.5 The switch statement

There is another mechanism provided in the C language to achieve selection – the `switch` statement. It doesn't really offer any extra functionality compared to the `if` statement, nor is it any more succinct. Indeed, the one way in which it differs from the `if` statement is capable of causing more confusion than it is worth, and you are advised to avoid any use of the `switch`.

Nevertheless, you may encounter the `switch` in programs that you are asked to maintain. The general form of it is:

```
switch ( integer expression ) {
case ( integer1 ) :
    statement1
    break;
case ( integer2 ) :
    statement2
    break;
        ...
case ( integer n ) :
    statement n
    break;
```

```
    default:
        statement
}
```

When executed, the value of the *integer expression* is calculated. That value is then compared in turn against the various `case` expressions, until either a match is found, or the `default` (if it exists) is reached. The corresponding statement or list of statements is then executed, continuing through until either the closing brace of the `switch` is encountered, or until a `break` statement is executed. Note that the general form shown here presumes that there is a `break` for each case. Unfortunately, it is not mandatory.

If there is a `break` after each group of statements, the behavior of the `switch` is the same as that of a corresponding cascading `if`. The following box shows a `switch` that is well structured in this regard:

```
switch (month) {
    case 2:
        length_of_month = 28 +
            (year%4==0 && (year%100!=0 || year%400==0));
        break;
    case  4:
    case  6:
    case  9:
    case 11:
        length_of_month = 30;
        break;
    default:
        length_of_month = 31;
        break;
}
```

Note how in this case the accumulation of cases is plausible – a bit like several different tests connected with "or" operations in an `if`-statement guard. In this fragment there are three mutually exclusive sets of statements controlled by the `switch`, and three matching `break` statements.

If the programmer does not follow the discipline of having one `break` for every group of statements, cases flow together in a chaotic and confusing manner. It is for this reason that the `switch` statement is to be distrusted. Program execution starts at the first `case` with a matching value, and moves through all subsequent statements until a `break` is encountered. Programmers trying to be "clever" then order the cases to exploit this flexibility. To see an example of this "cleverness", trace the `switch` statement in Figure 3.6 for each possible starting value of `x` between 1 and 10, and determine the final value of `x` that corresponds to each starting value. Confusing, isn't it! Should a programmer who writes things like this be rewarded?

> The `switch` statement offers a general form of the cascading `if`. Use it with caution, and maintain the discipline of having a `break` for each non-empty group of statements.

```
switch (x) {
    case 1:
        x += 4;
    case 4:
    case 7:
        x += 2;
        break;
    case 3:
    case 9:
        x += 3;
    default:
        x += 8;
}
```

Figure 3.6: A dangerous `switch` statement.

Exercises

3.1 Number each of the operators in this expression with the order in which it is applied. Then work out the value of the expression.

```
1 && - 2 * - 3 - 4 < 5 && 6 <= 7 >= 8 != 9 / 10 > ! 11
```

3.2 Trace the action of these statements, and determine the values printed out by each of the `printf` statements. Assume that all variables have been declared to be of type `int`. Be careful – some of them illustrate common errors.

a.

```
i = 3; j = 4;
if (i<j && j<6) {
    i = i+j;
} else {
    j = i+j;
}
printf("i=%d, j=%d\n", i, j);
```

b.

```
i = 3; j = 4; k = 7;
if ((i<j || j<k) && j<i) {
    i = i+1;
    if (i*i>k) {
        k = k+1;
    }
} else {
    j = j+1;
    if (i*i>k) {
        k = k+2;
    }
}
printf("i=%d, j=%d, k=%d\n", i, j, k);
```

c.
```
month = 7;
if (month == 2) {
    days = 28;
} else if (month == 4 || 6 || 9 || 11) {
    days = 30;
} else {
    days = 31;
}
printf("days=%d\n", days);
```

d.
```
x = 1; y = 2;
if (x>y)
    printf("x=%d, y=%d\n", x, y);
    x = x+1;
if (x<y)
    printf("x=%d, y=%d\n", x, y);
    y = y+2;
printf("x=%d, y=%d\n", x, y);
```

e.
```
x = 1; y = 2;
if (x>y); {
    printf("x=%d, y=%d\n", x, y);
    x = x+1;
}
if (x<y); {
    printf("x=%d, y=%d\n", x, y);
    y = y+2;
}
printf("x=%d, y=%d\n", x, y);
```

f.
```
x = 0; y = 0;
if (y<x) {
    printf("y is smaller\n");
} else if (y=x) {
    printf("x and y are equal\n");
} else {
    printf("y is greater\n");
}
```

3.3 The roots of the equation $ax^2 + bx + c = 0$ are given by

$$\frac{-b+\sqrt{d}}{2a} \quad \text{and} \quad \frac{-b-\sqrt{d}}{2a},$$

where d, the discriminant, is given by

$$b^2 - 4ac.$$

When $d = 0$ there is only one root; and when $d < 0$ there are no real roots. Special cases also arise when $a = 0$, and sometimes when $b = 0$. Write a program that reads three values, a, b, and c, and writes out the roots of the equation $ax^2 + bx + c = 0$. Handle as many of the cases as you can.

3.4 Write a program that reads a date in `dd/mm/yyyy` format and writes, in the same format, the date it will be tomorrow. For example,

```
mac: ./nextday
Enter date in format dd/mm/yyyy: 01/01/1999
Date read: 01/01/1999
Tomorrow:  02/01/1999
mac: ./nextday
Enter date in format dd/mm/yyyy: 31/12/1999
Date read: 31/12/1999
Tomorrow:  01/01/2000
mac: ./nextday
Enter date in format dd/mm/yyyy: 28/02/1999
Date read: 28/02/1999
Tomorrow:  01/03/1999
mac: ./nextday
Enter date in format dd/mm/yyyy: 28/02/2000
Date read: 28/02/2000
Tomorrow:  29/02/2000
```

Hint: the format control string `"%d/%d/%d"` can be used in a `scanf` to help de-format the input; and use of the format control "`%02d`" in the `printf` outputs numbers with leading zeros rather than leading blanks.

3.5 Write a program that reads a date in `dd/mm/yyyy` format and calculates the day number within the year:

```
mac: ./daynumber
Enter date in dd/mm/yyyy format: 31/12/2000
31/12/2000 is day number 366 in the year
mac: ./daynumber
Enter date in dd/mm/yyyy format: 1/5/2003
01/05/2003 is day number 121 in the year
```

Your program might be a bit clumsier than feels appropriate. The next chapter provides a mechanism that makes this exercise easier to manage.

3.6 Suppose that coins are available in denominations of 50c, 20c, 10c, 5c, 2c, and 1c. Write a program `calculatechange` that reads an integer amount of cents between 0 and 99 (your program might check that the input value falls within this range) and prints out the coins necessary to make up that amount of money:

```
mac: ./calculatechange
Enter amount in cents: 93
The coins required to make 93 cents are:
50, 20, 20, 2, 1
mac: ./calculatechange
Enter amount in cents: 69
The coins required to make 69 cents are:
50, 10, 5, 2, 2
```

Don't worry if your program again seems a bit clumsy, and not terribly general. There is a much more elegant way of handling this problem, but the necessary techniques are not covered for several more chapters.

3.7 In Exercise 2.8 on page 28 you were asked to write a program that converts temperatures from Fahrenheit to Celsius. Extend that program by adding in the reverse transformation:

```
mac: ./converter
Enter a temperature: 212F
The temperature 212.0F converts to 100.0C
mac: ./converter
Enter a temperature: 212C
The temperature 212.0C converts to 413.6F
```

If you wish to make your program even more useful, generalize it to additional units, and spell them out more fully:

```
mac: ./converter
Enter a quantity: 100M
The distance 100.0 miles converts to 160.9 kilometers
```

Use "M" for miles, "K" for kilometers, "P" for pounds, and "G" for kilograms. One mile is 1.609 kilometers, and one pound is 0.454 kilograms.

3.8 Suppose that an additional tax band is being introduced, with incomes over $250,000 now taxed at 47.5 cents in the dollar.

At the same time, a threshold is to be introduced into the Medicare levy, so that incomes over $100,000 are charged at 2.5 cents in the dollar.

Modify the program in Figure 3.5 to implement these two changes. You might find that the best strategy is to tackle the two changes one at a time.

Chapter 4

Loops

This chapter introduces loops. In English a "loop" is a circle of thread or some other flexible substance, and is closed off – the beginning and the end meet. In programming, the word loop has a slightly different meaning, and includes some of the connotations attached to the English word "spiral" – in which we go round and round, but also move downhill towards a desired endpoint. For example, a spiral staircase is more than just a loop around which we walk in a horizontal plane, it allows us to move vertically too.

In a computer program, we use loops to make vertical progress in a rather more abstract sense. We don't want to just keep on repeating some set of statements, since that would be a treadmill. Instead, we want to make progress in a vertical dimension, to move towards some goal, and to get off the staircase when we arrive at that goal. We want to *iterate* a group of statements, and, in the course of each iteration, make some definite movement towards a desired objective.

The language C provides two main types of loop structure: the `for` statement; and a restricted subset of it called the `while` statement. Both are examined in this chapter. Compared to the structures described in Chapter 3, they permit a quantum step in the expressive power of programs, and a corresponding leap in the difficulty of the type of problems that can be tackled and solved. For example, in this chapter you will encounter programs that handle arbitrary-sized sets of numbers, rather than the fixed input sets of previous example programs.

C also supplies a third kind of looping structure, the `do` statement. It belongs in the same category as the `switch` statement described in Section 3.5 – it needs to be known about, but has some drawbacks that mean that it should only be used with caution, and is best avoided by inexperienced programmers.

4.1 Controlled iteration

There are many circumstances in which a statement or set of statements is to be executed some fixed number of times. This is achieved with the `for` loop. The general form is:

`for` (*initialize* ; *guard* ; *update*)
    statement

where each of *initialize*, *guard*, and *update* are expressions. The *statement* is sometimes referred to as the *body* of the loop. Here is a first example of a `for` loop:

```
for (i=1; i<=NUM_LINES; i=i+1) {
    printf("%4d%10d\n", i, i*(i+1)/2);
}
```

This is what results when that loop is executed with `NUM_LINES` defined to be five:

```
   1         1
   2         3
   3         6
   4        10
   5        15
```

The key observation is that the `printf` has been executed repeatedly, controlled by the `for` statement above it.

Figure 4.1 shows the flow of execution through the various parts of a `for` loop. First, the expression denoted by *initialize* – normally an assignment statement – is evaluated, if it exists. Then the *guard*, which is an integer-valued expression, is evaluated. If the guard is non-zero (true), the *statement* that comprises the body of the loop is executed. As was the case with the `if` statement, the body can be either a single statement, or a compound statement – a list of statements enclosed in braces, considered to be a single entity. The *update* expression, which is again usually an assignment statement, is executed after the body has completed.

Once the *update* statement has executed, the guard is again checked, and if it is true, the loop executed again. This cyclic process continues until the guard is zero (false), at which time control passes directly to the next statement after the `for` statement.

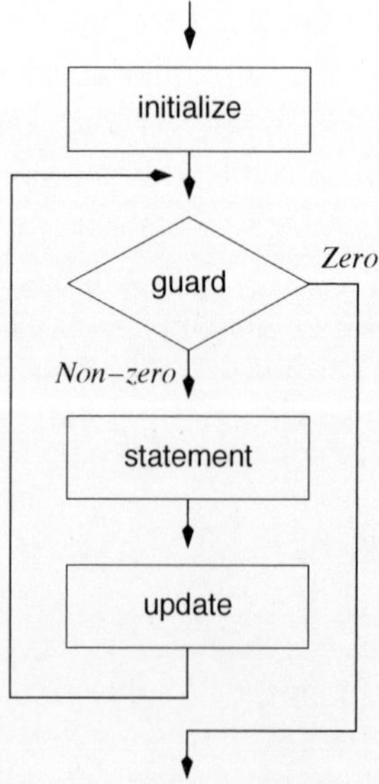

Figure 4.1: Execution flow through a `for` statement.

> In a `for` loop the body of the loop is executed only while the guard is non-zero. The update statement is executed after the body, and immediately prior to the guard being reevaluated.

Now look at that first `for` example again. The *initialize* part of the loop is the statement `i=1`. Once this statement has been executed, the guard – which is `i<=NUM_LINES` – is checked, and found to be true. So the `printf` statement that is the body of the loop is executed, which prints the number 1 and the corresponding value of `i*(i+1)/2`, which is also 1. At the end of the body, the *update* statement `i=i+1` is executed, giving variable `i` the value 2, and the guard is tested again. It is still true, so 2 and the second triangle number are printed, then the *update* statement executed for a second time. This continues until the *update* statement takes `i` beyond `NUM_LINES` (assumed in this example to be 5), at which time the loop exits.

Figure 4.2 shows a second example of a `for` loop, tackling the task that was set in Exercise 3.5 on page 42 (where some sample output is shown). This program fragment calculates the day number within the year for an input date, by iterating over the months up to (but not including) the specified month `mm`, adding up their lengths. The statement controlled by the loop – the body – is the entire `if` statement, which in turn contains three assignment statements. As always, February must be handled carefully. Note also the use of the postincrement assignment statement as the *update* component. The `++` increment operator is very common in `for` loops.

Figure 4.3 shows a more complex arrangement, in which two `for` loops are nested. The inner loop – controlling variable `j` – is executed in its entirety every time the outer loop (variable `i`) iterates. This gives an overall effect of the inner loop spiraling around very quickly, while the outer loop proceeds at a more sedate pace.

```
printf("Enter date in dd/mm/yyyy format: ");
if (scanf("%d/%d/%d", &dd, &mm, &yyyy) != 3) {
    printf("Invalid input\n");
    exit(EXIT_FAILURE);
}
length_of_feb = 28 + (yyyy%4==0 &&
            (yyyy%100!=0 || yyyy%400==0));
daynum = dd;
for (month=1; month<mm; month++) {
    if (month==2) {
        daynum += length_of_feb;
    } else if (month==4 || month==6 ||
               month==9 || month==11) {
        daynum += 30;
    } else {
        daynum += 31;
    }
}
printf("%02d/%02d/%04d is day number %d in the year\n",
    dd, mm, yyyy, daynum);
```

Figure 4.2: Calculate the day number within the year that corresponds to the current date given by the three variables `dd`, `mm`, and `yyyy`.

```
for (i=0; i<NTIMES; i++) {
    for (j=0; j<i; j++) {
        printf("i=%d,j=%d  ", i, j);
    }
    printf("\n");
}
```

```
i=1,j=0
i=2,j=0  i=2,j=1
i=3,j=0  i=3,j=1  i=3,j=2
i=4,j=0  i=4,j=1  i=4,j=2  i=4,j=3
```

Figure 4.3: A nested `for` loop. Constant `NTIMES` is assumed to be 5.

An analogy that you might find helpful is the various hands on a clock: the second hand (variable `j`) makes a full revolution for each step that the minute hand (variable `i`) makes; and if there were a third enclosing loop, it would proceed (like the hour hand) at an even more stately rate.

> In a nested loop the inner loop completes all iterations before the update statement in the outer loop is executed. Then, if the outer guard is still non-zero, the inner loop is commenced again, starting with the *initialize* component.

There is considerable flexibility in the choice of initialize, guard, and update components. For example, Figure 4.4 shows a loop in which the controlled variable is adjusted by multiplication rather than addition. Figure 4.4 also highlights the issue of integer overflow, mentioned as a problem in Section 2.2 on page 14, and examined in more detail in Section 13.2.

Any expressions are permitted as the initializing and updating components, a range of possibilities that includes the *empty expression*. As an extreme, "`for(;;);`"

```
for (i=3; i<100000000; i*=10) {
    printf("%8d x %-8d = %12d\n", i, i, i*i);
}
```

```
       3 x 3        =            9
      30 x 30       =          900
     300 x 300      =        90000
    3000 x 3000     =      9000000
   30000 x 30000    =    900000000
  300000 x 300000   =  -194313216
 3000000 x 3000000  =   2043514880
30000000 x 30000000 =  -1806942208
```

Figure 4.4: A `for` loop in which the controlled variable is adjusted by multiplication rather than by being incremented. The unexpected negative numbers result from integer overflow.

is a perfectly valid `for` loop, according to the rules of C. It does nothing before it starts, then it performs no test (and in doing so, arrives at the value "true"), then it does nothing and does the non-existent test again, and so on. Endlessly. Which brings us back to the distinction between treadmills and spirals.

Loops should spiral, and move at each iteration towards a goal. When a controlled variable is initialized, tested in the guard, and then updated, as has been the case in all of the examples shown so far, positive progress along the path of the spiral is pretty much guaranteed. But in the loop "`for(i=0;i<10;)`" there is no progress made, and no spiral. It is a treadmill – which in computing is called an *infinite loop* – and is an unwelcome addition to a program. In this simple case the error is reasonably obvious, and almost certainly there is an `i++` or similar statement missing. In more complex settings, writing a loop that doesn't make progress is an easy mistake to make, and all programmers have agonized over the "why" of an endless loop at some stage of their career.

So if you are faced with a program that appears to be "stuck" somewhere, the very first thing to check is the loops – ensure that every loop makes progress, in that whatever variable is being controlled in the loop moves towards the stopping condition, as expressed in the guard.

In most `for` loops the controlled variable will appear in all of the initialize, the guard, and the update parts.

The other reason why a program might get "stuck" is that it might be at a `scanf` waiting for you to enter some data, without you realizing. That is why you should always use `printf` to generate a prompt immediately prior to every `scanf` – to minimize this possible confusion.

Sometimes a loop appears to unexpectedly execute fewer times that you think it should. Look at the following code, and see if you can work out what it generates:

```
for (i=0; i<10; i++); {
    printf("i=%d\n", i);
}
```

It prints the numbers 0 to 9, right? Wrong. In fact, the third semi-colon in the first line of the fragment means that the `for` executes the *empty statement* ten times, and then goes on to do the `printf` once and write the message `i=10`.

Beware of loops that execute the empty statement.

4.2 Case study: Calculating compound interest

You are now ready to try an exercise that involves loops. Have a go at the following task before reading on:

Write a program that shows how, for interest rates of 2%, 3%, 4%, 5%, 6%, and 7%, a regular savings amount of $100 per month grows over periods of 1 to 7 years. Figure 4.5 shows the desired output.

```
Monthly savings of $100, with monthly compounded interest
Annual Rate    |   2%      3%      4%      5%      6%      7%
After 1 years  |  1211    1217    1222    1228    1234    1239
After 2 years  |  2447    2470    2494    2519    2543    2568
After 3 years  |  3707    3762    3818    3875    3934    3993
After 4 years  |  4993    5093    5196    5301    5410    5521
After 5 years  |  6305    6465    6630    6801    6977    7159
After 6 years  |  7643    7878    8122    8376    8641    8916
After 7 years  |  9008    9334    9675   10033   10407   10800
```

Figure 4.5: A two-dimensional table.

Figure 4.6 shows a complete program that makes use of nested loops to create a two-dimensional table. Each iteration of the outer loop – the one in which the control variable alters more slowly – generates one row of the table. Each iteration of the second loop generates a single number for the table. And to generate that value, a third loop is required, which calculates the number to be printed into that cell of the table. (The innermost loop could be replaced by a direct evaluation of a formula if we were prepared to investigate the mathematics involved, but for our purposes an iterative computation is perfectly valid.) After each row of values is generated, a newline character is required. The `printf` that generates that newline is the last statement in each iteration of the outermost loop. The two outer loops directly reflect the structure of the table – it is a two-dimensional report where each entry is a function of two parameters. A two-dimensional loop structure is thus the appropriate way of generating it.

A lot of the actual program (Figure 4.6) is concerned with output formatting. This is not uncommon – to make the output of a program look neat and tidy can be quite hard work, but as has already been noted, is well worth doing.

4.3 Program layout and style

A point to note in connection with programs in general is that tidy program layout is essential if human readers are to be able to access the structure of your program. Believe it or not, the jumble in the top box of Figure 4.7 has exactly the same functionality as the fragment in Figure 4.2 on page 47 – the C compiler doesn't care whether spaces or newlines or tabs are used to delimit the various components. But can you read it? And can you be sure that it does what it claims to? In this example, at least the variable names have been retained. Imagine if they were called `qxfgc` and `fczxp`, and so on. Indeed, there is a regular "obfuscated C" programming competition, see `http://www.ioccc.org/`, in which the objective is to write the most creative, but non-obvious, C program. When you are an expert programmer you can enter this competition if you wish; while you are learning, you should strive for simplicity and transparency.

The lower box in Figure 4.7 shows a third layout style that is preferred by some programmers. Supporters of this style argue that hiding the opening brace of a compound statement at the end of a line is misleading, and that both opening and closing

```
/* Print a table of numbers to show the effect of regular
   savings habits.
*/
#include <stdio.h>

#define MAX_YEARS 7    /* number of years to compute for */
#define MONTHLY 100    /* monthly savings amount */
#define MIN_RATE 2     /* minimum annual percentage rate */
#define MAX_RATE 7     /* maximum interest rate */

int
main(int argc, char *argv[]) {
    int month,
        rate,
        year;
    double balance,
        monthly_rate;

    /* print the table heading lines */
    printf("Monthly savings of $%d", MONTHLY);
    printf(", with monthly compounded interest\n");
    printf("Annual Rate    |");
    for (rate=MIN_RATE; rate<=MAX_RATE; rate++) {
        printf("%4d%%  ", rate);
    }
    printf("\n");

    /* and now the rows of the table, one by one */
    for (year=1; year<=MAX_YEARS; year++) {
        printf("After %1d years | ", year);
        for (rate=MIN_RATE; rate<=MAX_RATE; rate++) {
            /* compute one value */
            balance = 0.0;
            monthly_rate = 1.00 + ((rate/100.00)/12);
            for (month=1; month<=12*year; month++) {
                balance *= monthly_rate;
                balance += MONTHLY;
            }
            printf("%5.0f  ", balance);
        }
        /* end of one row */
        printf("\n");
    }
    return 0;
}
```

Figure 4.6: Using nested loops to generate a table. An example of the output generated by this program appears in Figure 4.5.

braces should be prominently displayed. Yet another style tucks the closing brace of each compound statement up at the end of the last statement. What is important is that you adopt a single style, and then stick with it. Consistency is more important that the particular style used. Indeed, to obtain consistency, organizations often

```
printf("Enter date in dd/mm/yyyy format: ");if(scanf(
"%d/%d/%d",&dd,&mm,&yyyy)!=3){printf("Invalid input\n")
;exit(EXIT_FAILURE);}length_of_feb=28+(yyyy%4==0&&(yyyy
%100!=0|| yyyy%400==0));daynum=dd;for(month=1;month<mm;
month++){if(month==2){daynum+=length_of_feb;}else if(
month==4||month==6||month==9||month==11){daynum+=30;}
else{daynum+=31;}}printf("%02d/%02d/%04d is day number"
" %d in the year\n",dd,mm,yyyy,daynum);
```

```
    printf("Enter date in dd/mm/yyyy format: ");
    if (scanf("%d/%d/%d", &dd, &mm, &yyyy) != 3)
    {
        printf("Invalid input\n");
        exit(EXIT_FAILURE);
    }
    length_of_feb = 28 + (yyyy%4==0 &&
                (yyyy%100!=0 || yyyy%400==0));
    daynum = dd;
    for (month=1; month<mm; month++)
    {
        if (month==2)
        {
            daynum += length_of_feb;
        }
        else if (month==4 || month==6 ||
                 month==9 || month==11)
        {
            daynum += 30;
        }
        else
        {
            daynum += 31;
        }
    }
    printf("%02d/%02d/%04d is day number %d in the year\n",
        dd, mm, yyyy, daynum);
```

Figure 4.7: Two further program layout styles. The top one is not recommended.

mandate a particular style for all programs their staff generate, so that any of their programmers can work readily with any of their programs. If you are employed in an organization like this, your own personal preference is unimportant.

> Neat and tidy program layout is as important as sensible choice of variable names if programs are to be readable and thus correct.

4.4 Uncontrolled iteration

The second type of C loop you need to be familiar with is the `while` loop. In fact, the `while` loop is really just a restricted kind of `for` loop, but it gets used sufficiently often that it cannot be ignored. Figure 4.8 shows the logical structure of the `while` loop, which has the general form:

> `while` (*guard*)
>   *statement*

When executed, the `while` loop has exactly the same semantics as an equivalent `for` loop in which the initialize and update statements have been omitted and are thus empty expressions:

> `for` (; *guard* ;)
>   *statement*

Despite this near identical behavior, there is a subtle convention followed by most programmers, which is that a `for` loop is used when the number of iterations is known in advance, and there is a control or "counting" variable; whereas a `while` loop is used when the number of iterations is not known at the time the loop commences, and there is no direct "count down" towards loop termination.

For example, consider the following problem: if a number is even, it should be halved; and if it is odd, it should be multiplied by three and then 1 added to it. Starting with a given number, what is the sequence of values traced out, and the largest value in that sequence? Figure 4.9 shows a program designed to explore this problem.

In Figure 4.9 a `while` loop seems to fit the nature of the problem. The loop `for(;n>1;)` is identical, and would have served equally well, but the use of the word `while` in some sense captures the open-ended nature of the computation – we are not actually in a position to demonstrate that this loop will terminate, since there is no guarantee that every path through the loop results in the guard moving closer to becoming false.

Note also that in this program a single nested loop has been used, despite the fact that the output of the program again appears as a table. In this case the tabular layout is purely a convenience, and the underlying computation is essentially one-dimensional. So a single loop is used, and the two-dimensional output is obtained through the use of an `if` statement within the loop that periodically inserts newline characters into the output character stream.

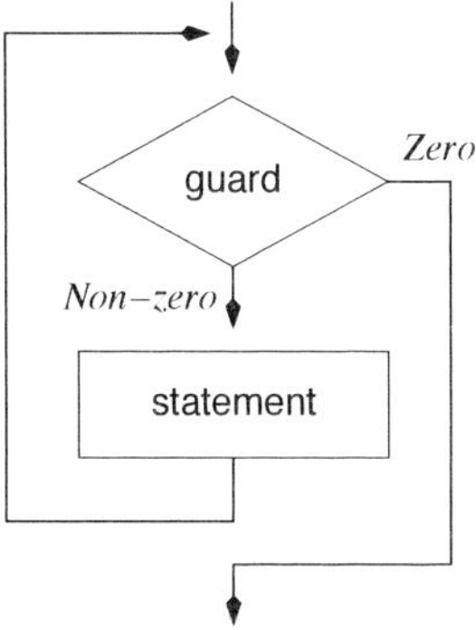

Figure 4.8: Execution flow through a `while` statement.

```
/* a value for n has been read */
max = n;
cycles = 0;
while (n>1) {
    printf("%5d ", n);
    if (n%2==0) {
        n = n/2;
    } else {
        n = 3*n+1;
    }
    if (n>max) {
        max = n;
    }
    cycles += 1;
    if (cycles%PERLINE == 0) {
        printf("\n");
    }
}
printf("\n%d cycles consumed, maximum was %d\n",
        cycles, max);
```

```
mac: ./threen
Enter starting value for n: 8
    8     4     2
3 cycles consumed, maximum was 8
mac: ./threen
Enter starting value for n: 9
    9    28    14     7    22    11    34    17
   52    26    13    40    20    10     5    16
    8     4     2
19 cycles consumed, maximum was 52
```

Figure 4.9: A program to explore some properties of the $3n + 1$ problem.

Both `for` statements and `while` statements share a common attribute – they test the guard prior to each and every iteration, and continue with that execution only if the guard is true. This means that they cannot terminate until the guard is false. More to the point, it means that when such loops do terminate, the guard is always false.

When a `for` or `while` loop terminates, the guard is false.

This observation means that one way of creating a loop guard is to decide what is supposed to be true at the end of the loop, and then make the guard the negation of that. For example, if `n==1` is required at the end of a loop, the guard should be `n!=1`. Every iteration of the loop should then move a step closer towards changing the guard from true to false. If you think about your loops as needing to make progress towards falsifying the guard, you will be less likely to get bogged down debugging infinite loops.

If a loop is to terminate, every iteration must move one step closer to making the loop guard false.

```
/* a value for n has been read */
isprime = 1;
for (divisor=2; divisor*divisor<=n; divisor++) {
    if (n%divisor==0) {
        isprime = 0;
        break;
    }
}
if (isprime == 1) {
    printf("%d is a prime number\n", n);
} else {
    printf("%d = %d * %d\n", n, divisor, n/divisor);
}
```

```
mac: ./isprime
Enter a number n: 100000003
100000003 = 643 * 155521
mac: ./isprime
Enter a number n: 100000007
100000007 is a prime number
```

Figure 4.10: Use of the `break` statement to abnormally terminate loop execution.

Achieving a negated guard is the usual way of exiting a loop. But there is a second way out, a kind of "beam me out, Scotty" that abruptly shifts the execution point from within the loop to the statement immediately following the loop. Figure 4.10 illustrates a situation in which use of this `break` statement might be considered.

In the program fragment in Figure 4.10, the number `n` is being tested, to see if there are any smaller numbers that divide evenly into it. If no numbers apart from 1 and `n` divide evenly into `n`, it is a *prime* number. Because the existence of any number as a factor means that `n` is not prime, once a factor (in variable `divisor`) has been determined, there is no need to continue the testing – the loop can be broken at that point. Breaking the loop has the useful side effect of leaving `divisor` as a known factor of `n` after the loop, because the update statement is not executed if the loop is aborted using a `break`. This fact is exploited in the final `printf`. Note how only numbers smaller than the square root of `n` need to be divided. Testing all the way up to `n-1` is not wrong, but it does make identification of prime numbers slower than is necessary. Note also that this program (erroneously) reports that all values less than two are prime numbers.

A second route out of the loop is created when a `break` statement is used in this way. To determine which pathway was taken, a loop with a `break` should always involve another variable, called a *flag*, that records whether a normal exit via the guard occurred, or whether the loop was broken. This is the role of variable `isprime` in Figure 4.10. A test involving the flag variable is then normally the first statement following the loop. Note that tests of the form "`if (isprime==1)`" that examine flag variables can be (and usually are) shortened to the equivalent form "`if (isprime)`".

> The `break` statement allows loops to be abnormally terminated. It should be used carefully, with a flag set before the loop is exited, and tested immediately after the loop.

When nested loops are involved, even greater caution is required – the `break` only causes one loop to be terminated, so a `break` from within an inner loop needs be followed by a test that includes a `break` to exit the outer loop. The resultant mess of conflicting pathways is unlikely to be pretty, and provides a natural tangle in which errors can thrive. So if you do use the `break` statement in a nested loop, take great care – it means that the loop has two exits, an ambiguity that is directly counter to the structure necessary in programs if they are to be demonstrably correct.

There is a third looping structure provided in C – the `do` statement, known in some other programming languages as the "repeat-until" statement. Like the `break` and `switch` statements, you should just write your programs without it. But because you may be obliged to read programs written by others, you do need to know about it. Figure 4.11 shows the logic flow, and its syntax is:

```
do
    statement
while ( guard )
```

In a `do` loop the body is always executed *at least once*, and it is not correct in the body to assume that the guard is always true. That fact is why the `do` statement is risky – the first iteration of a `do` loop has quite different properties to subsequent iterations. To return to the spiral staircase analogy, using a `do` loop is equivalent to changing from one floor to the next and only then checking to see which floor you want to get to – and you may have already been on it before you started.

> In a `do` loop the body of the loop is always executed at least once. It is a facility that needs to be used with caution.

4.5 Iterating over the input data

All of the examples so far in this chapter have used loops to control calculation. What happens if we want to use a loop to process multiple sets of input data? Can we use a `scanf` inside a loop?

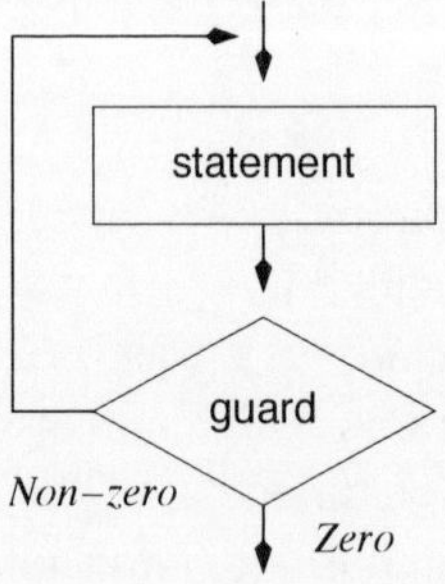

Figure 4.11: Execution flow through a `do` statement.

The answer to this question is, of course, yes. Figure 4.12 shows a program fragment that repeatedly reads numbers from the input, stopping only when the `scanf` fails. (Recall that the value returned by `scanf` is the number of items successfully read.) On the way through, each number read is processed – in the case of Figure 4.12, to simply find the maximum value and report it. In this particular example an initial value is read outside the loop, a technique known as *pump priming* or *pre-reading*. The pre-read is necessary because it is inappropriate to try and compute the maximum over an empty set of values, whereas (looking back at Figure 1.2 on page 8, which also includes a read loop) the sum of an empty set can be computed.

To indicate to the program that no more input is going to be provided from the keyboard, it is necessary to be able to provide an *end of file* indication. In most Unix shells, including in MacOS terminal windows, this is done by typing "control-D" after a newline, or two consecutive control-D characters if the last character in the input is not a newline character. On Windows machines it again depends on the shell being used to handle the command-line, but "control-Z" followed by "enter" is a common combination used to denote end of file. On most Unix shells "control-Z" suspends the current program without terminating it, and returning to the shell, so you do need to be aware of the distinction. Finally, note that most shells recognize "control-C" as a request that a running program be terminated. You will need this command if you suspect your program has an infinite loop.

There are also times when it is desirable to process the input stream character by character. This could be done using a "`%c`" format control in a `scanf`, but because it is a common operation, C provides another way of dealing with character input

```
printf("Enter values, control-D to end: ");
if (scanf("%d", &next)!=1) {
    printf("\nNo data entered\n");
    exit(EXIT_FAILURE);
}
n = 1;
max = next;
/* read further values and track the maximum */
while (scanf("%d", &next)==1) {
    if (next>max) {
        max = next;
    }
    n += 1;
}
printf("%d values read, maximum is %d\n", n, max);
```

```
mac: ./readloop1
Enter values, control-D to end: 1 2 3 2 6 5 27 15 4
^D
9 values read, maximum is 27
```

Figure 4.12: Use of `scanf` in a loop to process a set of input items of arbitrary size. The lower box shows an execution of the program fragment in the upper box.

```
    int ch, incomment=0, newlinelast=1;
    while ((ch=getchar()) != EOF) {
        if (ch == 'C' && newlinelast) {
            incomment = 1;
        }
        if (!incomment) {
            putchar(ch);
        }
        if (ch == '\n') {
            incomment = 0;
            newlinelast = 1;
        } else {
            newlinelast = 0;
        }
    }
```

```
mac: more data.txt
C a comment in the first line
but no Comment here
    or here
C but there is one here
mac: ./fortcomm < data.txt
but no Comment here
    or here
```

Figure 4.13: Use of `getchar` and `putchar` to process the input stream character by character. The program fragment removes lines that start with an uppercase "C". The lower box shows an execution of the program fragment in the upper box.

and output – the functions `getchar` and `putchar`. To show the use of these two functions, suppose that we are required to write a program that deletes all of the lines in a file that start with an uppercase "C". (This is the convention for indicating comments in Fortran programs.) Figure 4.13 shows a program fragment that achieves this goal. The first character of each line is the character after the previous newline character; and a newline always ends a comment.

Note the loop guard, and the way in which the guard both assigns to variable `ch` the integer ASCII value of the next input character, and then also tests to see if the assignment resulted in a valid value. This is one situation in which assignment side effects can be both tolerated and exploited, to make a recipe for reading that all C programmers know and use.

The predefined constant `EOF` takes on a value outside the ASCII set, and in most implementations has the value -1. The need to represent this non-character is why `ch` must be declared to be an `int` rather than a `char`.

> Functions `getchar` and `putchar` allow processing of the input as a stream of characters. The variable used must be declared to be an `int` in order for end of file value `EOF` to be manipulated properly.

And now for a challenge. Earlier in this book you saw a C program that read a set of numbers and printed out their sum. Without looking back at page 8, can you write an equivalent program using the C programming techniques described so far? If you can, you are doing well; if you can't, you should review Chapters 1, 2, and 3, before proceeding to the next chapter. Now might also be a good time to implement a solution to Exercise 1.3 on page 12.

Exercises

4.1 Trace the action of these loops, and determine the values printed out by each of the `printf` statements. Assume that all variables have been declared to be of type `int`. Be careful with the last two – they illustrate two common errors.

a.
```
for (i=0; i<20; i=i+3) {
        printf("%2d\n", i);
}
```

b.
```
for (i=1; i<2000000; i=2*i) {
        printf("%7d\n", i);
}
```

c.
```
sum = 0;
for (i=1; i<10; i++) {
    sum = sum+i;
    printf("S(%2d) - %2d\n", i, sum);
}
```

d.
```
for (i=0; i<8; i++) {
    for (j=i+1; j<8; j+=3) {
        printf("i=%d, j=%d\n", i, j);
    }
}
```

e.
```
for (i=0; i<8; i++) {
    for (j=i+1; j<8; j+=3) {
        if (i+j==7) {
            break;
        }
        printf("i=%d, j=%d\n", i, j);
    }
}
```

f.
```
j = 5;
for (i=0; i<j; i++) ; {
    printf("i=%d, j=%d\n", i, j);
}
```

g.
```
j = 5;
for (i=0; i<j; j++) {
    printf("i=%d, j=%d\n", i, j);
}
```

4.2 Give a general construction that shows how any `do` statement can be converted into an equivalent `while` statement.

4.3 The *Fibonacci numbers* have a range of interesting uses in Mathematics and Computer Science. For example, suppose that a single mould spore falls onto a loaf of bread. Suppose also that 48 hours after a spore is created, it is able to clone itself, and create a further fresh one every 24 hours thereafter. Finally. suppose also that 48 hours after it is created each new spore also starts cloning a fresh spore every day.

At the end of the first and second days there will be 1 spore present; by the end of the third day it has cloned and there will be 2; by the end of the fourth day the original spore has cloned again and there will be 3; by the end of the fifth day there will be 5, because two spores are now actively cloning; by the end of the sixth day there will be 8; and so on. In general, if $F(n)$ is the number of spores present at the end of the nth day, then $F(1) = 1$, $F(2) = 1$, and then $F(n) = F(n-1) + F(n-2)$ thereafter.

Write a program that prints out the number of spores present at the end of each day. Stop when the number of spores exceeds ten million.

4.4 Write a program that generates a table of the printable ASCII character set. The first printable character is blank, " ", with the integer value 32, and the last is the tilde character, "~", with integer value 126. Laying out the table in rows of eight shows the relationship between the uppercase letters and the lowercase letters:

```
        +0   +1   +2   +3   +4   +5   +6   +7
     +---------------------------------------
  32 |         !    "    #    $    %    &    '
  40 |    (    )    *    +    ,    -    .    /
  48 |    0    1    2    3    4    5    6    7
  56 |    8    9    :    ;    <    =    >    ?
  64 |    @    A    B    C    D    E    F    G
  72 |    H    I    J    K    L    M    N    O
  80 |    P    Q    R    S    T    U    V    W
  88 |    X    Y    Z    [    \    ]    ^    _
  96 |    `    a    b    c    d    e    f    g
 104 |    h    i    j    k    l    m    n    o
 112 |    p    q    r    s    t    u    v    w
 120 |    x    y    z    {    |    }    ~
```

Hint: start with a relatively simple program that writes the correct characters, and only when you have that program operating should you start working on getting the formatting right. Note also that the computation required is essentially one dimensional, so the program in Figure 4.9 on page 54 is a posible starting point.

4.5 Write a program that reads a sequence of integers and draws a simple graph. Assume that all of the values read are between 1 and 70. For example:

```
mac: ./grapher
Enter numbers: 20 25 30 28 26 22 17 14 13
^D
20 |********************
25 |*************************
30 |******************************
28 |****************************
26 |**************************
22 |**********************
17 |*****************
14 |**************
13 |*************
```

4.6 Write a program that counts the number of characters and lines in the input:

```
mac: ./mywc
Enter text:
Mary had a little lamb,
little lamb, little lamb;
Mary had a little lamb,
its fleece was white as snow.
^D
Lines:       4
Chars:     104
mac: ./mywc < mywc.c
Enter text:
Lines:      20
Chars:     314
```

Hint: use `getchar` to process one character at a time. Look for "`\n`" characters, and count them to determine the number of lines in the input.

4.7 Modify the program you wrote for the previous question so that it also counts the number of words in the input stream. You first need to decide on a suitable definition of what is meant by a "word". You program should then use a flag variable `inaword` that records whether the last character was part of a word. Count the number of times `inaword` gets changed from false to true.

4.8 Extend the program in Figure 4.9 on page 54 so that a value `nmax` is read, and each number between one and `nmax` is used as the seed to start the $3n + 1$ computation. Report the length of the longest cycle generated, and the seed that started that cycle. For example, when `nmax` is set to 50, the longest sequence is the one that starts at 27. It is the first one to take more than 100 cycles, and it passes through the value $9{,}232$ before converging. The first cycle of length greater than 200 starts at 2,463, and is of length 208; it grows as large as $250{,}504$ before diminishing back to one.

4.9 Using the program fragment shown in Figure 4.10 on page 55 as a starting point, write a program `nextprime` that calculates the next prime number after a given value:

```
mac: ./nextprime
Enter an integer value: 8
The next prime is     : 11
mac: ./nextprime
Enter an integer value: 87654321
The next prime is     : 87654337
```

4.10 As was noted in Chapter 1, the original 1989/1990 ANSI/ISO C standard only permits `/* */` style comments, whereas the 1999 ISO standard also provides for line-oriented comments starting with a `//` combination.

Starting with the program shown in Figure 4.13 on page 58, write a program that replaces each C99-style comment in the input text by an equivalent ANSI C comment. That is, each `//` pair that commences a comment should be replaced by `/*`, and then a `*/` combination should be inserted immediately prior to the next newline character.

4.11 The program you wrote for Exercise 4.10 probably doesn't work if a line contains `//` and then includes a `*/` combination as part of the comment.

Make further modifications so that all `/*` and `*/` combinations within any existing `//` comments are removed as part of the conversion process.

4.12 (*For a challenge*) Write a program that strips out ANSI C comments, so that all characters between `/*` and `*/` pairs are removed, including the four characters that make up the comment delimiters. For example, on the input file:

```
/* comment */ text /* comment * with an asterisk
that spans two lines */
a slash can appear / and might / or might // not ///*
start a comment */
and an */ can also appear anywhere outside
a comment **/***////*/**/*//*/ what does/* it */ mean?
```

your program should produce exactly this output:

```
 text
a slash can appear / and might / or might // not //
and an */ can also appear anywhere outside
a comment **//*/ mean?
```

Chapter 5

Getting Started with Functions

Three important programming techniques have now been introduced:

- Calculation – Chapter 2 described the fundamental arithmetic operations available in C, and the numeric data types they manipulate;
- Selection – Chapter 3 described the facilities provided by C for choosing alternative execution paths, and showed how to construct guards to enable those choices to be made; and
- Iteration – Chapter 4 examined the C looping structures, and gave examples that showed the notion of convergence towards a desired goal.

Taken together, these three concepts give great problem-solving power. Even the most complex programs – for example, the navigational software inside a GPS device – are composed using calculation, selection, and iteration.

But there is a fourth tool provided by all modern programming languages, including C, that has not yet been discussed:

- Abstraction – the process of creating self-contained units of software that allow the solutions to tasks to be parameterized, and hence made general-purpose.

In C, abstraction is provided by *functions*, the topic of this chapter.

> There are four important facets to all problem solving and programming tasks: calculation, selection, iteration, and abstraction.

5.1 Abstraction

Although it may sound rather contradictory, the best way to appreciate the role of abstraction is through a concrete example. Consider again the program shown in Figure 4.6 on page 51. That program uses two nested loops to control the two-dimensional structure of a table. Values for both `year` and `rate` are set, and then a table entry that is dependent upon those two values is calculated. The loops that set those two values are directly related to the principal task the program is solving

```
double
savings_plan(double amount, double ann_rate, int years) {
    int month;
    double monthly_mult, balance=0.0;
    monthly_mult = 1.00 + (ann_rate/100.00)/12;
    for (month=1; month<=12*years; month++) {
        balance *= monthly_mult;
        balance += amount;
    }
    return balance;
}
```

Figure 5.1: Function to calculate the result of a regular savings plan.

– which is constructing a table of values. But the innermost six lines, the ones following the "compute one value" comment, are independent of the table. They work out how much money would be accumulated for a given `rate`, `year`, and `MONTHLY` amount, and represent a *general* calculation that will be useful in other contexts too. Calculating those values in place also makes the program structure more complex than is desirable – three nested loops is always difficult to manage.

Now imagine this program as part of a banking environment. Variants of the same savings computation might be required in dozens of different programs, and while duplicating the code that many times would be possible, it would mean that every one of those programs took on an additional level of complexity. Also, imagine the headaches if a mistake was found in the loop, and it became necessary to search for every place that the code had been copied to, in order to apply a correction.

It would be much better if code fragments common to more than one application – or indeed, code fragments required more than once in even a single program – could be *abstracted*, and written only once. That is what a *function* does. Figure 5.1 shows the result. The first two lines are a *type declaration* that state that this function takes three *arguments*: a `double`, by the name of `amount`; another `double`, by the name of `ann_rate`; and then an `int`, by the name of `years`. The first type in the declaration, before the name of the function (which in the example is `savings_plan`), indicates that when the function has done something with the three values passed as arguments, it returns a value that is a `double`.

The next two lines declare three *local variables*, to be manipulated within the function, making a total of six variables available in the function. The *body* of the function follows the declarations, and indicates how the values supplied via variables `amount`, `ann_rate`, and `years` should be combined to calculate the required result. The last line of the function is a `return` statement. The expression associated with the `return` is passed back to the calling expression as the value of the function. In function `savings_plan`, the value returned is the final value of `balance`.

> A function has several components: a declaration for the return and argument types; local variable declarations; a body; and usually at least one `return` statement.

A function definition is passive, and the function does nothing on its own. To have it execute, a function must be *called*, and suitable argument values passed in to be used while it executes. For example, to use function savingsplan from the program in Figure 4.5 on page 50, the innermost loop would be replaced by:

```
balance = savings_plan(MONTHLY, rate, year)
```

It would even be possible to dispense with the variable balance, and just use

```
printf("%5.0f   ", savings_plan(MONTHLY, rate, year));
```

as the sole statement inside the doubly nested loop. That is, when supplied with three type-matching arguments, function savings_plan has exactly the same status in a program as a declared variable of type double, and can be used in the same places as a variable would be used, and in the same ways.

The value of the function is worked out in the following stages:

- The values of the argument expressions are calculated, evaluated using the context applicable at the point of call.
- Those values are assigned as the initial values of the corresponding argument variables listed in the type declaration for the function, with any necessary assignment type conversions carried out.
- The body of the function is executed, through until a return statement is reached.

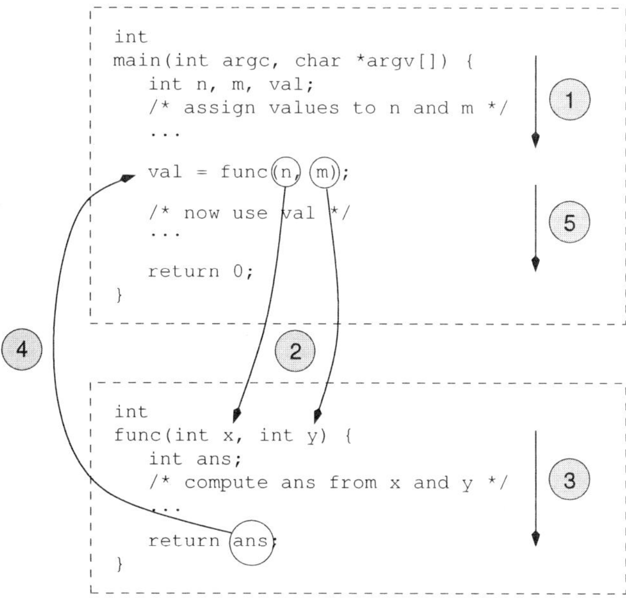

Figure 5.2: Sequence of operations that takes place when a function is called: (1) execution commences in the main program; (2) arguments are evaluated, and copied into function's argument variables; (3) function executes; (4) value is returned from the function to the calling environment as function ends; (5) execution is resumed in the calling environment.

- The expression associated with the `return` statement is calculated, evaluated using the context within the function.
- That value is passed back to the point from which the function was called.
- All local and argument variables in the function are destroyed.

Figure 5.2 illustrates this process. Each time the function name is used, the body of the function is executed, using whatever incoming values are passed to the argument variables. That is, instead of duplicating the code when similar tasks are to be carried out on different values, a function is created, and called multiple times, each time passing in different values as the arguments.

> When a function is called, the values of the argument expressions are assigned to the corresponding argument variables. The body of the function is then executed. When a `return` is encountered, a value is passed back to the point from which the function was called.

Figure 5.3 shows the use of the function defined in Figure 5.1. In this program the user is asked to enter three starting values, and the program makes three calls to `savings_plan` to show what happens to the final balance if the estimate of future interest rates is correct, a little under, and a little over.

To allow the C system to set up the correct communications with the function – both sending values in as arguments, and receiving a value back as the result of executing the function – its type must be declared *before* it is called. This is the purpose of the line after the `#include` line in Figure 5.3. No body is required in such a function *prototype*, and the semi-colon at the end of the argument list indicates that it is purely a type declaration, and not an actual definition of the function. Functions need only be defined once, but must be declared in every C program file in which they are going to be used.

> A function prototype declares the types involved in a function, and should be provided before any reference is made to the function.

5.2 Compilation with functions

How does the function get combined with the program wishing to call it? There are several ways. The easiest, and when programming at the introductory level presumed for most of this book, the commonest way, is to include the full definition of the function in the same file as the program that wishes to call it. Provided that a type declaration for the function – either as part of the function definition, or via a separate prototype – appears in the file before any references to it in other functions or in the `main` function, the correct linkage will be made when the function is called.

In practice this means that if prototypes for all functions are listed before any functions are defined, then their definitions can appear in any order, and can appear either after the definition of the `main` function, or before it. Figure 5.4 shows a complete program that includes a function `isprime`, derived from another program

```
/* Calculate the result of a regular savings plan.
*/
#include <stdio.h>

double savings_plan(double amount,
        double ann_rate, int years);

int
main(int argc, char *argv[]) {
    int years;
    double rate, per_month, answer;

    /* read in values to be processed */
    printf("Enter number of years    : ");
    scanf("%d", &years);
    printf("Enter annual rate (%%)    : ");
    scanf("%lf", &rate);
    printf("Enter monthly amount     : $");
    scanf("%lf", &per_month);

    /* and print out the desired answers */
    printf("Saving $%.0f per month for %d years\n",
            per_month, years);
    answer = savings_plan(per_month, rate-1, years);
    printf("\tat %.1f%% per year: $%.0f\n", rate-1, answer);
    answer = savings_plan(per_month, rate  , years);
    printf("\tat %.1f%% per year: $%.0f\n", rate  , answer);
    answer = savings_plan(per_month, rate+1, years);
    printf("\tat %.1f%% per year: $%.0f\n", rate+1, answer);
    return 0;
}
```

```
mac: ./savingsfunc
Enter number of years    : 40
Enter annual rate (%)    : 4.5
Enter monthly amount     : $200
Saving $200 per month for 40 years
        at 3.5% per year: $208933
        at 4.5% per year: $268230
        at 5.5% per year: $348208
```

Figure 5.3: Making use of the function `savings_plan` defined in Figure 5.1. The lower box shows the program being executed.

first developed in Chapter 4. In this example, the function is defined after the `main` function, with a prototype declaration prior to the `main` function.

Function `isprime` takes a single `int` argument, and returns a true/false `int` flag to indicate whether or not the argument is a prime number. This version also is correct for the special case when `n` is one.

There are three points to note in Figure 5.4. The first is that `return` statements can appear anywhere in a function, and in function `isprime` serve the role of the

```
/* Read a number and determine if it is prime.
*/
#include <stdio.h>

int isprime(int n);

int
main(int argc, char *argv[]) {
    int n;
    printf("Enter a number n: ");
    scanf("%d", &n);
    if (isprime(n)) {
        printf("%d is a prime number\n", n);
    } else {
        printf("%d is not a prime number\n", n);
    }
    return 0;
}

/* Determine whether n is prime. */
int
isprime(int n) {
    int divisor;
    if (n<2) {
        return 0;
    }
    for (divisor=2; divisor*divisor<=n; divisor++) {
            if (n%divisor==0) {
                /* factor found, so can't be prime */
                return 0;
            }
    }
    /* no factors, so must be prime */
    return 1;
}
```

Figure 5.4: A function `isprime`, and a `main` function that calls it. This program is complete within a single file.

`break` statement that was used in the earlier version of this computation (Figure 4.10 on page 55), terminating both the loop and the function. The second observation is that the returned value is used in place of the explicit `isprime` flag of the previous version. The third observation is that the calling program in Figure 5.4 is unable to access the value of the local variable `divisor` the way it did in Figure 4.10, and it is not possible for the program to print out a pair of factors of `n`. A function can only return a single value; and all local variables and argument variables are discarded at the time the function returns. If the function is then called a second time, the argument variables are re-initialized to the new argument expressions, and the local variables are recreated in an uninitialized state. They do *not* resume their final values from the previous call to that function.

```
mac: ls
func.c    prog.c
mac: gcc -Wall -ansi -c func.c
mac: gcc -Wall -ansi -c prog.c
mac: ls
func.c    func.o    prog.c    prog.o
mac: gcc -Wall -o prog prog.o func.o
mac: ls
func.c    func.o    prog      prog.c    prog.o
mac: ./prog
<<< whatever the program does >>>
mac:
```

Figure 5.5: Example showing separate compilation. After the three `gcc` commands, the file `prog` contains a self-contained and executable program. Neither `func.o` nor `prog.o` can be executed.

> The simplest way to manage a program that uses functions is to put all components of the program into a single file and then compile that file.

When a program is more complex, or when several programs are sharing a common pool of useful functions, inserting the text of the function definition in each file that needs it is wasteful. To avoid the redundancy, *separate compilation* is used. Figure 5.5 shows how this works, assuming (as in Section 1.3) that the `gcc` compiler is available. Two source files are manipulated in the interaction shown in the figure: `func.c`, which is assumed to contain one or more function definitions; and file `prog.c`, which is assumed to contain a program that uses those functions. For a program to be executable once it is compiled, whether it is all in a single file or spread across multiple files, exactly one `main` function should be present.

In the example, each of the two C files is first compiled separately. Use of the `-c` flag to the C compiler instructs it to simply compile the code in the file to make an *object file* (with a "`.o`" extension), without attempting to locate functions that are used but not defined. The third `gcc` instruction then combines the two "`.o`" files to build an executable program called `prog`. The complete compilation could also have been achieved using a single command-line:

```
gcc -Wall -ansi -o prog prog.c func.c
```

> Separate compilation allows efficient reuse of software modules. Each source file contains a group of logically related functions, and is compiled independently of other modules. A final linking step then creates the executable program.

If separate compilation is used, keeping track of which files have been edited can become a chore. And in a big program, split over a large number of separate source files, it is faster to only recompile files that have been edited since the last compilation, and then rebuild the final executable. Fortunately, there is a tool to help with this, called `make`, that examines the "last modified" time-stamps on a set of files and determines which components need recompilation. It is not possible to provide an explanation of make here, but when you start working with bigger programs, you are going to need to know about it, and how to structure the makefile that controls the process.

5.3 Library functions

If a collection of functions is to be used frequently, or in a wide range of programs, or by a wide range of different users, it is built into a *library*. Once a library of functions has been created, it can be used by any program that seeks to call a function in it, without the source code of that function needing to be recompiled.

Part of being a good C programmer is knowing how to use the various libraries that are provided as part of the standard C environment. Figure 5.6 shows a simple program that makes use of the library of mathematical functions. There are two points to be noted. First, another #include line is required – if functions from the math library are to be used, the compiler must know their types, and rather than have each

```
/* Show the use of math library functions and constants.
*/
#include <stdio.h>
#include <math.h>

int
main(int argc, char *argv[]) {
    double x;
    printf("Enter a value for x: ");
    scanf("%lf", &x);
    printf("sin(x)  = %.15f\n", sin(x));
    printf("log(x)  = %.15f\n", log(x));
    printf("fabs(x) = %.15f\n", fabs(x));
    printf("sqrt(x) = %.15f\n", sqrt(x));
    printf("M_PI    = %.15f\n", M_PI);
    printf("M_SQRT2 = %.15f\n", M_SQRT2);
    return 0;
}
```

```
mac: gcc -Wall -o usemathlib usemathlib.c -lm
mac: ./usemathlib
Enter a value for x: 2.0
sin(x)  = 0.909297426825682
log(x)  = 0.693147180559945
fabs(x) = 2.000000000000000
sqrt(x) = 1.414213562373095
M_PI    = 3.141592653589793
M_SQRT2 = 1.414213562373095
```

Figure 5.6: Using the functions and constants provided in the C mathematics library. The constants M_PI and M_SQRT2 are provided in many C systems, but are not part of the ANSI standard C.

programmer enter type declarations, prototypes are provided in a central file `math.h` installed as part of the C system. The `#include` directive instructs the compiler to go and read that file before reading any more of your program. Once the `#include` line has been processed by the compiler, a large set of mathematical functions is available for you to use in your program.

You can also read that file – after all, it just contains C program text. On many Unix machines the standard *header files* are in the directory `/usr/include/` (but might be a different directory on your computer). In the file `math.h` in that directory you will find a lot of rather complex C, and probably not any prototypes that you will recognize – they are in another file that in turn gets included from this one. But what you should be able to find (search with your editor) are lines like these three:

```
#define M_PI            3.14159265358979323846  /* pi */
#define M_PI_2          1.57079632679489661923  /* pi/2 */
#define M_PI_4          0.78539816339744830962  /* pi/4 */
```

They are there to provide precise numeric values for some of the commonly used mathematical constants. It is convenient to have these constants available, but be warned: they are not part of the ANSI C standard, and if you compile the program in Figure 5.6 with the `-ansi` command-line flag in `gcc`, error messages may arise, because strictly speaking they are not part of the ANSI/ISO 1989/1990 standard.

The second point to note in Figure 5.6 is the use of the `-lm` flag at the end of the `gcc` compilation line. Including the math library prototypes does not make the compiled definitions of those functions available; that has to be done when the executable is being built. Appending the `-lm` option tells `gcc` to make the compiled versions of the math functions available, so that the ones required can be linked in to the executable.

There is a large number of functions available, and Figure 5.6 shows the use of just a few of them, each doing the obvious job. Table 5.1 lists some (but still not all) of the other functions and constants provided in the math library. On a Unix or MacOS terminal shell you can find out details of any library functions – what the arguments are, what restrictions there are on their use, what bugs have been identified – using the Unix `man` command. For example, `man sqrt` provides information about the `sqrt` function, and `man getchar` provides a synopsis of the `getchar` function. Descriptions of library functions also appear in many locations on the internet.

> Libraries of functions are provided with every C system. The mathematics library contains useful constants and functions, and is described by the `math.h` header file, and linked using the `-lm` command-line flag.

Another useful library is described by `ctype.h`. This library includes a suite of functions called `isalpha`, `isascii`, `isdigit`, `islower`, `isspace`, `isupper`, and so on, each of which takes an `int` argument representing a character value, and returns true or false to indicate whether or not that character is of the type being queried. The same library also includes two other functions that are useful: `toupper(c)`, which returns the uppercase equivalent of character `c`, if `c` is a lowercase alphabetic

Function or constant	Purpose
`int abs(int n)`	Absolute value (integer)
`double acos(double x)`	Inverse cosine
`double asin(double x)`	Inverse sine
`double atan(double x)`	Inverse tangent
`double cos(double x)`	Cosine
`double exp(double x)`	Raise e to the power of `x`
`double fabs(double x)`	Absolute value (double)
`double log(double x)`	Logarithm base e
`double pow(double b, double x)`	Raise `b` to the power of `x`
`double sin(double x)`	Sine
`double sqrt(double x)`	Square root
`double tan(double) x`	Tangent
`double M_E`	The value of e
`double M_PI`	The value of π
`double M_SQRT2`	The value of $\sqrt{2}$

Table 5.1: A subset of the functions and constants provided in the C math library. The three constants are not part of the ANSI C standard.

character; and `tolower`, which does the reverse transformation. Exercise 5.7 on page 80 asks you to write two of the functions described by `ctype.h`.

5.4 Generalizing the abstraction

In some situations it is quite clear what task a function should perform, and what the arguments to that function should be. Function `isprime` in Figure 5.4 falls into this category – there is no other sensible way of constructing the interface between the calling program and the function.

In other cases the interface may not be so clear cut, and a design decision is required. Consider the savings plan example again. Suppose that in the bank's investment division we also wish to provide financial estimates to people who already have some money saved, and, in the mortgage division of the bank, we wish to advise people who currently owe the bank money. The function in Figure 5.1 on page 64 assumes that the savings process starts with a zero balance, and cannot be used in either of these two scenarios.

However, with further abstraction, and the addition of another argument, a more versatile function can be constructed. Figure 5.7 shows this extension. Now an initial (positive or negative) account balance is provided as an argument. Adding another argument in this way makes the function more general, and if that generality is not required in some applications, zero can just be passed as an argument.

The revised function assumes that the bank pays the same rate of interest on savings as it charges on loans, which is clearly not correct. So yet another argument should probably be added, being the interest rate charged on debit balances, so that

```
double
savings_plan(double initial, double amount,
        double ann_rate, int years) {
    int month;
    double monthly_mult, balance = initial;
    monthly_mult = 1.00 + (ann_rate/100.00)/12;
    for (month=1; month<=12*years; month++) {
        balance *= monthly_mult;
        balance += amount;
    }
    return balance;
}
```

```
mac: ./savingsfuncgen
Enter number of years     : 25
Enter annual rate %       : 7
Enter monthly amount      : $1250
Enter initial balance     : $-175000
Saving $-175000 plus $1250 per month for 25 years
        at 6.0% per year: $84873
        at 7.0% per year: $10641
        at 8.0% per year: $-95748
```

Figure 5.7: A generalized version of function `savings_plan`. The lower box shows an execution using a modified version (not shown) of the program in Figure 5.3. Paying $1,250 per month for 25 years against a $175,000 mortgage is sufficient if the interest rate stays at 7%, but is problematic if interest rates rise by one percent.

it can be greater than the interest rate paid on credit balances. Adding such a fifth argument again adds generality – the two rates can be made the same if necessary, and made different if that is what is required.

As a rule of thumb, the more arguments a function is passed, the more general-purpose the function can be.

There is one final point to be made with regard to the functions: modifying an argument variable within the function has no effect whatsoever on the value passed as an argument, even if that argument expression happens to be a single variable, and even if that variable happens to have the same name as the corresponding argument variable within the function. It is the *value* of the argument expression that is passed in to the argument variable via the initial assignment, and all changes to that variable are lost when the function terminates. The only way changes to an argument or local variable can be preserved is if the final value of that variable is passed back via a `return` statement. This seems very restrictive. But the next chapter describes a mechanism for bypassing this constraint without actually violating it.

Changes made to argument variables are not reflected in the argument expressions used to call the function, even when the argument expression is a single variable.

5.5 Recursion

There is one aspect of functions that is rather surprising when it is first encountered, which is that they can replace iteration in programs. Indeed, this flexibility is sufficiently general that some languages the functional and logic families have no explicit looping constructs at all, and rely entirely upon functions to obtain iteration.

To see how a function can replace iteration, consider the two functions in Figure 5.8. Both calculate the same value, namely, the nth triangle number $T(n) = 1+2+\cdots+(n-1)+n$. The first function, `t_itr` uses direct iteration to compute the required sum, expressed as a `for` loop.

The second function is the interesting one. It is based upon the realization that the function $T(n)$ can also be defined as a recurrence, with a base case given by $T(0) = 0$, and an inductive case given by $T(n) = n + T(n-1)$. This recurrence relation translates into the function `t_rec` in Figure 5.8. And the surprise is that the function calls itself. Such a function is said to be *recursive*.

> A recursive function is one which, as part of its definition, makes reference to itself.

The trick to understanding how this can possibly work is to note that, at each recursive call, the argument expression for the next call is one less than the current argument variable. And when the argument variable has the value zero, an answer of zero is immediately returned, without any computation being required. So if `n` is a positive integer, the recursion will always "bottom out" at some point, and arrive at the base case in the first branch of the `if` statement. Once that happens, answers start getting returned. The bottoming-out process is equivalent to the spiraling convergence that was discussed in Chapter 4 in connection with loops. Just as a loop must

```
/* Calculate the n'th triangle number using iteration. */
int
t_itr(int n) {
    int sum, i;
    sum = 0;
    for (i=1; i<=n; i++) {
        sum += i;
    }
    return sum;
}

/* Calculate the n'th triangle number using recursion. */
int
t_rec(int n) {
    if (n==0) {
        return 0;
    } else {
        return n + t_rec(n-1);
    }
}
```

Figure 5.8: Iterative and recursive functions for summing the numbers from 1 to `n`.

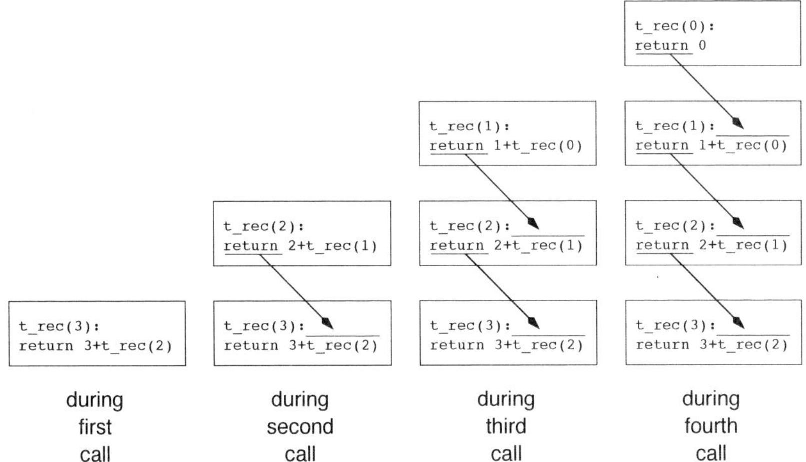

Figure 5.9: Tracing the sequence of stack frames built up during the evaluation of `t_rec(3)`.

converge towards the negation of its guard, so too a recursive function must converge towards its base case at each recursion.

To see how recursion is implemented, suppose `t_rec(3)` is to be evaluated. The argument `n` is 3, and differs from zero, so the second branch of the `if` is taken, and the expression `3+t_rec(2)` is to be returned. But to evaluate it, `t_rec(2)` must be computed. So the function starts executing again, using variables that have the same names as in the first execution, but are stored in a different part of memory. The first execution is temporarily suspended, and the second execution commenced on top of it, in a *stack* of pending tasks.

In the second call, the argument `n` is 2, which again differs from zero, so the second branch of the `if` is taken, and the expression `2+t_rec(1)` is to be evaluated and returned. So the function starts executing for a third time, and another call is stacked on top of the second, which is suspended and stacked on top of the first call, which is also still suspended.

In the third call, the argument `n` is 1, and differs from zero, so the second branch of the `if` is taken for a third time, and the expression `1+t_rec(0)` must be calculated and returned. But to do so requires that `t_rec(0)` be evaluated, so the function starts executing for a fourth time, and a fourth call is stacked on top of the third. Figure 5.9 shows how the stack of pending executions builds up frame by frame until this point.

In the fourth call, the argument `n` is 0, and the first branch of the `if` statement is selected. So the `return` statement is executed; the fourth call terminates; its stack frame is peeled off the stack and discarded; and the value 0 returned to the third call.

On receipt of the returned 0, the third call can now add it to the waiting 1, and can return 1 as its value. Another stack frame is popped off the stack, and the second call to `t_rec`, which is now once again at the top of the stack, is resumed, with the value 1 available to be added to the 2 that has been waiting.

That makes the number 3 available to be returned to the first call, and another frame is popped off the stack. Now the original call is resumed, and the arriving 3 added to the 3 that has been waiting, and the number 6 returned to whatever place that very first call was made from. It seems an incredibly laborious process, just to work out $3+2+1+0$. But remember, computers are good at repetitive calculations; and recursive functions are still very fast in practice.

The original call might have been as part of an evaluation of `t_rec(4)`, which was perhaps called from `t_rec(5)`, and so on. This is an important point – when it is executing, a function does not have any knowledge of where it was called from, or how deep the execution stack of pending evaluations is below it. Each call just has to complete its own assigned task, which is dictated solely by statements in the function definition and the arguments it was supplied with. Carrying out that task may involve suspensions while other functions are called and other stack frames are pushed on top, but eventually this function will be back on top of the stack, and will be executed through to completion and a `return` statement. At that moment its stack frame is popped and discarded, and a value, plus a wake-up signal, sent back to the function execution that has been patiently sitting just underneath it on the stack.

> Each time a function is called a new stack frame for that function is pushed onto a stack of such records. When the function returns, its frame is popped off the stack, and the function corresponding to the stack frame underneath it is resumed.

One last comment: the recursive function discussed here, and the one considered in Exercise 5.13 below, are rather trivial – looking at them, it may be hard for you to see why recursion is such an exciting possibility. Indeed, you are probably aware that it is also possible to calculate $T(n)$ directly using the closed form $T(n) = n(n+1)/2$. Most other recurrence relations also have such a closed form. But sometimes finding a closed form can be difficult, and from a time effectiveness point of view, it may be better to write a recursive function that evaluates the specific values required, than to try and mathematically solve the general case, or even find an iterative calculation. Other examples of recursive functions appear later in this book, and in some of them the advantage of a recursive solution is quite overwhelming. Until then you have to trust that recursion is indeed an important technique in computing, and accept that this section is intended to do nothing more than start you thinking about the topic.

> Recursion is an important technique in programming. In some languages function recursion replaces explicit iterative control structures.

5.6 Case study: Calculating cube roots

Suppose that you need to calculate cube roots in a program. (And that you are unaware that the cube root of a value v can be obtained by calculating $v^{1/3}$.) You approach a mathematician friend who knows about the Newton Raphson method for finding roots of equations, and are told that if x is an approximation of the cube root of v, then $x' = (2x + v/x^2)/3$ is a better approximation. Your friend also tells you that, for the range of values v you are interested in, which is between $10^{-6} \leq |v| \leq 10^{6}$, a total of 25 iterations of this formula is enough to give good accuracy in the final approximation, starting from $x = 1.0$. Try the following exercise now, before going on to look at the solution:

> Write a function `cube_root` that receives a `double` argument and calculates and returns an approximate cube root for it. You should also write a main program that allows you to test your function.

In this description the number of iterations to be performed is an externally specified constant. An alternative – and more general – approach is to add an `int` argument to the function to limit the number of iterations to be performed, and pass in the constant 25 for use in this particular application.

Figure 5.10 shows a function that meets this specification. Three constants are defined as part of the module. Constants `CUBE_LOWER` and `CUBE_UPPER` might also be usefully employed in the main program that calls this function – a different method might be used for extreme values, for example.

Computing a fixed number of iterations of a converging approximation is risky, especially so when the arithmetic being undertaken is floating point, and the impact of accumulated rounding effects hard to quantify. It is more sensible to keep iterating until either a "good" answer has been found, where good is expressed as an accuracy constraint; or until it is clear that the accuracy constraint is too demanding, and that no answer that accurate can be identified. Exercise 5.8 on page 81 explores this issue further, and more examples of approximate computations appear in Chapter 9.

```
#define CUBE_LOWER 1e-6
#define CUBE_UPPER 1e+6
#define CUBE_ITERATIONS 25

/* Return an approximate cube root calculated
   by a converging iterative mechanism.
*/
double
cube_root(double v) {
    double next=1.0;
    int i;
    if (fabs(v)<CUBE_LOWER || fabs(v)>CUBE_UPPER) {
        printf("Warning: cube root may be inaccurate\n");
    }
    for (i=0; i<CUBE_ITERATIONS; i++) {
        next = (2*next + v/(next*next))/3;
    }
    return next;
}
```

Figure 5.10: Calculating an approximate cube root using a converging iteration based upon the Newton Raphson approximation. More than 25 iterations might be required for very large or very small values.

```
#include <stdio.h>
#include <math.h>

double cube_root(double v);

int
main(int argc, char *argv[]) {
    double val, croot;
    printf("Enter a value: ");
    while (scanf("%lf", &val)==1) {
        croot = cube_root(val);
        printf("%16.9e, croot=%16.9e, ^3=%16.9e\n",
            val, croot, croot*croot*croot);
        printf("Enter a value: ");
    }
    return 0;
}

double
cube_root(double v) {
    /* just return any old value at first... */
    return 1.0;
}
```

Figure 5.11: Scaffolding and stub for a simple function.

5.7 Testing functions and programs

Figure 5.11 shows a simple program intended solely to call the function described in Figure 5.10, and allow it to be tested and debugged. Such a program is called *scaffolding*, like the scaffolding that surrounds a building site while work is in progress.

Figure 5.11 also shows a place holder for a function – just a declaration, and a `return` statement – that is included so that the main program can be compiled even before the function is written. Such a function is called a *stub*. To develop a program, the sequence of operation is usually to establish some scaffolding, then start writing individual functions, one at a time. Any other required functions are installed as stubs. Use of the scaffolding allows the function that is currently being developed to be tested. Once a function is working, it is "signed off", and the next function started, possibly using re-designed scaffolding. You must then refrain from tinkering further with the completed function, and if you do have to alter it, be sure to re-test it thoroughly, even if that means reinstating the original scaffolding.

> When designing and implementing functions, use scaffolding and stubs, and concentrate on getting one function operational at a time.

Tackling the programming task this way minimizes the possibility of confusion, and is far more likely to lead to a successful outcome than an approach in which all functions are written and tested concurrently. Note also that the function checks that its input meets the design specification. Such *validation* may seem tedious, but self-defense is important. It cannot be reiterated too many times that you should always assume that a person using your software will, by accident or design, abuse it.

> Design software to either abort, or give warnings, when inappropriate inputs are supplied – programs that silently continue their computations based upon erroneous values are dangerous.

Choice of suitable test data is also a critical part of program development. Boundary cases at the various extremes of normal operation should be tested, as well as a range of more normal inputs. Testing should also explore possible error situations, to ensure that the parts of your software that are defensive in nature are operating correctly too. Nor should you just test simple values – look for complex situations, and verify that the output is correct in all of them. In the case of `cube_root`, that verification is easy. With other functions you may need to be more creative, and to compare with alternative automatic or manual calculations.

Never just assume that a program is operating correctly, based on a small number of tests. A wide-ranging test regime can build your confidence in the usefulness of a program or function, but no amount of testing can *guarantee* that a program is correct. Because of this stark fact, in a professional software engineering environment, designing suitable tests is treated as being of equal importance as writing the program in the first place. The testing team is also sometimes insulated from the coding team so as to avoid cross-infection of misconceptions or incorrect assumptions about the desired behavior.

> Comprehensive testing is essential if a program is to be relied on. Tests should cover simple cases, complex cases, absurd cases, inputs just inside the design boundaries of the software, and inputs that lie outside the design parameters.

Exercises

5.1 Write a function `max_2_ints` that expects two `int` arguments, and returns the larger of them. Test your function using some suitable scaffolding.

5.2 Write a function `max_4_ints` that expects four `int` arguments, and returns the largest of them. The obvious way of doing this is somewhat heavy-handed. Can you think abstractly? Is there a role for your previous function, `max_2_ints`?

5.3 Write an `int` function `int_pow` that raises its first argument to the power of its second argument, where the first argument is an `int`, and the second argument is a positive `int`.

For example, `int_pow(3,4)` should return the value 81.

5.4 The number of different ways of selecting a k item subset of n distinct items is given by

$$C_k^n = \frac{n!}{(n-k)!\,k!}\,,$$

where $n! = 1 \times 2 \times \cdots (n-1) \times n$.

Write a function `int n_choose_k(int n, int k)` that calculates and returns this value.

Hint: what other function might you want to use?

5.5 A number is *perfect* if it is equal to the sum of its factors (including one, but excluding itself). The first perfect number is 6, since $1+2+3=6$. The next is 28, with $1+2+4+7+14=28$.

Write a function, `int isperfect(int n)`, that returns true if its argument `n` is a perfect number, and false otherwise. Then write another function, `int nextperfect(int n)` that returns the next perfect number greater than its argument `n`. Finally, use these two functions in a program that searches for and prints perfect numbers.

Don't leave your program running too long looking for perfect numbers. There are just four that are less than 10,000, and the fifth is 33,550,336. It took a 2.7 GHz Macbook Pro nearly ten minutes to find that fifth number (in the first edition of the book, the corresponding time was two hours, using a 700 MHz Pentium computer). The next one after that, according to the list at `http://en.wikipedia.org/wiki/List_of_perfect_numbers`, is 8,589,869,056, and is too large to be represented using `int` arithmetic.

5.6 Two numbers are an *amicable pair* if their factors (excluding themselves) add up to each other. The first such pair is 220, which has the factors [1, 2, 4, 5, 10, 11, 20, 22, 44, 55, 110], adding to 284; and 284, which has the factors [1, 2, 4, 71, 142], the sum of which is 220. The next amicable pair is 1,184 and 1,210; and then 2,620 and 2,924

Write a function that takes two `int` arguments and returns true if they are an amicable pair.

Write some scaffolding to allow you to test your function by reading pairs of numbers. Or, if you want a challenge, write a main program that searches for such pairs and prints them when it finds them.

5.7 Use the on-line manual to find out about the functions `isupper` and `tolower`, described by `ctype.h`.

Implement your own versions of them as `my_isupper` and `my_tolower`. Then write scaffolding that allows you to test your versions of these two functions against the system ones.

5.8 The rounding errors that accumulate in floating point numbers mean that when they are being compared for equality, a small tolerance should be allowed.

Write a function `int near_equal(double x1, double x2)` that returns true if the two argument values are either both exactly equal to zero, or are within 0.01% of each other.

For example, `near_equal(0.0,0.00001)` should be false, whereas both `near_equal(0.0,0.0)` and `near_equal(1.01567,1.01568)` should be true.

Using `near_equal` in a `while` loop guard, rewrite function `cube_root` in Figure 5.10 so that the loop stops when an answer is determined such that `next` cubed is "nearly equal" to `v`.

Add a temporary `printf` to `cube_root`, and check that the values converge. For the various test values shown in the middle box of the figure, how many iterations are required to obtain convergence? Can you find any arguments for which convergence does not appear possible?

5.9 Take your solution to Exercise 5.5 (or another similar exercise that you have done) and split it into multiple files, one per function. Then follow the instructions indicated in Figure 5.5 on page 69 and verify that it is possible to create a single executable program.

5.10 Add a fifth argument to function `savings_plan` (Figure 5.7 on page 73) to allow for the possibility that the interest rate levied on debit balances might be different to the interest rate paid on credit balances, as was discussed at the end of Section 5.4. Write some suitable scaffolding so that you can test your function.

5.11 Write a function `double sum_sequence(int n)` that calculates and returns the sum

$$\frac{1}{1} + \frac{1+2}{1\times 2} + \frac{1+2+3}{1\times 2\times 3} + \frac{1+2+3+4}{1\times 2\times 3\times 4} + \cdots + \frac{1+2+\cdots+n}{n!},$$

where n is a positive integer argument passed to the function. For example, `sum_sequence(3)` should return the value $(1/1) + (3/2) + (6/6) = 3.5$.

5.12 Consider the two functions in Figure 5.8 on page 74. What happens in each when the argument `n` is -2?

Modify function `t_rec` so that it has exactly same behavior as `t_itr`.

5.13 You probably wrote an iterative function for Exercise 5.3. Now write a recursive one for the same task.

5.14 The function $\log^*$, pronounced "log star", is defined as being the number of times that you can take the logarithm of its argument before getting a value less than one. For example, using base two logs, $\log^* 10 = 3$, because $\log_2 10 = 3.322$ (one application); $\log_2 3.322 = 1.732$ (second application); and $\log_2 1.732 = 0.792$ (third application, and now less than one).

Write a function that calculates $\log^*$ for a `double` argument. Test your function using some suitable scaffolding.

5.15 Two functions that call each other are said to be *mutually recursive*. Consider these two functions:

```
int
eeee(int n) {
    if (n==0) {
        return(1);
    } else {
        return oooo(n-1);
    }
}

int
oooo(int n) {
    if (n==0) {
        return(0);
    } else {
        return eeee(n-1);
    }
}
```

Calculate by hand the values of `eeee(5)` and `oooo(5)`.

What do these two functions do? Can you give a simpler implementation?

Chapter 6

Functions and Pointers

Chapter 5 introduced functions, a method of abstracting. Appropriate use of functions allows the sensible re-use of software, in that libraries of related functions can be collected together and exploited by a range of programs. Thinking in terms of functions also aids in the program design process – a problem can be decomposed into smaller tasks, and then each of those smaller tasks either represented as a function, or further refined into components that are eventually function-sized.

This chapter considers some of the finer points you need to know about functions, and also introduces pointer variables and pointer operations. Chapters 7 and 8 build your skills further, and introduce two important data aggregation techniques – arrays, and structures. Only then will it be time, in Chapter 9, to bring all of this knowledge together and examine solutions to a range of problems that are more compelling than the ones examined so far.

6.1 The main function

You have probably realized that the `int main` that has been inserted at the beginning of every program as a component of the standard recipe introduced in Chapter 1 is part of a function definition; and that the `return` that appears at the end of the rote recitation is part of the same function.

C is structured so that every section of executable code is a function. When a program is compiled and linked, there must be exactly one `main` function present if an executable file is to be generated, and if there is not the compiler will generate an error message, unless the `-c` compilation flag has been used. Then, when the program in that file is executed, the operating system transfers control to the first statement in the `main` function, and creates a stack frame to house the variables it declares.

When a `return` statement is encountered in the `main` function, program execution is terminated, the stack frame is popped, and control is passed back to the operating system, together with the value of the corresponding return expression. The usual convention in a C program is that a zero return value from a program marks "successful termination, all ok"; and that non-zero values indicate "an error situation has arisen". The symbolic constants `EXIT_FAILURE` and `EXIT_SUCCESS` are defined to be one and zero respectively in the header file `stdlib.h`, and can be used with the `return`. Other program-specific values can also be returned if required.

The return status flag can be interrogated at the operating system level to determine the outcome of the program. Most Unix commands return such a flag, and you should write your programs to observe the same convention. Exercise 6.1 on page 96 explores the issue of program flags.

The `exit` function, introduced in Section 3.2, follows the same convention on return values, but is more powerful. A `return` terminates program execution only when `main` is the active function, as `return` pops a single stack frame. On the other hand, `exit` is an abrupt termination that strips from the stack all frames associated with your program before returning control to the operating system, regardless of how deeply the function calls have been built up.

> The `main` function is called by the operating system when a program commences execution. A `return` from the `main` function returns control to the operating system. Use of `exit` returns control to the operating system from anywhere in a program.

So what are the two arguments to main, the `argc` and `argv` variables that are part of the same standard recipe? They are parameters passed in from the operating system, and allow your program to inspect command-line arguments. Section 7.11 on page 124 explains how to make use of these two variables.

6.2 Use of void

The reserved word `void` is used in situations where a type or list of types and identifiers is expected, but none is being given. For example a function whose task is to print an argument in a specified manner might not need to return a value at all. Other functions might not require any arguments. Figure 6.1 shows examples of the use of `void` in these two ways.

Functions that do not return a value (that is, functions that return `void`) do not require an explicit `return` statement – when execution passes beyond the last statement in the body of the function, control automatically returns to the calling function. This facility is made use of in the definition of `print_double` in Figure 6.1. If an explicit return is required in a `void` function, perhaps because of some condition that allows early exit, then the `return` statement can be used without an associated expression being necessary.

Functions with no return value are called *procedures* in some languages, and declared using a different syntax than are functions. The early language Fortran called the same concept a *subroutine*, and you might still hear this word used from time to time. C does not make a distinction between functions and procedures, and every section of a C program is a "function", whether it returns a value or not.

> Functions that have no arguments are declared with the argument list `void`; functions that do not return a value are declared with a return type `void`.

```
void fatal_error(void);
void print_double(double x);

void
fatal_error(void) {
    printf("Aaaarrrgggh, cannot recover, program abort\n");
    exit(EXIT_FAILURE);
}

void
print_double(double x) {
    printf("%10.6f", x);
}
```

Figure 6.1: Using `void` in function declarations.

Functions that have no return value are called as stand-alone statements, rather than as part of an expression. They are to execute, but there is no sense of "using" their result. In C, functions that do have return values can also be used as statements rather than expressions. This can be convenient when the returned value is uninteresting, or of no further use. For example, when `scanf` was first introduced in Chapter 2, it was used as a statement. Only later was it explained that it returned a count of the number of values successfully read, and that the returned value could be captured and tested. The statement "`sqrt(x);`" could also be used in a program, although it is not clear why you would want to. In this case what would happen is that the value of `x` would be passed into the `sqrt` function; the value $\sqrt{x}$ would be calculated by the function and returned; and then the calling program would throw that value away. The overall effect would, be the same as if the statement had not been there.

Indeed, *any* expression can be used as a statement, with the calculated value discarded and not used: "`1+M_PI;`" is a perfectly valid statement that causes no change to any variables and may as well not be there.

6.3 Scope

In the functions that have been used so far as examples, the sole communication between the calling function and the called function has been through the set of arguments going in, and the value returned back out. The sets of declared variables in caller and callee are quite distinct, and because they are allocated space in different stack frames, do not conflict even when they are declared to have the same name. If a function declares a variable called `x`, and so too does the main program, then while that function is executing there are two variables named `x` in existence, but only the one in the top stack frame is available for use.

Figure 6.2 illustrates this idea. Both `main` and `func` declare variables `x` and `z`. Each time `func` is called, the values of `x` and `z` are modified. But both these variables are *local* to the function, as one is an argument variable, and the other is declared within the body of the function. So changes to them have no effect on the variables whose values were passed as arguments at each call, and the variables that are local to the `main` function remain stubbornly set at `x=3` and `z=5` each time the `printf` in `main` is executed.

The rules of *scope* – determining which variable is referenced by the use of a given identifier – mean that no confusion is possible. The only variables accessible are the local ones. Whether they have the same names or not, a function cannot access another function's local variables, even when their values are passed as arguments to the function.

> It is not possible for any function to access – either to use the value of, or to modify – any variable that is local to another function.

Does this mean that we are hopelessly restricted in what can be achieved by a function? Is there no way – aside from returning a computed value from the function – that a function can influence the world in which it operates?

There are two answers to this question. The first is to say "yes, functions are all there is, you must operate within this restriction". This first answer leads directly to the family of *functional languages* that was described briefly in Chapter 1. As it turns out, this "restriction" is not terribly restrictive at all, and functional programming has some quite distinct advantages over the procedural family, of which C is a member.

```
int
main(int argc, char *argv[]) {
    int x=3, z=5;
    printf("main: x=%2d, z=%2d\n", x, z);
    func(x);
    printf("main: x=%2d, z=%2d\n", x, z);
    func(z);
    printf("main: x=%2d, z=%2d\n", x, z);
    return 0;
}

void
func(int x) {
    int z=7;
    x = x+1;
    z = x+z+1;
    printf("func: x=%2d, z=%2d\n", x, z);
}
```

```
main: x= 3, z= 5
func: x= 4, z=12
main: x= 3, z= 5
func: x= 6, z=14
main: x= 3, z= 5
```

Figure 6.2: A program fragment showing that local variables in functions are distinct, even if they have the same names. The lower box shows an execution of the program.

Which bring us to the second answer to the question posed above – the C answer – which is "no, there are facilities that allow functions to alter the environment in which they are operating". Such changes are called *side effects*. C provides a number of mechanisms whereby functions can alter the state of the calling context. There is a certain element of risk in writing functions that have side effects, and in particular, the facilities described in the next section should be used with great care – a better way of doing it is described in Sections 6.6 and 6.7. It is also worth noting that in a sense the whole of C is based upon the use of side effects, since every assignment statement has the side effect of altering the value of the left-hand-side variable.

In a functional language, all functions, including arithmetic operations, are pure, and side effects are not possible. In C, functions that cause side effects are both possible and necessary.

6.4 Global variables

Variables declared within a function are local to that function. Variables declared outside of any function are *global* to all functions that are physically defined within the same source code file. Figure 6.3 gives an example of such a variable, and shows how it can be altered by functions within the file.

```
int z=2;

int
main(int argc, char *argv[]) {
    int x=3;
    printf("main: x=%2d, z=%2d\n", x, z);
    func(x);
    printf("main: x=%2d, z=%2d\n", x, z);
    func(z);
    printf("main: x=%2d, z=%2d\n", x, z);
    return 0;
}

void
func(int x) {
    x = x+1;
    z = x+z+1;
    printf("func: x=%2d, z=%2d\n", x, z);
}
```

```
main: x= 3, z= 2
func: x= 4, z= 7
main: x= 3, z= 7
func: x= 8, z=16
main: x= 3, z=16
```

Figure 6.3: A program fragment showing that all functions in a file have access to global variables. The lower box shows an execution of the program.

In Figure 6.3, variable `z` is declared prior to any of the functions, and given an initial value of 2. That initialization happens even before the `main` begins executing. So the first `printf` executed shows `z` with the value 2. The calls to the function alter that global variable, and the modified value is available for use in `main` after the function returns. On the other hand, variable `x` in `func` is still a local variable, and its changed value is always lost when the function returns.

> Global variables can be accessed and modified from within any function defined in the same file as the variable.

All of the functions declared in a file are also global. They can be called from within any other function in the same file, and can also be called (using separate compilation) by functions declared in other files.

The ability to declare global variables does raise one problem: it is possible to have multiple variables declared with the same name. To resolve this ambiguity, the rules of scope stipulate that any reference to a multiply declared variable applies to the local one; and a global variable can only be referred to if there is no local variable of the same name (irrespective of type) that *shadows* it. The same rule applies to function names, and can be a cause for confusion – declaring a variable called `sqrt` in a function automatically makes the `sqrt` routine from the mathematics library unavailable in that function. If you do declare a variable called `sqrt`, and then later call the function `sqrt`, the compiler objects at that point with a message something like "called object is not a function", because, in the scope in question, `sqrt` is not a function and hence cannot be called.

> Local variable declarations in a function shadow global variables and functions of the same name, and render them inaccessible to the function.

More subtle errors arise from the unexpected shadowing of global variables, or even of argument variables, when there is no such type clash identified by the compiler. For example, it is legal in C to declare a local variable that has the same name as an argument variable in the same function, in which case the argument variable is shadowed. A good C compiler will issue a warning message in this situation (`gcc -Wall` certainly does); nevertheless, you should remain alert to the possibility that you may have inadvertently shadowed a global or argument variable.

Does this mean that if we want to write functions that have side effects, we must make use of global variables? Fortunately, the answer is "no". Sections 6.6 and 6.7 describe a rather more elegant way of allowing a function to alter the environment it got called from, and that is the mechanism that should be used when side effects are required.

> Global variables should be used only with extreme caution. Relying on them for communications to and from a function makes the function less general, less robust, and harder to reuse.

It is also worth repeating some advice that was given earlier: always read the warning messages issued by the compiler. Warning-free code may be hard to achieve in some circumstances, but for the programs being written in this book, should be possible. And even if you are unable for some reason to eliminate all of the warnings, you must at least make sure you understand why they are arising.

Pay attention to compiler warning messages – they indicate things that might go wrong.

6.5 Static variables

If a global variable is being used exclusively by one function, as a kind of "internal" memory, then having it accessible to other functions is unnecessary. To handle this requirement, C provides a third *storage class*, and allows the declaration of `static` variables. A static variable is local to the function it is declared in, but retains its value between calls to that function. Because it is to retain its value, it is not allocated in the stack frame for the function, and is instead given space within a separate area of memory reserved for static and global variables. Figure 6.4 shows a simple program that makes use of a static variable. As with the other example programs in this chapter, you are encouraged to trace through the function calls to ensure that you understand why the various `printf` statements produce the values that they do.

```
int
main(int argc, char *argv[]) {
    int x=3, z=5;
    printf("main: x=%2d, z=%2d\n", x, z);
    func(x);
    printf("main: x=%2d, z=%2d\n", x, z);
    func(z);
    printf("main: x=%2d, z=%2d\n", x, z);
    return 0;
}

void
func(int x) {
    static int z=7;
    x = x+1;
    z = x+z+1;
    printf("func: x=%2d, z=%2d\n", x, z);
}
```

```
main: x= 3, z= 5
func: x= 4, z=12
main: x= 3, z= 5
func: x= 6, z=19
main: x= 3, z= 5
```

Figure 6.4: A program fragment showing the declaration and use of a static variable. The lower box shows an execution of the program.

Static variables allow functions to maintain state from one call to the next without that information being accessible outside the function.

Static variables provide a relatively sound way of having functions retain internal information. But a warning is warranted – mixing recursive functions and static variables almost inevitably leads to tears. Recursive functions are sensible only when all of their local variables are stack-based – which is formally referred to as the storage class *automatic* – and are created afresh for each call in the recursive stack. Having multiple active functions all referring to the same underlying static variable is likely to result in considerable confusion.

6.6 Pointers and pointer operations

Each variable that is declared in a program is stored in a location in the computer's memory, and when accessing that variable, the hardware uses the address of that location rather than the variable name. One of the tasks of the compiler is to convert symbolic names into addresses in memory, so that variables can be accessed.

Typical modern computers have around a billion of *words* of memory, and, roughly speaking, each word can hold one `int` or `float` variable. A word usually consists of either four or eight *bytes*, where a byte holds one `char` character value; and to hold a character, eight *bits* are required. A bit (standing for *b*inary dig*it*) is the fundamental unit of storage, and is represented as "0" or "1". Current computers have memory allocations of around 4 GB, or approximately 4 billion bytes. To put this capacity into some kind of perspective, the text of a relatively long book occupies around one million bytes; and this one is a bit over half a million bytes. So the memory of a modern computer can hold the text of between 4,000 and 8,000 books.[1]

Each byte in memory has an *address*, and for our purposes we can visualize the computer memory as a long list of byte-sized boxes, each with a number, and each capable of storing a single character. The addresses count upward at the rate of one per byte. So if each `int` occupies four bytes, and one `int` is stored at address n, then the next `int` is stored at address $n + 4$.

A *pointer* is a C variable that stores an address. Because we don't know whereabouts in memory a program will be loaded when it is executing, it makes no sense to try and read and write pointer values, as a program may execute in quite a different part of memory each time it is executed. Instead, pointers are assigned after a program has commenced execution; and when a program terminates, the values of pointer variables are lost.

A pointer variable stores the memory address of another variable.

There are two important operations that make pointer variables useful. The first is the operator "`&`", which means "the address of". This operator can only be applied

[1] In the first edition of the book, this section said "Current computers have memory allocations of around 256 MB". The difference corresponds to a 16-fold growth in around 10 years, which corresponds to a *doubling* of typical memory every two and a half years. Meanwhile, the price of entry-level computers continues to drop.

to variables, and returns the location in memory that is currently allocated to that variable. For example, consider this program fragment:

```
static int w;
int x, y, z;
printf("&w = %16p\n&x = %16p\n&y = %16p\n&z = %16p\n",
    &w, &x, &y, &z);
```

In it, the addresses of variables w, x, y, and z are printed as base-16 hexadecimal integers using the "%p" format descriptor that is specific to pointers. When executed on a machine with 8-byte pointers the following output might be produced:

```
mac: ./pointer1
&w =        0x10676a068
&x =    0x7fff6636a874
&y =    0x7fff6636a870
&z =    0x7fff6636a86c
```

Round about half of the digits represent memory addresses, and for our purposes the 7fff part of these values can be ignored. Note how the addresses are multiples of four (in hexadecimal, digit "c" has the value 12), and x, y, and z are located at intervals of four bytes. These variables have all been stored in four-byte words. And while there is no requirement that the compiler assigns adjacent words when allocating variables, nor is it surprising that it has happened, although, as it turns out, z is stored before y, and y is stored before the word allocated to x. The static variable w is stored in a quite different part of memory – x, y, and z are stored on the stack, while w is with the other static and global variables. Note also that every time this program is executed the addresses can change. The allocation of a program to a particular part of memory during execution is an ephemeral process, and except for the purposes of trying to explain pointers to students learning programming, there is no benefit at all in printing out their values.

The second critical operation is the pointer dereference operator "*". It is also a unary operator, and takes as its operand a pointer-valued expression. That expression is usually, but not always, a pointer variable; and the "*" operator has the meaning "use this address to access the underlying variable stored at the indicated memory location". The symbol "*" is also used as a binary operator for multiplication, but the C compiler is able to differentiate between the two uses, and there is no confusion.

To declare a *pointer variable*, more syntax is required. Every pointer variable must be given a definite type: "pointer to int", or "pointer to double", or similar, so that the compiler knows how to interpret the memory word indicated by the pointer. Hence, if p is an expression of type "pointer to T", then *p is an expression of type T. Similarly, if a variable x is of type T, then &x is of type "pointer to T".

Figure 6.5 gives a simple example of pointer declaration, assignment, and manipulation: variable pi is of type "pointer to int", and variable pd is of type "pointer to double". Once they have been set to the addresses of underlying variables of the corresponding base type, they can be used to manipulate the values of those variables through use of the dereferencing operator. Figure 6.6 shows diagrammatically the relationship between the four variables declared in Figure 6.5.

```
int n=123, *pi;
double x=456.789, *pd;
printf("   n = %3d,    x = %7.3f\n", n, x);
pi = &n;
pd = &x;
printf("*pi = %3d, *pd = %7.3f\n", *pi, *pd);
*pi = *pi+1;
*pd = *pd / *pi;
printf("*pi = %3d, *pd = %7.3f\n", *pi, *pd);
printf("   n = %3d,    x = %7.3f\n", n, x);
```

```
   n = 123,    x = 456.789
 *pi = 123, *pd = 456.789
 *pi = 124, *pd =   3.684
   n = 124,    x =   3.684
```

Figure 6.5: A program fragment showing the declaration of pointer variables, and the use of the pointer operators "&" and "*". The lower box shows an execution of the program.

There are several points to note in connection with Figure 6.5. The first is that, like all declared variables, pointers do not have an initial value assigned – they must be given a value before they can be used. So use of pi before a value has been assigned to it is as meaningless as a reference to variable n would have been if no initializer had been given in the declaration. And if pi does not have a value, then *pi is doubly meaningless. If you are lucky, the runtime system will give an error message when you make such a gaffe: "Segmentation fault" being the usual bland (and at first, rather unhelpful) summary of what went wrong. If you are *un*lucky, the reference through the pointer will succeed, and you will scribble over a random spot of memory that might (perhaps much later during the execution) cause your program to mysteriously calculate incorrect results, or simply come to a screeching halt.

> Pointers provide a mechanism for *aliasing* – referring to the same variable by two different names. Like all aliasing mechanisms, pointers must be treated with respect.

The second point to note in connection with Figures 6.5 and 6.6 is that the pointer variables can have any valid name. In the example, they are given names related to

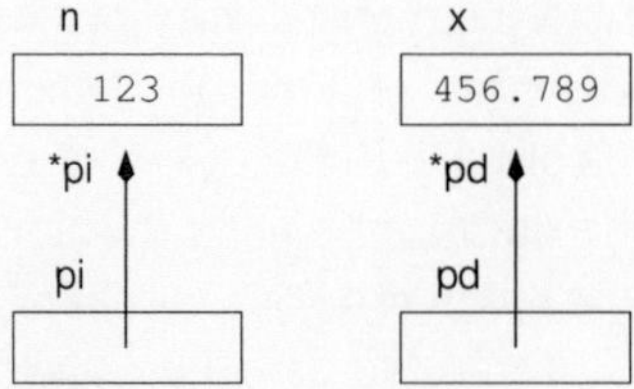

Figure 6.6: The pointer variables declared in Figure 6.5, and the initial values of their targets.

what they are pointing at, but there is no obligation or necessity to do this. If a second `int` variable `sum` was declared in the program, the assignment `pi=&sum` part way through the program would be perfectly valid, and would result in subsequent references to `*pi` being to the value of variable `sum`.

The third point to take note of in Figures 6.5 and 6.6 is that the address-of and dereferencing operators are both unary operators, and like all unary operators, have high precedence (see Table 3.3 on page 31).

Finally, note that the dereference operator can be used on the left-hand side of an assignment statement: the expression `*pi=*pi+1` means that the value of the expression `*pi+1` (as an `int`, since `pi` is of type pointer to `int`) should be stored into the memory location currently indicated by the value of variable `pi`.

> The dereferencing operator `*` can be used to alter the value of an underlying variable whose address is stored in a pointer variable.

You are probably asking yourself "so what?", as all that seems to have been achieved by the introduction of pointers is the ability to change a variable without mentioning its name. But that is a powerful facility, and the next section shows how use of pointers adds considerable flexibility to the design of functions.

6.7 Pointers as arguments

Towards the end of Chapter 5 it was pessimistically concluded that a function was unable to alter its arguments except by assigning a returned value back into one of them. Strictly speaking, this is true – since it is always an *expression* that is passed into a function, there is no chance of altering a variable in the calling function. But suppose the argument expression is a *pointer* value, and suppose that in the function the corresponding pointer variable is used to reach out across memory and access the underlying memory location. Then we can create an effect where it *looks* like the argument is being altered, even though the real argument is unchanged. Figure 6.7 gives the classic example – a simple function that exchanges the values of two arguments. This function is taught to every C programmer at some stage of their apprenticeship.

In Figure 6.7 all the parts mesh together in a carefully coordinated manner. The prototype for `int_swap` says that its arguments are both of type pointer to `int`. Each time `int_swap` is called, function `main` passes over two integer pointers, constructed using the address-of operator "`&`" and pointing to `int` variables local to `main`. And within function `int_swap`, the arguments `p1` and `p2` are manipulated using the "`*`" operator, to access and modify the variables underlying the pointers that were passed.

The net effect is that the function swaps the values of the two variables underlying the pointers passed in to the function – and at a superficial level it looks like the arguments are being swapped. Figure 6.8 shows the situation during the first call to `int_swap` in the program in Figure 6.7.

> When a function needs to alter its arguments, it should be designed to receive pointers, and when it is called, pointers should be passed. The function is then able to use those pointers to alter the variables underlying them.

```
void int_swap(int *p1, int *p2);

int
main(int argc, char *argv[]) {
    int x=2, y=3, z=4;
    printf("main: x=%2d, y=%2d, z=%2d\n", x, y, z);
    int_swap(&x, &y);
    printf("main: x=%2d, y=%2d, z=%2d\n", x, y, z);
    int_swap(&x, &z);
    printf("main: x=%2d, y=%2d, z=%2d\n", x, y, z);
    int_swap(&y, &x);
    printf("main: x=%2d, y=%2d, z=%2d\n", x, y, z);
    return 0;
}

/* exchange the values of the two variables indicated
    by the arguments */
void
int_swap(int *p1, int *p2) {
    int tmp;
    tmp = *p1;
    *p1 = *p2;
    *p2 = tmp;
}
```

```
main: x= 2, y= 3, z= 4
main: x= 3, y= 2, z= 4
main: x= 4, y= 2, z= 3
main: x= 2, y= 4, z= 3
```

Figure 6.7: A function and program showing the flexibility achieved when pointers are passed into a function. The lower box shows an execution of the program.

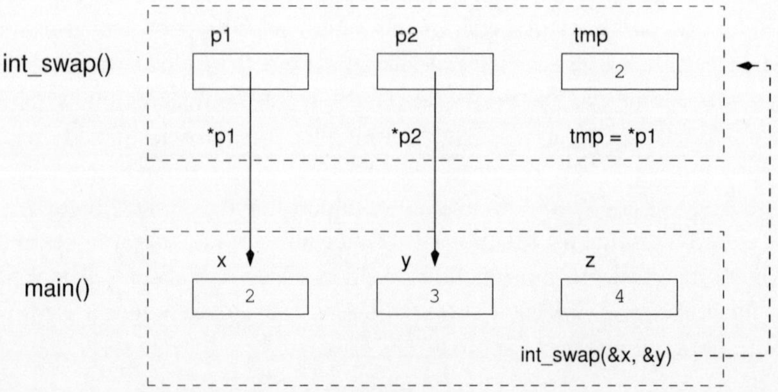

Figure 6.8: After `tmp=*p1` is executed in the first call to `int_swap` in Figure 6.7.

Because int_swap is expecting pointer arguments, it cannot be passed integer constants or expressions. It makes no sense to write int_swap(70,&n), for example, as 70 is a constant, not an address. And while it might be tempting to try to print the word at memory address 70 using printf("%d",*70), the memory protection mechanisms embedded in modern operating systems will, for security reasons, prevent you from accessing memory areas that have not been allocated to your program. A "segmentation fault" run-time error is almost certain to occur when you try.

6.8 Case study: Reading numbers

Consider the following specification:

> Write a function that reads integers until it obtains one in the range given by its first two arguments. When a suitable value is read, it stores that value using its third argument, and returns the predefined constant READ_OK. If no suitable value is located, the predefined constant READ_ERROR should be returned.

The desired function is to repeatedly read numbers until it finds one that is within range, where the range is expressed by the first two arguments, lo and hi. The number found – if one exists – is stored into the variable underlying the third argument, which is a pointer. For example, if a value between -100 and $+100$ is required in variable valu, this code fragment could then be used:

```
if (read_num(-100, +100, &valu) != READ_OK) {
    printf("Read error, program abort\n");
    exit(EXIT_FAILURE);
}
/* ok, can now go ahead and use the number in valu */
```

In this fragment, appropriate arguments are passed into the function, and the value returned from the function is checked before any use is made of the variable valu.

Figure 6.9 shows the required function. As per the specification, it returns a flag that indicates whether or not it executed correctly, as well as modifying a variable in the calling environment. This is a very common technique; and the various status codes that might be returned as status flags should always be set up using the #define facility.

Apart from the use of a pointer argument to allow a second value to be returned from the function, there is relatively little to note in Figure 6.9, and it should now be within your ability to write this function. Several of the exercises that follow ask you to write functions that have pointer arguments. You are encouraged to work through those problems and check that your functions operate correctly by also writing suitable scaffold programs, and then testing them using a wide range of argument values.

```
#define READ_OK 0
#define READ_ERROR 1

int read_num(int lo, int hi, int *num);

/* Read numbers until one in the desired range from lo
   to hi is entered. Return that one as num. */
int
read_num(int lo, int hi, int *num) {
    int next;
    printf("enter a number between %d and %d inclusive: ",
            lo, hi);
    while (scanf("%d", &next) == 1) {
        /* got a number, so take a look at it */
        if (lo <= next && next <= hi) {
            /* this number is within range */
            *num = next;
            return READ_OK;
        }
        printf("%d is not between %d and %d\ntry again: ",
                next, lo, hi);
    }
    /* no valid numbers found, and scanf has failed */
    return READ_ERROR;
}
```

Figure 6.9: A function that reads numbers until it gets one within a specified range.

Exercises

6.1 If you have access to a Unix machine, try and reproduce the following sequence, where `helloworld.c` is any simple C program:

```
mac: grep "main" helloworld.c
main(int argc, char *argv[]) {
mac: echo $status
0
mac: grep "jhgfd" helloworld.c
mac: echo $status
1
mac: ./helloworld
Hello world!
mac: echo $status
0
```

What is happening?

Now modify the program in `helloworld.c` so that it returns 1, and then recompile it. What do you expect to happen? Does it?

6.2 For each of the three marked points in the following program write down a list of all of the program-declared variables and functions that are in scope at that point, and for each such identifier, its type. Don't forget `main`, `argc`, and `argv` (which has the type `(char*) []`, but you don't know what that means yet). Where there is more than one choice for a given name, be sure to indicate which one you are referring to.

```
int bill(int jack, int jane);
double jane(double dick, int fred, double dave);

int trev;

int
main(int argc, char *argv[]) {
    double beth;
    int pete, bill;
    /* point #1 */
    return 0;
}

int
bill(int jack, int jane) {
    int mary;
    double zack;
    /* point #2 */
    return 0;
}

double
jane(double dick, int fred, double dave) {
    double trev;
    /* point #3 */
    return 0.0;
}
```

6.3 The following two functions are both legal according to the rules of C (although, to be fair, the `gcc` compiler does give a warning message for the second one, saying "declaration of 'dumber' shadows a parameter").

```
int
dumb(int dumb) {
    return dumb+1;
}

int
dumber(int dumber) {
    int dumber=6;
    return dumb(dumber+1);
}
```

What do the two functions return?

What should be done to the programmer who wrote them?

6.4 Back in Chapter 2, when the `scanf` function was introduced, it was stressed that each variable being read should be prefixed with an ampersand character "`&`". Why is it required? What does the following code fragment (try) to do?

```
n = 123456;
scanf("%d", n);
```

What happens when you execute it?

6.5 Write a function `int_sort2(int *p1, int *p2)` that orders its two arguments so that the numerically smaller value is placed into the underlying variable corresponding to the first argument pointer, and the larger into the variable corresponding to the second argument pointer. Do not use the `int_swap` function discussed in Section 6.7.

6.6 Write a function `int_sort3(int *p1, int *p2, int *p3)` that orders its three arguments from smallest to largest. This time you may make use of `int_swap` function. If you do, be sure to think carefully about the types, and what the arguments should be when it is called. You may also make use of `int_sort2`, if you wish.

How about an `int_sort4` function? And `int_sort5`? Would you like a generalized mechanism for handling arbitrary-sized sets of numbers? If so, read on, the answer is just over the page in Chapter 7.

6.7 Write a main program to test the function `read_num` shown in Figure 6.9. What does the function do when `lo` is greater than `hi`? How could it be altered to better handle this case?

6.8 Write a function:

```
void int_divide(int numerator, int denominator,
    int *quotient, int *remainder)
```

that calculates the integer quotient and remainder when the numerator is divided by the denominator using integer division..

Write suitable scaffolding so that you can test your function.

6.9 Consider again the problem described in Exercise 3.6 on page 43. Write a function `int try_one_coin(int *cents, int coin)` that reduces the current `cents` amount by the value of the current `coin` as many times as is possible, altering the value of `cents` appropriately, and returning the number of coins of that denomination that should be issued.

Then write a function `void print_change(int cents)` that tests each different coin denomination in the correct ordering, and uses `try_one_coin` to tell it how to generate the required change.

In the late 1980s in Australia, 1c and 2c coins were abolished, and $1 and $2 coins were introduced. Write a further function `int round_to_5(int cents)` that returns a value rounded off to the nearest multiple of five. For example, 12c of change is rounded to 10c; whereas 23c is rounded to 25c.

Finally, write a driver program that allows you to test your functions on monetary amounts up to $10.

Chapter 7

Arrays

The exercises at the end of Chapter 6 raised the issue of ordering a set of values. If a small, fixed, number of values are to be sorted into order, then a function can be tailored to do the job. But what if 100 items – or more – are to be sorted? How can a general-purpose function be written if it is unclear how many objects there will be?

This chapter provides the answers to these questions, and introduces a data aggregation technique called the *array*. Using arrays, it is possible to read large collections of data, then process them as a whole – for example, to sort them into order, or compute some other holistic result – and then print them out again in a modified form.

An important point worth noting is that an array is a *data structure*, whereas until this point discussion has revolved entirely around *control structures*. The `if` and `for` statements, for example, allow clustering and grouping of the fundamental statements for input, output, and assignment. Similarly, the array is a powerful mechanism that provides grouping of the fundamental data objects – `int`, `double`, and so on.

7.1 Linear collections of like objects

It was observed in Chapter 6 that variables are sometimes assigned adjacent memory words. When that example was being discussed, the point was made that it cannot be assumed that variables are assigned to consecutive words of memory. But suppose that a mechanism is available to force a collection of same-type variables to be allocated to consecutive slots in memory. And suppose also that it is possible to access the individual variables in the collection based on their position relative to the start of the collection – dealing with them as the "first", the "second", and so on.

This is what an array is – a collection of same-type variables that is guaranteed to be laid out in memory in a regular pattern, in such a way that the individual objects in the collection can be identified by their ordinal position. Figure 7.1 shows a first – and somewhat boring – example of the use of arrays.

In Figure 7.1, an array `A` containing `N` variables is declared (in this case `N` is 5), each of which is an `int`. The first variable has the name `A[0]`, the second the name `A[1]`, and the last the name `A[4]`. The array name can be any valid identifier, and multiple arrays of different sizes and underlying variable types can be declared in a program, just as multiple simple (or *scalar*) variables can be declared.

```
#define N 5

int
main(int argc, char *argv[]) {
    int A[N], i;
    for (i=0; i<N; i++) {
        A[i] = i*(i+1)/2;
    }
    for (i=0; i<N; i++) {
        printf("A[%d]=%d  ", i, A[i]);
    }
    printf("\n");
    return 0;
}
```

```
A[0]=0  A[1]=1  A[2]=3  A[3]=6  A[4]=10
```

Figure 7.1: Declaring and using arrays. The lower box shows an execution of the program.

Note carefully that the array *subscripts* in the square brackets "`[]`" start at zero, not one. These names can be used directly if required, and the assignment `A[3]=17` is perfectly valid. Note also that the whole collection is `A`, but `A` is not any single one of them, and there is no circumstance under which `A` alone can be used on the left-hand side of an assignment.

> An array is a collection of same-type variables, accessed via the use of an integer subscript. The first variable in an array is at subscript zero.

The power of arrays arises from the fact that the subscript value used to select an array element can be any integer-valued expression. In the figure, this flexibility allows the use of one loop to assign values to each of the five array elements, and then a second loop to print them out. The number of items in the array is always controlled by some upper *limit* (in the example, the constant `N`), meaning that the loop used to access the elements of an array is most naturally a `for` loop, with the structure `for(`*var*`=0;`*var*`<`*limit*`;`*var*`++)`. If you use this standard recipe, the variable used as the *var* will correctly count through all of the *limit* items in the array. In this sense, an array is a controlled repetition of data, in the same way that a `for` loop offers controlled repetition of program statements.

> The array data structure corresponds closely to the `for` loop control structure.

In ANSI C the declared size of an array must be known at the time the program is compiled. This requirement means that a `#define` constant should always be used to set the array size, so that if a change becomes necessary, all of the loops that manipulate the array inherit the altered value. Later versions of the standard relax this requirement, and allow arrays to be declared based on `int` variables that already have values. For example, in C99, a function can declare an array of size given by an `int` argument to the function.

Once an array is declared it is not necessary to use all of the variables in it, and there is little harm caused if arrays are declared too big. If an array is over-declared, because it is not known how many values will be required while the program is executing, the *limit* that controls the operation of `for` loops manipulating the array should be a variable in the program, and should store the number of variables in the array (starting at index position zero) that are in use at that time.

Finally, note that the output of the program in Figure 7.1 could have been achieved without an array – a simple loop would have sufficed. The point of that program is simply to show how arrays are declared, and how the individual variables within the array are accessed. The next two sections show a "real" application of arrays – one in which an arbitrary-sized set of values is read, modified, and then written in altered form. Without the use of an array, that would be all but impossible.

7.2 Reading into an array

Figure 7.2 shows a program fragment that carries out a rather more complex array operation – it prompts the program user for input, and then reads values into an array until either the array is full, or the user signals end of file. On a Unix system, end of file is indicated by typing control-D, shown in the examples as `^D`.

Because the number of iterations of the loop is unknown, it is natural to use a `while` loop rather than a `for` loop. The limit `maxvals` is dictated by the array size, and might be 10 (as is shown in the lower part of Figure 7.2), or 100, or 12,345. The exact value doesn't affect the logic of the program – even the prompt is adjusted automatically.

It is an error to refer to array elements that have not been declared. In particular, in most situations use of a negative subscript, or of a subscript greater than or equal to the dimensioned size (remember, the valid subscripts vary from 0 to `maxvals-1`) is erroneous, and you can expect such a program to fail. Unfortunately, arrays are another form of aliasing; and worse, most C systems do not provide run-time array bounds checking. So the assignment `A[-1]=5` is likely to get executed without complaint on the C system you are using, and if it does, has the effect of setting to 5 whatever is stored one memory word before the first word in array `A`. That assignment will happen irrespective of whether or not the memory word in question is a variable in your program, and irrespective of whether or not it actually stores an `int`. The unexpected alteration might never show up as a program error; or it might cause an immediate "segmentation fault" run-time error; or it might, for example, mean that your program computes incorrect drug dosage values, and permanently disables someone. Of these three possibilities, the immediate segmentation fault is the most desirable – at least then you got lucky, and have clear evidence that there is a serious mistake that needs to be identified.

> It is an error to refer to array elements that do not exist. Guarding against such errors is the responsibility of the programmer, as most C systems do not implement run-time array bounds checking.

```
printf("Enter as many as %d values, ^D to end\n",
        maxvals);
n = 0; excess = 0;
while (scanf("%d", &next)==1) {
    if (n==maxvals) {
        excess = excess+1;
    } else {
        A[n] = next;
        n += 1;
    }
}
printf("%d values read into array", n);
if (excess) {
    printf(", %d excess values discarded", excess);
}
printf("\n");
```

```
mac: ./readarray
Enter as many as 10 values, ^D to end
1 2 3 4 3
^D
5 values read into array
mac: ./readarray
Enter as many as 10 values, ^D to end
1 2 3 4 3 4 5 4 3 4 5 6 7
^D
10 values read into array, 3 excess values discarded
```

Figure 7.2: A program fragment that shows how to read values into an array. Care must be taken to not exceed the bounds of the array, which can only be guaranteed if each value is first read into a temporary variable before being placed into the array. The lower box shows two executions of a program containing the fragment.

To protect against this kind of insidious error, you must be very careful to only assign using valid subscripts. In Figure 7.2, the values read using the `scanf` are counted into the array, and a test made on the array subscript to be used before it is actually allowed as an index. Note also that it is prudent to first read into a temporary variable (`next`) before assigning into the next vacant word of `A` – only when the `scanf` has succeeded is it appropriate to assign another array element and alter `n`. Finally, notice that variable `n` is initialized to zero; used as an array index to store the next item read; and then immediately incremented. It is thus always a correct count of the number of objects in the array, regardless of whether or not the array gets filled up. Subsequent operations that iterate over the array elements then have the structure `for(i=0;i<n;i++)` – the standard recipe that is always used.

The logic of Figure 7.2 should be mimicked every time a variable number of items are to be read into an array, and is the only secure way of performing this task.

7.3 Sorting an array

Once an array of numbers has been read into memory, a wide range of operations can be contemplated. For example, it is easy to calculate the sum or the mean of the numbers, or to compute the most frequently appearing value. One transformation that is useful in a variety of applications is that of *sorting* the array – rearranging the items so that they are in ascending (or, at least, non-descending) order. Many subsequent information processing tasks are made much simpler if their input data is ordered, and this fact makes the task of sorting fundamental to computing. (Recall that in Chapter 1 computer science was defined as a discipline that treats information as its raw material, and studies ways in which it can be stored and transformed.)

Before considering the problem of sorting an array, a new concept needs to be introduced: an *algorithm* is a set of steps that provides a general description of how instances of some problem can be solved. There may be multiple algorithms for tackling any particular task, and some of them may be more useful than others. For example, given a name, and a sorted list of name-value pairs such as appears in an old-style telephone directory, one algorithm for searching for the value corresponding to the name is to start at the beginning, and scan every name until the one being sought is located. In computing, this approach of trying everything, one by one, until a match is found, is called *linear search*. It works even if the list is not sorted, but if the list is long is likely to be slow. Nobody ever used the phone book this way.

An alternative algorithm – one you probably mastered when you were young, when using hard-copy dictionaries – is to check round about the middle of the list, and go either forwards or backwards from that middle position, depending respectively on whether the thing being looked up comes before or after the contents of that middle page. This *binary search* algorithm only works when the list is sorted. But when that condition is met, it is enormously faster than linear search.

> An algorithm is a set of steps for solving a problem. There may be multiple algorithms for solving a given problem, each with different advantages and disadvantages.

There are many different algorithms for sorting, the topic of this section. Figure 7.3 presents a C implementation of the *insertion sort* algorithm. Insertion sort is a relatively crude mechanism – a tractor rather than a Ferrari. But, despite its crudeness, insertion sort is an important technique for you to learn, and is perfectly acceptable when the size of the array being sorted is small, less than around a thousand or so items.

The program fragment shown in Figure 7.3 assumes that `n` values (indexed from zero to `n-1`) have already been read into array `A` by a loop such as that shown in Figure 7.2; and the example execution shown in the lower box of the figure also presumes that some more program statements that write out "before" and "after" values for the contents of the array have been wrapped around the fragment shown.

The key idea behind insertion sort is that elements are added one by one to an initial part of the array that is kept sorted. At first, that initial part has just one element in it, `A[0]`, and is so is already sorted. Then `A[1]` is looked at, and swapped with `A[0]` if that is what it takes to get the two items into order. More generally, if

```
/* assume that A[0] to A[n-1] have valid values */
for (i=1; i<n; i++) {
    /* swap A[i] left into correct position */
    for (j=i-1; j>=0 && A[j+1]<A[j]; j--) {
        /* not there yet */
        int_swap(&A[j], &A[j+1]);
    }
}
/* and that's all there is to it! */
```

```
mac: ./insertionsort
Enter as many as 10 values, ^D to end
1 8 15 3 17 12 4 8 4
^D
9 values read into array
Before:    1   8  15   3  17  12   4   8   4
After :    1   3   4   4   8   8  12  15  17
```

Figure 7.3: Program fragment showing how to sort an array from smallest to largest using the insertion sort algorithm. Function `int_swap` is defined in Figure 6.7 on page 94. The lower box shows an execution of a program containing the fragment.

`A[0]` to `A[i-1]` is already sorted, then `A[i]` is "added" in, and swapped leftward over `A[i-1]`, `A[i-2]`, and so on, until it is either placed between two elements in the correct order, or until it reaches `A[0]` and is the (new) smallest element in the array. Note the use of the function `int_swap` from Figure 6.7 on page 94 – there is no point not making ongoing use of functions that were written for other initial purposes. Good software design facilitates this kind of re-use.

The name "insertion sort" comes about because of the way that the next unsorted item is inserted into a sorted prefix at each iteration of the main `for` loop. This is the spiraling convergence referred to in Chapter 4 – each time the main `for` loop repeats, the sorted array prefix is one element longer than it was previously. Indeed, looking at the structure of the implementation in Figure 7.2, it is clear that the array is sorted after exactly `n-1` iterations of the main `for` loop.

As an example, suppose that the seven numbers $\{22, 14, 17, 42, 27, 28, 23\}$ are to be sorted. Table 7.1 illustrates process that takes place. Values to the right of the zig-zag line have yet to be sorted; ones to the left of it are part of the sorted prefix. Each cycle takes the item just to the right of the boundary, and places it in sorted position to the left of the line, shown in grey. At first, only one item is sorted. But by the end, the final item has been put in place, and the whole array is sorted.

The discussion in this chapter is more about arrays than about sorting, and while the exercises at the end of this chapter introduce other sorting algorithms, they too are of the "agricultural" quality of insertion sort rather than being "formula one" performers. Sorting algorithms that can be used to efficiently sort very large sets of values – the Ferraris of sorting – are discussed in detail in Chapter 12. Those clever algorithms are to insertion sort what binary search is to linear search, and mean that sorting is not usually a bottleneck operation in data processing applications.

	A[0]	A[1]	A[2]	A[3]	A[4]	A[5]	A[6]
Initially	22	14	17	42	27	28	23
After i=0	**22**	14	17	42	27	28	23
After i=1	**14**	22	17	42	27	28	23
After i=2	14	**17**	22	42	27	28	23
After i=3	14	17	22	**42**	27	28	23
After i=4	14	17	22	**27**	42	28	23
After i=5	14	17	22	27	**28**	42	23
After i=6	14	17	22	**23**	27	28	42

Table 7.1: Tracing the action of insertion sort on the array $\{22, 14, 17, 42, 27, 28, 23\}$. In each phase the item in grey is moved left into sorted position, using a sequences of swaps of adjacent elements.

To understand why insertion sort is considered to be slow, consider what happens if the input array happens to be sorted in the *reverse* order when the algorithm commences. In this case, as the ith item is added to the sorted prefix, a sequence of $i - 1$ swaps is required, and the inner `for` loop in Figure 7.3 executes all the way from $j = i - 1$ down to $j = 0$. So to sort n elements might take $0 + 1 + 2 + 3 + \cdots + (n - 2) + (n - 1) = (n - 1)n/2$ comparisons and swaps. To make this concrete, if we are unlucky with the input sequence we are provided with, sorting $n = 100$ objects might take as many as $99 \times 100/2 \approx 5{,}000$ comparisons. Even so, it can be carried out in far less than a second of computation time (recall from Chapter 1 that a rule of thumb for current computers is around 100 million steps per second). But to sort $n = 1{,}000{,}000 = 10^6$ items will take rather longer: as many as 5×10^{11} comparisons, or perhaps 5,000 seconds, over an hour.

At the other end of the spectrum, if we are lucky the input sequence is already sorted (or very close to sorted), and just n comparisons, and a few swaps, might be required. In between these two extremes is a somewhat nebulous "average" case to be thought about; if we assume that on average each execution of the inner `for` loop executes $i/2$ times, then the total cost will on average be proportional to $n^2/4$ rather than the worst-case of $n^2/2$. The key point to note is that except in special circumstances, the execution cost for insertion sort grows quadratically in the number of objects in the array. This point is returned to in Chapter 12 when more efficient sorting algorithms are introduced.

> Insertion sort is one of many different sorting algorithms. It has the advantage of being simple to understand and to implement, but is slow to execute if more than a few thousand objects are being sorted.

7.4 Arrays and functions

This section discusses one of the genuinely insightful decisions that was made during the development of the C language. It concerns the relationship between arrays and pointers, and the way arrays are handled in functions.

Suppose that `A` is an array of `n` integer values. The first variable in `A` is `A[0]`, and is stored at location `&A[0]`. Similarly, the second variable is `A[1]`, stored at `&A[1]`. The developers of C specified that the array itself, `A`, is defined to be a *pointer constant* whose value is the address of the first variable in the array, that is, `&A[0]`. As an example, if `p` is a variable of type pointer to `int` (that is, `p` is of type `int*`), then the assignment `p=A` has exactly the same effect as `p=&A[0]` – it leaves `p` pointing at the first variable in `A`.

The identifier used as an array name is a constant of type pointer to T, where T is the type underlying the array.

This relationship makes it easy to pass arrays into functions. Since the array name is a pointer constant, if the array is passed into a function, what is transferred into the corresponding argument variable is a pointer expression. It can either be declared as a pointer in the function header, or as an undimensioned array using the notation `A[]`. If the argument is declared as a pointer, and then altered within the function (by being assigned to), it is only the local variable that is changed – the original address constant is not altered in any way. In this sense, array arguments are treated exactly the same as integer arguments – the value of the expression is copied over into a local argument variable that can then be altered, but the original expression cannot be altered.

Array argument variables can be declared as either arrays, or as pointers of the same underlying type. The number of elements in the array does not need to be part of the declaration of that argument, and the function can accept array arguments of any size, provided the underlying type is the same.

Functions that receive the argument as a pointer variable are shown later in the chapter, and in the remainder of this section the functions shown declare the argument to be an undimensioned array. For example, consider the program in Figure 7.4. That program is the one presumed to have been executed in the lower box of Figure 7.3, and makes use of a total of four functions. Because an array is a pointer to the first of its elements, changes made in the function via that pointer are directly reflected in the underlying array. That means that use of an array within a function follows an identical pattern to use of the array in the scope in which it was declared, and the bodies of functions `read_int_array` and `sort_int_array` are exactly as discussed already in Figures 7.2 and 7.3. The third function, `print_int_array`, similarly uses the argument variable `A` to access elements of the array declared in the `main` function, in this case to print them out.

Access from within a function to array elements via a pointer passed as an argument directly alters the underlying variables in the original array.

Note the manner in which the reading function is instructed of the maximum number of values that the array can hold (10 in the example execution shown in

```
/* Read an array, sort it, write it out again.
*/
#include <stdio.h>

#define MAXVALS 10

int read_int_array(int A[], int n);
void sort_int_array(int A[], int n);
void print_int_array(int A[], int n);
void int_swap(int *p1, int *p2);

int
main(int argc, char *argv[]) {
    int numbers[MAXVALS], nnumbs;
    nnumbs = read_int_array(numbers, MAXVALS);
    printf("Before: ");
    print_int_array(numbers, nnumbs);
    sort_int_array(numbers, nnumbs);
    printf("After : ");
    print_int_array(numbers, nnumbs);
    return 0;
}

int
read_int_array(int A[], int maxvals) {
    int n, excess, next;
    /* the body of this function is in Figure 7.2 */
    return n;
}

void
sort_int_array(int A[], int n) {
    int i, j;
    /* the body of this function is in Figure 7.3 */
}

void
print_int_array(int A[], int n) {
    int i;
    for (i=0; i<n; i++) {
        printf("%4d", A[i]);
    }
    printf("\n");
}
```

Figure 7.4: A complete program for sorting a set of integers. The body of function `read_int_array` is shown in Figure 7.2, and the body of function `sort_int_array` is shown in Figure 7.3. The lower box of Figure 7.3 shows an execution of the completed program.

```
typedef double vector_t[SIZE];

void
vector_add(vector_t A, vector_t B, vector_t C, int n) {
    int i;
    for (i=0; i<n; i++) {
        C[i] = A[i] + B[i];
    }
}
```

Figure 7.5: Function showing the use of user-defined array types.

Figure 7.3), via the transfer of the constant `MAXVALS` into the argument variable `maxvals`. The function returns the number of values that were actually read. Thereafter, every time `numbers` is passed into a function, the value of `nnumbs` accompanies it, so that each function can guard its loops accordingly, and avoid straying into sections of the array that have not been initialized.

> Unless an array always contains the dimensioned number of valid values, a variable that records the number of initialized values in the array must accompany the array at all times.

Figure 7.5 shows another function making use of array arguments. It also illustrates the use of a new declaration mode: the *typedef*. Instead of being a variable declaration, the first line in Figure 7.5 is a declaration of a new *type*. The use of the keyword `typedef` prior to the type `double` is what denotes this mode, and the modified statement is interpreted by the compiler as meaning "every time you see the identifier `vector_t` used as a type in a declaration, it means an array of `double` containing `SIZE` values". The `typedef` statement does not actually declare a variable, so a subsequent variable declaration is always required – `vector_t X`, for example – when memory space is to be allocated.

In Figure 7.5 it makes sense to use the `typedef` facility, as there are three arguments to the function `vector_add`, all of the same type. Use of `typedef` also brings flexibility. For example, if it was later decided to alter the base type of the whole computation from `double` to `float`, the change is easily implemented by changing only the `typedef` statement. In a sense, the `typedef` is to types what the `#define` is to values.

> The `typedef` declaration defines a new type. It can be an alias for a simple type, or a compound type. Typedefs should be used for all important recurring types in a program.

Any type can be given a name using a `typedef`. For example, if a program manipulates several variables all of type pointer to `int`, then the statement `typedef int *intptr` might be used, so that all of those variables can be uniformly declared to be of type `intptr`. It even makes sense to sometimes `typedef` simple types – `typedef double data_t` is perfectly reasonable, and allows `data_t` to be subsequently used as a type throughout the program, and easily altered if changes to circumstances subsequently warrant it.

Any identifier can be used as the name of the new type that is being introduced. But just as it makes sense to choose variable identifiers appropriately, it is also prudent to be systematic in the choice of type names. One convention – and the one used throughout this book – is to add a "`_t`" suffix to all type identifiers, to prevent them being confused with variable names.

Once the use of `typedef` has been absorbed, the details of Figure 7.5 are as expected: three array pointers are passed into the function, together with an integer `n` that indicates how many values in each of the arrays is valid. The function manipulates the arrays using a `for` loop, and in using the argument pointers, alters the values in the array that was passed as the third argument. For example, if `V` has been declared as a `vector_t` and assigned some initial values, then the function call `vector_add(V, V, V, num)` doubles each of the first `num` elements in `V` and leaves any remaining elements unchanged.

7.5 Two-dimensional arrays

So far, the examples of arrays have only used `int` and `double` types for the underlying variables. But any type can be used as the base type. In other sections of this chapter arrays based on `char` variables, and arrays based on pointer variables, are examined. This section looks at the complex issue of using an array type as a base type for another array to create a *two-dimensional array*.

Consider these two declarations:

```
int X[10];
int (Y[5])[10];
```

The first declaration says that the identifier `X` is a pointer constant, and has as its value the address of the first of a continuous set of 10 variables of type `int`. Similarly, the second declaration says that the identifier `Y` is a pointer constant, and has as its value the address of the first of a continuous set of 5 variables. But in `Y`, each of those component objects is an "array of 10 `int`". That is, the second declaration allocates memory space for a total of 50 integers.

The first component of `X` is `X[0]`, and is of type `int`. The first component of `Y` is `Y[0]`, and is of type `int[10]`. The first component of `Y[0]` is thus at `(Y[0])[0]`, and is an `int`. Similarly, the last component of `Y` is at `Y[4]` and is of type `int[10]`; and its last component is at `(Y[4])[9]`, and is of type `int`. In practice, the precedence hierarchy allows the parentheses to be dropped, and `Y` can be declared as `int Y[5][10]`, with its "first component of first component" accessed via `Y[0][0]`, and its "last component of last component" accessed via `Y[4][9]`.

> A two-dimensional array is an array of one-dimensional arrays. When one subscript is supplied, a one-dimensional array is obtained.

A two-dimensional array is naturally dealt with using nested `for` loops. Figure 7.6 shows a simple example, in which an array is initialized and then printed. In

```
/* Manipulate a two-dimensional array.
*/
#include <stdio.h>

#define ROWS 5
#define COLS 10

void assign_2d(int A[][COLS], int nrows);
void print_2d(int A[][COLS], int nrows);

int
main(int argc, char *argv[]) {
    int Y[ROWS][COLS];
    assign_2d(Y, ROWS);
    print_2d(Y, ROWS);
    return 0;
}

void
assign_2d(int A[][COLS], int nrows) {
    int i, j;
    for (i=0; i<nrows; i++) {
        for (j=0; j<COLS; j++) {
            A[i][j] = 100 + 10*i + j;
        }
    }
}

void
print_2d(int A[][COLS], int nrows) {
    int i, j;
    for (i=0; i<nrows; i++) {
        for (j=0; j<COLS; j++) {
            printf("%4d ", A[i][j]);
        }
        printf("\n");
    }
}
```

```
 100  101  102  103  104  105  106  107  108  109
 110  111  112  113  114  115  116  117  118  119
 120  121  122  123  124  125  126  127  128  129
 130  131  132  133  134  135  136  137  138  139
 140  141  142  143  144  145  146  147  148  149
```

Figure 7.6: Manipulating a two-dimensional array. The argument type declarations in the functions must specify a constant value for the second dimension, so that element offsets can be correctly calculated.

```
typedef vector_t sqmatrix_t[SIZE];

void
sqmatrix_add1(sqmatrix_t A, sqmatrix_t B, sqmatrix_t C,
        int n) {
    int i,j;
    for (i=0; i<n; i++) {
        for (j=0; j<n; j++) {
            C[i][j] = A[i][j] + B[i][j];
        }
    }
}

void
sqmatrix_add2(vector_t A[], vector_t B[], vector_t C[],
        int n) {
    int i;
    for (i=0; i<n; i++) {
        vector_add(A[i], B[i], C[i], n);
    }
}
```

Figure 7.7: Functions showing the use of two-dimensional arrays. The type `vector_t` and function `vector_add` defined in Figure 7.5.

both of the functions the number of rows to be dealt with – the number of elements in argument `A` – is specified as a second variable argument rather than as part of the type of `A`. But the number of elements in each row of the array (the constant `COLS`) must be specified, as it is part of the type declaration of `A`. As with all array arguments, the *size* of each of the base elements in the array must be declared to the function, even if the *number* of elements is indicated by a companion variable.

> When two-dimensional arrays are passed to functions, only the dominant dimension can be left unspecified.

To see why, consider how the memory address of array cell `A[i][j]` is calculated. Within the `i`'th row, the `j`'th value is at address `&(A[i])+4*j`. The constant 4 in that calculation arises because each underlying `int` variable (on most computers) occupies four bytes. Then, to work out the address of `A[i]` to plug in to this computation, a similar calculation is performed: it is `A+(4*COLS)*i`, where `COLS` is the number of `int` variables in each element of the array `A`. So the overall address of the `int` in `A[i][j]` is given by `A+4*(COLS*i + j)`, where, as before, the constant four represents the size of each underlying `int`. Hence, knowledge of `COLS` is essential if elements in the array are to be correctly accessed.

Figure 7.7 shows how this growing complexity is managed through the judicious use of `typedef`. A new type, `sqmatrix_t` is defined using the previously defined `vector_t` type (Figure 7.5 on page 108), and then used as the argument type for two functions. The two functions, `sqmatrix_add1` and `sqmatrix_add2`, carry out exactly the same task as each other, but do so in different ways: in `sqmatrix_add1` the argument arrays are handled as two-dimensional objects, and two subscripts are supplied in order that the underlying `double` variables can be accessed; whereas in `sqmatrix_add2` the three arguments are treated as one-dimensional arrays, and each of their components handed over to the previous `vector_add` function for addition. This second function shows the subtle difference between the C approach, of declaring an "array of arrays", and the alternative approach of having a single array that requires two subscripts.

There is no reason to stop at two dimensions, and higher dimensional arrays can be constructed in exactly the same way – by declaring them to be an array of objects, where each of the objects is an array. Provided the right number of subscripts is supplied (usually through a set of `for` loops nested to the dimension of the array) , the individual elements in the array can always be accessed.

One thing to be careful of is that, as the dimensionality grows, so does the space required. The four-dimensional array `double Z[200][200][200][200]` has over a billion elements in it, and requires more than 12 GB of memory. Such a declaration will fail on current desktop and laptop computers.

> When large arrays are being declared, the difference in cost between using `double` and `float` base variables, and between using `int` and `char` base variables (and other integer types) may become significant.

7.6 Array initializers

Scalar variables can be initialized on declaration using a first assignment: `int n=0` both declares `n`, and assigns an initial value of zero. Static variables (Section 6.5 on page 89) must always be initialized this way, since any other assignment is executed at every call to function that declares the variable.

Arrays can be similarly initialized on declaration, using a variant assignment in which all of the values to be assigned are listed:

```
#define MONTH_ARRAY 13
    int month_days[MONTH_ARRAY] =
        {0,31,28,31,30,31,30,31,31,30,31,30,31};
```

This statement both declares a thirteen-element array of `int`, and assigns initial values. In this particular case it makes sense to use subscripts in $1 \ldots 12$, and so the declared type must be `int[13]`. If insufficient values are provided for the declared size of the array, the remaining entries are assigned to zero. Hence, the declaration `int A[SIZE]={0}` initializes every element of `A` to zero. If too many elements are supplied, the surplus ones are (possibly silently) discarded by the compiler.

> Arrays can be initialized on declaration by supplying a list of values in braces.

When an array is being initialized, the compiler infers the number of elements required if no bound is supplied:

```
int month_days[] =
    {0,31,28,31,30,31,30,31,31,30,31,30,31};
```

This statement has exactly the same effect as the one above, but has the drawback not providing the programmer with a variable or constant that can be used for loop control. One work-around, which is used in Section 7.8 below in connection with arrays of `char`, is to insert a *sentinel* value at the end of the array, and write all loops so that they terminate when the sentinel is reached:

```
int data_vals[] =
    {17,5,8,16,68,54,33,-1};
```

The array `data_vals` can be controlled by the loop:

```
for (i=0; data_vals[i]!=-1; i++)
```

If fresh values are inserted into array `data_vals` prior to the sentinel, and the program recompiled, the array is automatically enlarged, and the loop iterates to cover the added entries. But be careful – this approach can only be used if the sentinel value is never, ever, going to be a valid data value. Using a separate variable or constant to specify the size of the array is less susceptible to errors than the use of a sentinel. An elegant way of controlling loops when the size of the array is not set by the programmer is discussed in Section 10.4.

Multi-dimensional arrays are initialized by supplying the correct number of components, with nested braces indicating the subdivisions within the components. Can you work out how the programmer intends this array to be used?

```
int month_days[2][13]
    = {{0,31,28,31,30,31,30,31,31,30,31,30,31},
       {0,31,29,31,30,31,30,31,31,30,31,30,31}};
```

As with all array initializers, rows which are short are padded to length with zeros.

One issue that arises in connection with array initializers is the size of the compiled, or executable, version of the program. If a global array is declared and initialized, the executable file on disk usually stores each of the initial values. For example, in many C systems the declaration `int B[10000000]={0}` adds 40 MB to the size of the executable program. Compared to this cost, initialization via an explicit loop may be an attractive option. And stack-based automatic arrays of this size may have their own problems – there might be insufficient memory available in the stack for them to be created. Section 10.1 on page 163 examines the problem of large arrays, and shows another way of creating them that avoids these difficulties.

7.7 Arrays and pointers

Earlier in this chapter it was explained that an array name was regarded as being equivalent to a pointer constant. The flip-side of this ingenious relationship is that a pointer can be used to access an array, a possibility that is best illustrated with an example. Suppose that the declarations `int A[5]` and `int *p` have been made.

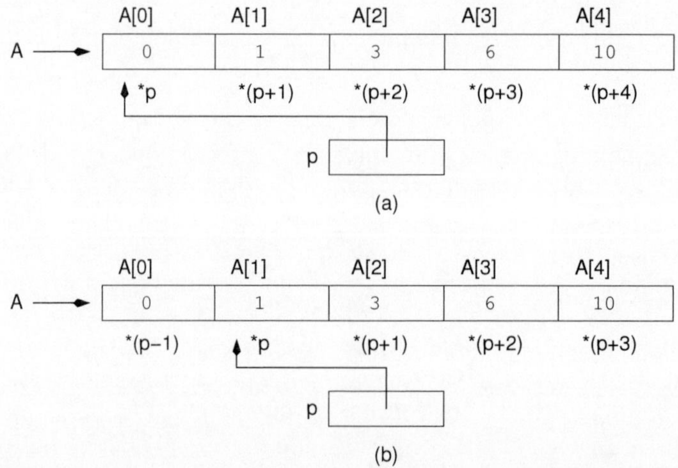

Figure 7.8: Pointer variables and pointer constants (arrays) can refer to the same underlying memory: (a) after the assignment `p=A`, and then (b) after the subsequent assignment `p=p+1`. The array `A` is assumed to have been assigned values by the program fragment shown in Figure 7.1 on page 100.

Then the assignment `p=A` assigns to `p` the address of the first element in `A`. And if `p` points at the first element of `A`, then `*p` is exactly the value `A[0]`. This situation is illustrated in Figure 7.8(a).

To further exploit the duality between arrays and pointers, C offers a useful facility called *pointer arithmetic*. Memory is a sequence of bytes, with each byte having an address. A pointer variable holds an address, at which a variable of the type underlying the pointer is presumed to be stored. The rules of pointer arithmetic stipulate that if n is an integer expression, then the expression `p+`n is a pointer of the same type as `p`, but to an address that is $n \times b$ bytes further along in memory, where b is the number of bytes occupied by each variable of the type of pointer `p`.

For example, when `p` is of type pointer to `int`, the numeric value of `p+1` is exactly one integer storage unit (usually four bytes) greater than the numeric value of `p`, which makes `p+1` a pointer to the next `int` after the one pointed at by `p`. Similarly, `p-1` is a pointer to the integer before `p`.

> Pointer addition allows the construction of pointer expressions that reference adjacent (or otherwise related) variables of the same underlying type as the initial pointer.

In other words, if `A` is the base address of an array, then the notation `A[i]` is just a convenient shorthand for the alternative expression `*(A+i)` – create a pointer to the `i`'th unit after the address `A`, and then use that pointer to access an array element. The duality between arrays and pointers works both ways – if `p` is a pointer, then `p[i]` can be used to access the `i`'th object after the one currently pointed at by `p`.

Pointer *assignment* captures the result of pointer addition or subtraction. Figure 7.8(b) shows the effect of adding "one" to the pointer `p` of Figure 7.8(a). Now `*p` is the second element of A, and if the first element of the array is to be accessed, the expression *(p-1) must be used.

Pointers can be compared for both equality and relative order. In Figure 7.8(a) the equality test p==A would be true, and in Figure 7.8(b), would be false. The order test A<=p would be true in both situations, since p stores an address at least as great as the address constant A in both arrangements. It is important to understand that these comparisons operate on the address values of A and p, and have nothing to do with the contents of the memory words they are indicating. The comparison p==A can only be true if both p and A are pointing at the same word of memory, whereas the test *p==*A is true any time p points at a value that is the same as the value stored in A[0].

Pointers can be tested for equality and relative order. A common mistake is to test the values the pointers are pointing at, rather than the pointers themselves.

A further operation on pointers is that of *pointer difference*. If p and q are both of type pointer to T for some type T, then the expression p-q is of type int and indicates the number of variables of type T that lie between the one pointed at by p and the one pointed at by q.

Pointer difference can be used to determine how many objects of some base type T lie between two pointers of type pointer to T.

The program fragment in Figure 7.9 mirrors the situation in Figures 7.1 and 7.8, and further explores the relationship between arrays and pointers. The initial situation is as shown in Figure 7.8(a), but, because p is a variable rather than a constant, it can

```
int A[N], *p, i;
for (i=0; i<N; i++) {
    A[i] = i*(i+1)/2;
}
printf("A = %10p\n", A);
p = A;
for (p=A; p<A+N; p++) {
    printf("p = %10p, *p = %2d\n", p, *p);
}
```

```
A = 0xbffff5e4
p = 0xbffff5e4, *p =  0
p = 0xbffff5e8, *p =  1
p = 0xbffff5ec, *p =  3
p = 0xbffff5f0, *p =  6
p = 0xbffff5f4, *p = 10
```

Figure 7.9: Using a pointer to step through an array. In this example the constant N has the value 5. Figure 7.8(a) shows the arrangement after the assignment p=A. The lower box shows an execution of the program fragment in the upper box.

be stepped through the array. For example, the third output line in the lower box corresponds to the situation shown in Figure 7.8(b).

Notice how, using pointer addition and pointer comparison, the controlled variable in the `for` loop is the pointer `p`. Each time `p` is incremented, four is added to the byte address it points at, making the next element of array `A` accessible via the pointer indirection `*p`. Had the base type of the array been `double`, eight would have been added to the byte address in `p` at each increment, but the loop would still operate correctly, as the guard tests the pointer in relative terms, and not according to the exact number of bytes involved.

> A pointer variable can be used to step through the elements of an array. The guard on the controlling loop must test the pointer against another pointer value, not a constant.

Pointers can also be used to step through the rows, and elements within the rows, in two-dimensional arrays. But it is critical that you distinguish between pointers that point to whole array rows, and pointers that point to elements within a row. In particular, it is easy to make mistakes, and step a pointer forward only one element, when the intention was to step to the next row. Unless you are very confident, you should always access elements in two-dimensional arrays using double subscripts, rather than via pointers.

7.8 Strings

Arrays of type `char` play a special part in the language C – they are used to store *strings*, which are sequences of characters. To make manipulation of these special arrays easy, C imposes a requirement on strings that does not apply to arrays in general, and stipulates that the last element be a zero, which is represented by the character constant `'\0'`. This *null byte* acts as a sentinel, and allows a wide range of string handling functions to be written.

Consider the following set of declarations, each of which has an initializer:

```
char s1[5] = {'H', 'e', 'l', 'l', 'o'};
char s2[6] = {'W', 'o', 'r', 'l', 'd', '\0'};
char s3[100] = "Goodbye";
char s4[] = "Pluto";
char *s5 = "Farewell Neptune";
```

In a broad sense, all of `s1` to `s5` are arrays of characters, and so can be loosely categorized as strings. But there are also some important differences. Array `s1` stores a set of characters, but does not include a null byte. It can be manipulated on a per-character basis using standard array techniques, and can be printed character by character using the "`%c`" format descriptor, for example. But the "`%s`" format descriptor cannot be used on it.

String `s2` includes an explicit null byte, and the array has to be sized accordingly – the null byte does actually occupy a `char` variable. With the sentinel, `s2` is a proper C string, and can, for example, be printed out in its entirety using a "`%s`" format descriptor: `printf("%s\n",s2)` works just fine.

In C, strings are stored as null-terminated arrays of `char`. The null byte must be counted when space allocations are being made.

The third and fourth strings in the example, `s3` and `s4`, show further options. Both are initialized to string values, and are properly terminated in the same way that `s2` is. C automatically supplies a terminating null byte to every string constant created using double quotes. The declaration of `s3` allocates many more bytes than are required for the initially assigned value `"Goodbye"`, and means that there is room for longer strings – up to 99 characters – to be stored if required. The declaration of `s4` says that the underlying array should be made long enough to store the initial value, and in this example a total of six bytes are allocated, with `s4[5]=='\0'`.

String `s5` is different again. That declaration causes two regions of memory to be allocated – one, either four bytes or eight bytes long (depending on the number of bytes required by pointers in your computer hardware) to a variable named `s5` of type `char*`, and the second, seventeen bytes long, to an array of `char` in which the letters `'F'`, `'a'`, and so on, are stored. The pointer variable `s5` is given an initial value, and points at the first `char` in the constructed string, the one holding the `'F'`.

Because `s5` is a pointer variable (rather than a pointer constant, as is the case with `s1` to `s4`), it can be changed within the program – the assignment `s5=s4` is perfectly valid, whereas `s4=s5` is not. Also worth noting is that the underlying string associated with `s5` might be allocated by the compiler to a section of memory that for security reasons is tagged as being read-only, and an attempt to change the string with an assignment statement `s5[0]='f'` might cause a runtime error to occur. On the other hand, the assignment `s4[0]='f'` is always valid, since array `s4` is a collection of declared variables. Figure 7.10 illustrates the distinction between `s4` and `s5`.

Character arrays and character pointers can be initialized to strings. If a character pointer is initialized, the string it points at might be allocated in read-only memory.

If variable `s5` is modified via an assignment statement, the string `"Farewell Neptune"` is irrevocably lost. It exists in memory somewhere, but if nothing is pointing at it, cannot be accessed by the program except by guesswork or luck. The technical name for such regions of memory that can no longer be accessed by a program is *garbage*, and in some programming languages an operation called *garbage collection* is periodically undertaken to recover unreachable memory. In C there is no

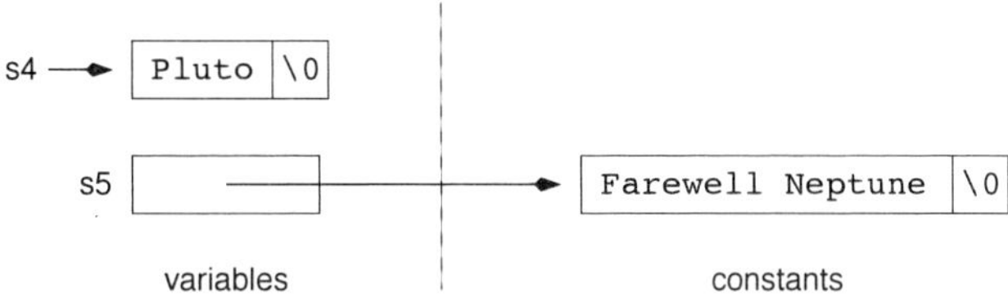

Figure 7.10: Array and pointer declarations for strings. The runtime system may prevent modification of the string underlying the pointer variable `s5`.

```
    char *p = "Cheshire:-)";
    while (*p) {
        printf("p = %12p, string at p = %s\n", p, p);
        p = p+1;
    }
```

```
p =  0x10cc5ef38, string at p = Cheshire:-)
p =  0x10cc5ef39, string at p = heshire:-)
p =  0x10cc5ef3a, string at p = eshire:-)
p =  0x10cc5ef3b, string at p = shire:-)
p =  0x10cc5ef3c, string at p = hire:-)
p =  0x10cc5ef3d, string at p = ire:-)
p =  0x10cc5ef3e, string at p = re:-)
p =  0x10cc5ef3f, string at p = e:-)
p =  0x10cc5ef40, string at p = :-)
p =  0x10cc5ef41, string at p = -)
p =  0x10cc5ef42, string at p = )
```

Figure 7.11: Accessing a string via a pointer variable.

garbage collection, and a program that permanently loses track of sections of memory by altering the pointers that (used to) point to them is said to have a *memory leak*.

Figure 7.11 gives another perspective on strings. The pointer p is a variable, and so can be changed in the loop. Each time it is incremented, the string that it points at appears to get one character shorter, and when printed using the "%p" format descriptor, it is clear that the pointer has advanced by one. The "%s" format descriptor follows the null byte convention, and prints characters starting at the address indicated by the corresponding pointer variable, until a null byte is encountered. So the string is not really getting shorter as p is incremented – it is just that more and more of the characters are to the left of p, and printf has no reason (or permission) to look at those characters. The null byte acts as a sentinel to control the loop, and when p points at the null byte, *p is zero, and the guard is false. This type of guard is very common in functions that manipulate strings, but can be reasonably cryptic. If you have any doubts, you should write the longer form in your programs: *p!='\0'.

> The format descriptor "%s" prints a string, starting at the byte indicated by a char* argument, and continuing until a null byte is encountered.

There is an important library of string manipulation functions that you need to be familiar with, described by the header file string.h. Table 7.2 summarizes the more useful ones. As with all library functions, the on-line help facility can be used to obtain more details – man strcmp gives details of strcmp, for example. In some C systems an extended set of functions is provided in the library described by strings.h.

Most of the functions listed in Table 7.2 are relatively straightforward to implement, and the writing of strlen, strcmp, and strcat makes a useful exercise to help consolidate your understanding of strings. Figure 7.12 shows how the string "assignment" function strcpy is implemented. Two alternative versions are shown,

Function	Purpose
`int strlen(char *s)`	Returns the number of characters in `s`, not including the null byte.
`char *strcpy(char *dest, char *src)`	Copies `src`, including the null byte, into the array space indicated by `dest`. No bounds checking is done, and `dest` must be large enough to accommodate `src`, plus a null byte. This makes it risky. Be careful!
`char *strncpy(char *dest, char *src, int n)`	As for `strcpy`, except that `n` indicates the number of characters to be copied. Less risky than `strcpy`, but note that `dest` must be (at least) `n` bytes long, even if the string in `src` is shorter than `n`.
`int strcmp(char *s1, char *s2)`	Compares `s1` and `s2`, and returns negative, zero, or positive when `s1` is less than, equal to, or greater than, `s2`. The ASCII ordering shown on page 60 is used, with the uppercase letters preceding lowercase.
`int strncmp(char *s1, char *s2, int n)`	As for `strcmp`, except that `n` supplies a limit on the number of characters examined.
`int strcasecmp(char *s1, char *s2)`	As for `strcmp`, except that upper and lower case alphabetic characters are considered to be equal.
`char *strcat(char *dest, char *src)`	Appends a copy of `src` to the string `dest` by overwriting its null byte, copying characters, and then writing a new null byte. The string `dest` must be large enough to accommodate the extended string. Risky.
`char *strncat(char *dest, char *src, int n)`	As for `strcat`, except that `n` provides a limit on the number of characters of the second argument that may be copied. Safer than `strcat`.
`int atoi(char *s)`	Returns the integer value represented by the characters of `s`.
`double atof(char *s)`	Returns the `double` value represented by the characters of `s`.

Table 7.2: A subset of the string handling functions provided in the C library described by `string.h`. Functions `strcpy`, `strncpy`, `strcat`, and `strncat` return a pointer to the start of the copied string. The last two functions (`atoi` and `atof`) are described in the header file `stdlib.h`.

```
char *strcpy1(char dest[], char src[]) {
    int i=0;
    while (src[i]!='\0') {
        dest[i] = src[i];
        i = i+1;
    }
    dest[i] = '\0';
    return dest;
}

char *strcpy2(char *dest, char *src) {
    char *p=dest;
    while ((*p++ = *src++))
        /* nothing */ ;
    return dest;
}
```

Figure 7.12: Two equivalent implementations of the function strcpy. In the second, the loop guard has the side effect of copying the characters, including the null byte. The two postincrement assignment statements also involve side effects that are exploited. The additional parentheses in the loop guard are not necessary, but serve to tell the compiler that yes, the use of a single "=" in the loop guard really is what is intended, silencing the warning message that might otherwise arise.

one rather more succinct than the other. The brevity arises through a quite complex reliance on assignment side effects during expression evaluation, and it is regarded as something of a "classic" in C circles. Note the use of an empty body in the while loop, and the reliance on the fact that the postincrement operator alters its operand only after the operand value has been used in the expression the operand is part of. You should not be trying to write such terse code, and for most purposes the approach of strcpy1 is the more reasonable one, and certainly so for novice programmers.

One difficulty that new programmers always have with strings is caused by the fact that it is necessary to distinguish between the strings, and the pointers that point at them. The assignment p=q assigns a *pointer* to p; and the test p==q tests the *pointers* for equality. So if you want to assign a *string*, or test two *strings* for equality, the library functions strncpy and strcmp must be used.

> The operators "=" and "==" apply to variables, including pointer variables. The functions strncpy and strcmp apply to the strings pointed at by character pointers.

Table 7.2 also lists two additional string functions, atoi and atof. These two convert strings representations such as "123" and "45.341" into the internal int and double representations needed for arithmetic. That is, they convert a character string into a number, in the same way that scanf converts character strings typed on the keyboard into internal numbers. They are used to good effect in Section 7.11.

7.9 Case study: Distinct words

Try this exercise before reading any further:

> Design and implement a program that reads text from the standard input, and writes a list of the distinct words that appear. Words may be limited to a maximum of 10 alphabetic characters. Assume that as many as 1,000 distinct words might appear.

Figures 7.13 and 7.14 describe a complete program that meets the specification. It makes use of a two-dimensional array of characters to store a set of words. As required, a word is defined to be a sequence of as many as ten alphabetic characters (constant `MAXCHARS`), and the program is configured to handles inputs that contain as many as 1,000 distinct words (constant `MAXWORDS`). Many of the ideas discussed in this chapter come together in this program, and it is worth detailed study. The following features should be noted:

- In Figure 7.13, the inclusion of the header file `ctype.h`, to get access to the function `isalpha`, which returns true if its argument is an alphabetic character, and false otherwise.
- The early return of `EOF` if no alphabetic character can be found with which to start a new word.

```
#include <stdio.h>
#include <ctype.h>

/* Extract a single word out of the standard input, of not
   more than limit characters. Argument array W must be
   limit+1 characters or bigger. */
int
getword(char W[], int limit) {
    int c, len=0;
    /* first, skip over any non alphabetics */
    while ((c=getchar())!=EOF && !isalpha(c)) {
        /* do nothing more */
    }
    if (c==EOF) {
        return EOF;
    }
    /* ok, first character of next word has been found */
    W[len++] = c;
    while (len<limit && (c=getchar())!=EOF && isalpha(c)) {
        /* another character to be stored */
        W[len++] = c;
    }
    /* now close off the string */
    W[len] = '\0';
    return 0;
}
```

Figure 7.13: Function for reading the next alphabetic string from the standard input stream.

```
#include <stdio.h>
#include <string.h>

#define MAXCHARS 10        /* Max chars per word */
#define MAXWORDS 1000      /* Max distinct words */

typedef char word_t[MAXCHARS+1];
int getword(word_t W, int limit);

int
main(int argc, char *argv[]) {
    word_t one_word, all_words[MAXWORDS];
    int numdistinct=0, totwords=0, i, found;
    while (getword(one_word, MAXCHARS) != EOF) {
        totwords = totwords+1;
        /* linear search in array of previous words... */
        found = 0;
        for (i=0; i<numdistinct && !found; i++) {
            found = (strcmp(one_word, all_words[i]) == 0);
        }
        if (!found && numdistinct<MAXWORDS) {
            strcpy(all_words[numdistinct], one_word);
            numdistinct += 1;
        }
        /* NB - program silently discards words after
           MAXWORDS distinct ones have been found */
    }
    printf("%d words read\n", totwords);
    for (i=0; i<numdistinct; i++) {
        printf("word #%d is \"%s\"\n", i, all_words[i]);
    }
    return 0;
}
```

```
Mary had a little lamb, little lamb, little lamb,
Mary had a little fourleggedwhitefluffything.
```

```
16 words read
word #0 is "Mary"
word #1 is "had"
word #2 is "a"
word #3 is "little"
word #4 is "lamb"
word #5 is "fourlegged"
word #6 is "whitefluff"
word #7 is "ything"
```

Figure 7.14: Main program to call the function `getword` defined in Figure 7.13. Linear search is used to step through an array of the distinct words, to see if the next word is different. The bottom box shows an execution of the program when presented with the input shown in the middle box.

- The carefully engineered guard on the second `while` loop in Figure 7.13, which allows `getchar` to be called only if the word has not yet reached its length limit, and then looks at `c` only if a character was successfully read, and then allows that character to be added to the word only if it is alphabetic.

- The explicit insertion of a null byte at the end of the string, once the word has been found.

- In Figure 7.14, the inclusion of the header file `string.h`, to gain access to `strcmp` and `strncpy`.

- The use of a `typedef`, to create a type called `word_t`, and the fact that the `word_t` type allows space for null bytes, by allocating `MAXCHARS+1` characters to each word.

- The use of a linear search within the `while` loop, to check the current word against words stored previously in array `all_words`, and the check of the flag variable `found` once the inner `for` has terminated.

- The check that `numdistinct` is less than `MAXWORDS`, before a new word is copied into the next vacant slot in the array, to avoid over-running array `all_words` and scribbling over memory that is used for other purposes.

In short, it is a rather complex program, and you need to invest a non-trivial amount of time to fully understand it.

7.10 Arrays of strings

Figure 7.14 manipulates an array of fixed-length character arrays, and uses them to store a set of words. The fact that the two-dimensional array is rigidly structured so that every row has the same number of underlying elements is wasteful if the strings to be stored are of widely varying length. For example, if words of up to 100 characters were to be allowed, then 101 bytes of storage would be allocated to every word in `all_words`, even though the majority of the words are likely to be shorter.

In Figure 7.14 the set of strings is dynamic and created at runtime, and it is hard to see how anything other than a two-dimensional rectangular array could be used. On the other hand, when the set of strings is static, a better arrangement is possible – a one-dimensional array of pointers to strings can be used to record the addresses of strings, with each of the strings now able to be of a different length. It doesn't actually matter where in memory the strings are – all that matters is that each of the pointers in the array correctly indicates the corresponding string, and that each is terminated by a null byte. Such a structure would be of type `(char*)[]`, or alternatively, `char**`.

One further point to be noted in connection with strings, arrays of strings, and pointers in general, is the role of `NULL`. Like all variables, when pointers are declared they must not be assumed to have any initial value. The value `NULL` is a pointer constant that is used in programs to assign values to pointers that do not currently point at anything. That is, the declaration `int *p` declares a pointer, and leaves it uninitialized; whereas the declaration `int *p=NULL` declares the pointer `p` and gives it a valid value that is an *in*valid address. When an array of pointers to strings is being declared, it is conventional to add a `NULL` pointer after the last string, to act as a sentinel. That is, each of the strings in the array is terminated by a null byte; and the array itself is ended with a null pointer. The actual value of `NULL` is "0".

Use of a `NULL` pointer as a sentinel is commonplace in programs that manipulate arrays of strings. An example is given shortly.

> The constant `NULL` is used to signify pointer values that have been initialized, but do not currently point at an underlying object.

Finally in this section, note that Chapter 10 shows how arrays of strings can be created while a program is executing, so that the waste associated with two-dimensional rectangular arrays like `all_words` in Figure 7.14 can be eliminated.

7.11 Program arguments

The final section in this chapter deals with the two arguments to the `main` program. Variables `argc` and `argv` have been used so far as part of a formula, without any discussion. Now is the time for an explanation – they communicate options from the command-line used to initiate the program, and let the operating system pass information for the program to make use of. Figure 7.15 gives a simple program that makes use of `argc` and `argv` to print out the command-line that called it, and at the same time, shows how an array of strings is manipulated.

The `int` variable `argc` indicates the *number* of command-line arguments, including the name of the program itself. The argument `argv` is an array of pointers to strings, of exactly the `(char*) []` or `char**` type described in the previous section. Each of the strings in the array is one of the command-line arguments. So `argv[0]` is always the name of the currently executing program; if `argc` is greater than one, then `argv[1]` is the first argument on the command-line; and so on. Note the use of quotes on the command-line to construct argument strings that include blanks.

Figure 7.16 illustrates the structure that is passed to the `main` function in connection with the first example execution in Figure 7.15. The second example execution shows a different possibility – the shell expansion `po*.c` takes place before the program is initiated, so the program sees a list of filenames that match the pattern.

Because of the `NULL` sentinel stored in `argv[argc]`, the loop in Figure 7.15 can be controlled in several different ways. The one shown in the figure simply counts up to `argc`. An alternative is to step through until the sentinel, and structure the loop as `for (i=0; argv[i]!=NULL; i++)`. That second version can then be further condensed, to get `for (i=0; argv[i]; i++)`.

> The program arguments `argc` and `argv` describe an array of strings, with each string in the array one of the arguments supplied on the command-line when the program was initiated.

The facility provided by command-line arguments can be used in many different ways. For example, a filename might be supplied, to be processed by the program; or an initial value for a variable might be supplied:

```
int
main(int argc, char *argv[]) {
    int i;
    printf("argc = %d\n", argc);
    for (i=0; i<argc; i++) {
        printf("argv[%d] = \"%s\"\n", i, argv[i]);
    }
    return 0;
}
```

```
mac: ./progargs filename.txt "String with blanks in it" -ansi
argc = 4
argv[0] = "./progargs"
argv[1] = "filename.txt"
argv[2] = "String with blanks in it"
argv[3] = "-ansi"
mac: ./progargs po*.c
argc = 5
argv[0] = "./progargs"
argv[1] = "pointer1.c"
argv[2] = "pointer2.c"
argv[3] = "pointer3.c"
argv[4] = "pointer4.c"
```

Figure 7.15: Using `argc` and `argv` to access the command-line arguments supplied when the program was called. String `argv[0]` is the name of the program being executed.

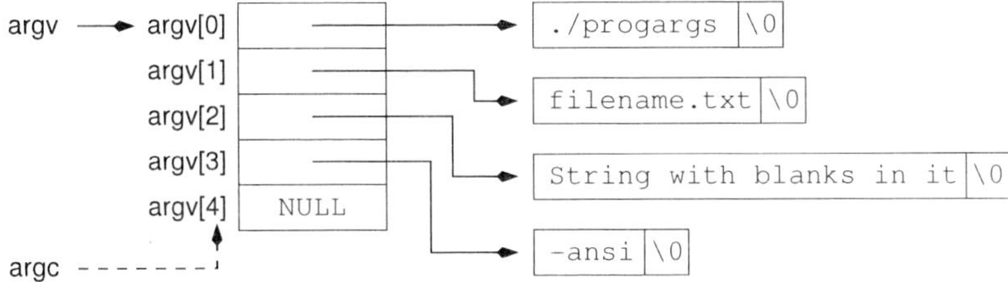

Figure 7.16: The array of strings created and passed to the `main` program in the first example execution in Figure 7.15.

```
    int n=DEFAULT_N;
    if (argc>1) {
        n = atoi(argv[1]);
    }
    printf("Using n=%d\n", n);
```

This code fragment achieves the latter task – variable `n` is given an initial default value as part of its declaration, but if a program argument is available, that value is converted from a string to an integer by the library function `atoi` mentioned earlier, and used to overrule the default. Several of the programs presented in the remainder of this book make use of command-line arguments.

Exercises

7.1 Write a function `int all_zero(int A[], int n)` which returns true if the elements `A[0]` to `A[n-1]` are all zero, and false if any of them are non-zero.

7.2 Modify the program of Figure 7.3 on page 104 so that the array of values is sorted into decreasing order.

7.3 Modify the program of Figure 7.3 on page 104 so that after the array has been sorted only the distinct values are retained in the array (with variable `n` suitably reduced):

```
mac: ./distinct
Enter as many as 1000 values, ^D to end
1 8 15 3 17 12 4 8 4
^D
9 values read into array
Before:     1    8   15    3   17   12    4    8    4
After :     1    3    4    8   12   15   17
```

7.4 Write a program that reads as many as 1,000 integer values, and counts the frequency of each value in the input:

```
mac: ./freqcnt
Enter as many as 1000 values, ^D to end
1 3 4 6 4 3 6 10 3 5 4 3 1 6 4 3 1
^D
17 values read into array
Value    Freq
   1        3
   3        5
   4        4
   5        1
   6        3
  10        1
```

There are two quite different algorithms for this problem. Can you identify both of them? One of them imposes an upper limit on the input values, and so is less general than the other. Does it have any compensating advantages?

7.5 Suppose that a set of "student number, mark" pairs are provided, one pair of numbers per line, with the lines in no particular order. Write a program that reads this data and outputs the same data, but ordered by student number. For example:

```
    823678   66
    765876   94
    864876   48
    785671   68
    854565   89
```

On this input, your program should output:

```
765876  94
785671  68
823678  66
854565  89
864876  48
```

Hint: use two parallel arrays, one for student numbers, and one for the corresponding marks. You may assume that there are at most 1,000 pairs to be handled.

7.6 An alternative sorting algorithm that you might be familiar with goes like this: scan the array to determine the location of the largest element, and then swap it into the last position. Then repeat the process, concentrating at each stage on the elements that have not yet been swapped into their final position. This strategy is called *selection sort*.

Write a function `void selection_sort(int A[], int n)` that orders the `n` elements in array `A`.

(*For a challenge*) Write your function using recursion rather than iteration.

7.7 Write a function that takes as arguments an integer array `A` and an integer `n` that indicates how many elements of `A` may be accessed, and returns the value of the integer in `A` that appears most frequently. If there is more than one value in `A` of that maximum frequency, then the smallest such value should be returned. The array `A` may not be modified.

7.8 Write a function that takes as arguments an integer array `A`, an integer `n` that indicates how many elements of `A` may be accessed, and an integer `k`; and returns the value of the `k`'th smallest integer in `A`. That is, the value returned should be the one that would move into `A[k]` if array `A` were to be sorted. The array `A` may not be modified. Be sure that you handle duplicates correctly.

7.9 One way of quantifying how close an array is to being sorted is the number of ascending *runs*. For example, in the array $\{10, 13, 16, 18, 15, 22, 21\}$ there are three runs present, starting at 10, at 15, and at 21. Write a function that returns the number of runs present in the integer array `A` of size `n`.

7.10 Another way of quantifying sortedness is to count the number of *inversions* – pairs of elements that are out of order. For example, on the sequence in the previous question, there are three inversions: two caused by 15, and one caused by 21. Write a function that returns the number of inversions present in the integer array `A` of size `n`.

7.11 Consider the following program, which makes use of the types and functions declared in Figures 7.5 and 7.7, assuming that `SIZE` is 5:

```
vector_t A, B;
sqmatrix_t C;
int i;

for (i=0; i<SIZE; i++) {
    A[i] = 0.5*i;
    B[i] = 1.0/(i+1);
}
vector_add(A, B, C[0], SIZE);
for (i=1; i<SIZE; i++) {
    vector_add(A, C[i-1], C[i], SIZE);
}
sqmatrix_add2(C, C, C, SIZE);
```

What are the final values stored in matrix `C` at the end of this program?

7.12 Write a function `int is_palindrome(char*)` that returns true if its argument string is a palindrome, that is, reads exactly the same forwards as well as backwards; and false if it is not a palindrome. For example, "rats live on no evil star" is a palindrome according to this definition, while "A man, a plan, a canal, Panama!" is not. (But note that the second one is a palindrome according to a broader definition that allows for case, whitespace characters, and punctuation characters to vary.)

The web site at `http://www.palindromelist.net/` lists many hundreds more, including several variants of the Panama one ("A man, a plan, a cat, a ham, a yak, a yam, a hat, a canal - Panama!", for example). Two of the more interesting ones listed at that site are "Sex at noon taxes" and "Are we not drawn onward, we few, drawn onward to new era?"

7.13 Write the functions `strlen` and `strcat` described in Table 7.2 on page 119.

7.14 Write the function `int atoi(char*)` that converts a character string into an integer value.

7.15 Write a function `int is_anagram(char*,char*)` that returns true if its two arguments are an anagram pair, and false if they are not. An anagram pair have exactly the same letters, with the same frequency of each letter, but in a different order. For example, "luster", "result", "ulster", and "rustle" are all anagrams with respect to each other.

Rather more fun can be had if spaces can be inserted where required. A nice page at `http://www.wordsmith.org/anagram/` discovered that "programming is fun" can be transformed into both "prof margin musing" and "manuring from pigs".

7.16 Modify the program of Figures 7.13 and 7.14 so that the frequency of each distinct word is listed too.

Chapter 8

Structures

The array mechanism that was introduced in Chapter 7 creates collections of variables all of the same type, and accesses the members of those collections by specifying ordinal offsets. This chapter examines a second data aggregation mechanism – the *structure*. A structure combines underlying variables of differing types, and provides access to the components via an explicit name for each. It allows a bag of objects that are of mixed types, but related to each other in some logical sense, to be handled via a single name when it is appropriate to do so, and handled as individual components at other times.

8.1 Declaring structures

Suppose that a program is to manipulate information about the planets and their moons. Each body must have information recorded pertaining to its name and the name of the body it orbits, both stored as character strings; plus a mean orbital distance, a mass, and a radius, all stored as `double` variables. Suppose also that the two character strings may be presumed to be at most 20 characters long.

Information about a planet can be held in the variable `one_planet` declared via the mechanism shown in Figure 8.1. The compound variable `one_planet` has five components, accessed by name using the "`.`" component selection operator. Hence,

```
#define PLANETSTRLEN 20

typedef char pstr_t[PLANETSTRLEN+1];

struct {
    pstr_t name
    pstr_t orbits;
    double distance;        /* million km */
    double mass;            /* kilograms */
    double radius;          /* kilometers */
} one_planet;
```

Figure 8.1: Declaration of a single structure variable.

one possible initialization of the variable `one_planet` is:

```
strncpy(one_planet.name, "Earth", PLANETSTRLEN);
strncpy(one_planet.orbits, "Sun", PLANETSTRLEN);
one_planet.distance = 149.6;
one_planet.mass = 5.9736e+24;
one_planet.radius = 6378.1;
```

Each of the five components of `one_planet` is a variable in its own right. For example, `one_planet.distance` is a variable of type `double` and can take part in any operation where a `double` is permitted; similarly, after the assignments shown in the box, variable `one_planet.orbits[0]` is a `char` and has the value `'S'`.

To avoid having to reproduce verbatim the entire structure definition each time a compound variable of the same type is required, structures can be named for later reuse by supplying a *tag*:

```
struct planet_s {
    pstr_t name, orbits;
    double distance;            /* million km */
    double mass;                /* kilograms */
    double radius;              /* kilometers */
};
```

Doing it this way allows the structure tag `planet_s` to be used in later declarations:

```
struct planet_s big_planet, big_moon;
```

More succinct than both these styles is to use `typedef` to create a full type name `planet_t` for the structure being presented, and thereafter simply use that name. Figure 8.2 shows how to do this, and declares two initialized variables of the new type. One initializing value of the correct type should be supplied for each component of the structure being declared.

Structure types allow related variables to be grouped together into a single compound value.

```
typedef struct {
    pstr_t  name, orbits;
    double  distance;            /* million km */
    double  mass;                /* kilograms */
    double  radius;              /* kilometers */
} planet_t;

planet_t the_earth =
    {"Earth", "Sun", 149.6, 5.9736e+24, 6738.1};
planet_t the_moon =
    {"Moon", "Earth", 0.3844, 7.349e+22, 1738.1};
```

Figure 8.2: Declaration of a structure using a `typedef`. All planetary data is drawn from `http://nssdc.gsfc.nasa.gov/planetary`.

8.2 Operations on structures

In Chapter 7, the only operation permitted on an array was subscripting – or alternatively dereferencing, treating the array name as a pointer. It is not possible, for example, to copy an array `B` into an array `A` with the assignment `A=B`, and the individual elements must be copied instead. Nor is it possible to compare two arrays for equality, `A==B`; and whole arrays cannot be passed to functions as arguments – instead, a pointer to the first element of the array gets passed, and the function thus always has the power to alter the underlying array.

With structures, some of these restrictions are relaxed. If `A` and `B` are declared to be of the same type, then `A=B` copies over each component of `B` to `A`. This copying includes any arrays that are declared as part of the structure type. For example, the assignment `another_planet=one_planet` is valid, and transfers the string `"Earth"` into the array `another_planet.name` as if a call to `strncpy` had been made. Assignment of structures is possible because the exact type and size of any arrays within structures are always known. On the other hand, arrays cannot be assigned because the number of elements in them is, in many situations, unknown. When arrays are passed into a function, for example, the function receives them as pointers, and has no knowledge of the size of the array, or even whether or not the pointer is pointing at the first element. Hence the refusal to countenance operations that might require knowledge of exact array sizes.

Structures cannot be compared for equality, even of they have the same type. This also makes sense – think about the strings that are stored in `one_planet` and `another_planet` after the assignments:

```
another_planet = the_earth;
another_planet.name[6] = 'X';
```

The string `another_planet.name` is still `"Earth"`, but the two `name` arrays are not identical, since the one in `another_planet` now has the letter `'X'` stored after the null byte that terminates the string. This ambiguity over interpretation means that it is safer to not allow the comparison at all. If structures must be compared, then the fields should each be compared in turn, under the control of the programmer.

> Structures of the same type can be assigned, but not compared. Arrays cannot be assigned, even if they are declared to be of exactly the same base type and number of elements.

To print a structure, the various individual components are formatted according to their natural types. For example, the `printf` statement in Figure 8.3 formats the various parts of a `planet_t` variable `one_planet`. It makes no sense to try and print the entire structure at once, just as there is no facility to format and print an array.

Similarly, structures must be read one component at a time, as shown in Figure 8.4. When executed, and then followed by a corresponding `printf` statement as shown in Figure 8.3, the program fragment in Figure 8.3 yields the interaction shown in the lower box. Note how the character arrays into which the strings are being read with the "`%s`" format control are automatically pointers, and only the scalar variable names must be prefixed by the address operator "`&`" in the `scanf`.

```
    printf("%s orbits %s\n", one_planet.name,
        one_planet.orbits);
    printf("\torbital distance is %.2e million km\n",
        one_planet.distance);
    printf("\tmass is %.2e kg\n", one_planet.mass);
    printf("\tradius is %.2e km\n", one_planet.radius);
```

```
Earth orbits Sun
        orbital distance is 1.50e+02 million km
        mass is 5.97e+24 kg
        radius is 6.74e+03 km
```

Figure 8.3: Printing a structure, one component at a time. The structure declaration appears in Figure 8.2. The lower box shows an execution of the program fragment in the upper box.

Structures are read and written component by component.

Structure declarations can make use of other structures, a facility which greatly enhances their usefulness. Figure 8.5 sketches the data types that might be used in a program that is to manipulate information about staff and students in a university. Each staff member (type `staff_t`) has their full name recorded, plus an employee number, a date of birth, a date on which they commenced service, a status flag, and an annual salary; and each student (type `student_t`) also has a full name, plus a student number, a date of birth, and then a list of as many as eight subjects in which they are currently enrolled. Finally, each subject enrollment (type `subject_t`) involves a subject code, a commencement date, a status flag, and a final mark.

Only two variables are declared at the end of the sequence in Figure 8.5, but both contain a large number of fields. Table 8.1 lists some of those components; each has a corresponding type that is determined by tracking the declarations. Note how the common elements have been abstracted out into separate declared types: `fullname_t`, `date_t`, and so on. Components in different structures can have the

```
#define PLANETPROMPT \
    "name, orbits, distance, mass, radius"

    planet_t new_planet;
    printf("Enter %s:\n", PLANETPROMPT);
    scanf("%s %s %lf %lf %lf",
        new_planet.name,
        new_planet.orbits,
        &new_planet.distance,
        &new_planet.mass,
        &new_planet.radius);
```

Figure 8.4: Reading a structure, one component at a time. The structure declaration appears in Figure 8.2. The lower box shows an execution of the program fragment in the upper box, assuming a `printf` statement of the kind shown in Figure 8.3.

```
#define NAMESTRLEN 40
#define MAXSUBJECTS 8

typedef char namestr[NAMESTRLEN+1];

typedef struct {
    namestr     given, others, family;
} fullname_t;

typedef struct {
    int         yy, mm, dd;
} date_t;

typedef struct {
    int         subjectcode;
    date_t      enrolled;
    int         status;
    int         finalmark;
} subject_t;

typedef struct {
    fullname_t  name;
    int         employeenumber;
    date_t      dob;
    date_t      datecommenced;
    int         status;
    int         annualsalary;
} staff_t;

typedef struct {
    fullname_t  name;
    int         studentnumber;
    date_t      dob;
    int         nsubjects;
    subject_t   subjects[MAXSUBJECTS];
} student_t;

staff_t     jane;
student_t   bill;
```

Figure 8.5: Declaration of nested structures.

same name – for example, the components `name` and `dob` are common to both `staff_t` and `student_t`. Indeed, when components in two different structures have the same interpretation, it makes perfect sense for them to be named alike.

Note also that this is just a sketch – in real systems there are dozens of other types and fields involved (address, entrance marks, payroll history, annual leave records, next of kin, tax paid, applications for special consideration, enrollment history for previous years of study, and so on) and the structures would be correspondingly more complex. But the same overall rules apply – *data abstraction* is used to create a hierarchical structure to the information that must be maintained, in the same way that function abstraction allows grouping of repeated execution patterns on that data.

Variable	Type
`jane`	`staff_t`
`jane.name`	`fullname_t`
`jane.datecommenced.mm`	`int`
`jane.annualsalary`	`int`
`bill`	`student_t`
`bill.dob`	`date_t`
`bill.dob.mm`	`int`
`bill.name.given`	`char[41]`
`bill.name.given[3]`	`char`
`bill.subjects`	`subject_t[8]`
`bill.subjects[1].enrolled`	`date_t`
`bill.subjects[1].enrolled.yy`	`int`
`bill.subjects[1].finalmark`	`int`

Table 8.1: Some of the variables that are part of the structures described in Figure 8.5

.

Finally in connection with Figure 8.5, note again the use of the "`_t`" convention for type names that was mentioned in Section 7.4. There are other possible conventions, including the use of initial uppercase letters for types, `Fullname`, `Date`, `Subject`, and so on. In some languages this latter approach is mandatory. There is no requirement in C that types be differentiated in any particular way; nevertheless, without some kind of convention like this, you are quickly going to lose track of which identifiers are being used for types and which are being used for variables. Use of the "`_t`" convention, or some similar rule, allows declarations of the form `date_t date`, which is probably more helpful than (say) using `typedef` to create a type `date`, and then hunting for an alternative name for the actual variable being declared: `date dte`, for example.

> Type names for structures and other types can be any valid identifier. But for readability, and ease of maintenance, you should adopt a sensible convention and use it methodically.

Another way of thinking about structures, and nested structures, is to imagine that you are going on a skiing holiday. Your toothbrush, toothpaste, and other toiletries get packed into a small bag, and then it gets zipped closed. It corresponds to one sub-structure. Your passport, foreign cash, and credit cards then get sealed into a document wallet – another sub-structure. Perhaps some underclothes get put into yet another package; your gloves, goggles, and hat into another; and some pairs of shoes into yet another special purpose bag. Finally, all of these components, plus some shirts and trousers and jackets, get assembled together, put into a suitcase, and the suitcase closed – the main structure. Then, when you check-in at the airport for your flight, and they ask "just one bag?", you answer "yes", because by now you do have just one bag. In the same way, structures allow us to manipulate a suitcase full of variables without having to list every object individually. In particular, we are able to take structures into and out of functions – the equivalent of taking a suitcase on holiday, and then bringing it back home again.

8.3 Structures, pointers, and functions

Structures are passed into functions in exactly the same manner as scalar variables of type `int` or `double` – the value of the argument expression is copied into a local argument variable of the same type, and within the function the local variable is manipulated. Function `print_planet` in Figure 8.6 shows this mode of argument passing, where the types are as declared in Figure 8.2. Within the function, variable `one_planet` is local, and changes made to it are not reflected in the passed variable `planet` declared within the scope of function `main`. In the case of `print_planet` (the body of which consists of the `printf` in Figure 8.3), this is not a problem.

> Structures are passed into functions in the same way as scalar arguments are – the value from the argument expression is copied into a local argument variable.

Functions can also return structures. The second of the three functions in Figure 8.6, function `read_planet`, demonstrates this approach. A local structure variable `new_planet` is declared, assigned values using the `scanf` statement given in Figure 8.4, and then returned in its entirety to the calling location for use in an assignment statement.

> Functions can return structure values.

The third function in Figure 8.6, function `read_planet_ptr`, uses a pointer to access the underlying variable in the `main` function. This style of use again follows the pattern already established for scalar `int` and `double` variables. Within the function the structure pointer `planet` is of type `planet_t*`. When `planet` is dereferenced, it yields an object of type `planet_t`. So to access the `mass` field, the expression `(*planet).mass` could be used. The address of that `mass` component would then be `&(*planet).mass`, with the parentheses necessary. But because the notation `(*`*pointer*`).`*component* ends up being both relatively common and relatively tedious, C offers a shortcut, and the operator "`->`" combines dereferencing and component selection. That is, *pointer*`->`*component* means "the *component* variable of the structure pointed at by *pointer*". It is still necessary to pass the addresses of the component variables into `scanf`, but no parentheses are required when doing so.

Use of a pointer argument and modification of a variable via that argument allows the function `read_planet_ptr` to return an integer "success or failure" flag, a considerable benefit. This is the usual manner in which functions and structures are used together – the value returned from the function is a status flag, and if a structure is to be created, it is done via an argument pointer.

Even when the function is not modifying the structure, passing a pointer rather than the whole structure is usually desirable. Passing a pointer can certainly save on memory space, since the structure might occupy hundreds or thousands of bytes in total (compared to four or eight bytes for a pointer argument); and also has the potential to save on execution time, as there is no need to copy over the structure value into the corresponding local variable. Note also that a structure variable is in most cases the only possible way in which a structure expression can be constructed,

```
void print_planet(planet_t one_planet);
planet_t read_planet(void);
int read_planet_ptr(planet_t *one_planet);

int
main(int argc, char *argv[]) {
    planet_t planet;
    planet = read_planet();
    print_planet(planet);
    if (read_planet_ptr(&planet) != EOF) {
        print_planet(planet);
    }
    return 0;
}

void
print_planet(planet_t one_planet) {
    /* the body of this function is in Figure 8.3 */
}

planet_t
read_planet(void) {
    planet_t new_planet;
    /* the body of this function is in Figure 8.4 */
    return new_planet;
}

int
read_planet_ptr(planet_t *planet) {
    int nvals_read;
    printf("Enter %s:\n", PLANETPROMPT);
    nvals_read = scanf("%s %s %lf %lf %lf",
        planet->name,
        planet->orbits,
        &planet->distance,
        &planet->mass,
        &planet->radius);
    if (nvals_read != 5) {
        return EOF;
    } else {
        return 0;
    }
}
```

Figure 8.6: Program showing use of structure arguments in functions. Function `read_planet` returns a structure; whereas function `read_planet_ptr` is passed a pointer to a structure, and uses that pointer to fill in the fields of the structure. The structure declaration appears in Figure 8.2. The body of function `print_planet` appears in Figure 8.3, and the body of function `read_planet` appears in Figure 8.4.

meaning that requiring that a pointer to a variable (rather than a general expression) be present in the argument list is not likely to be restrictive in any way.

For most purposes, it is appropriate to pass a structure pointer rather than a structure. Passing a pointer allows the function to alter the components in the underlying compound variable.

8.4 Structures and arrays

There is one last, but very important, way in which structures can be used – they can be replicated in arrays. Consider again the example `typedef` shown in Figure 8.2 on page 130. A program manipulating planetary data is unlikely to be dealing with the earth alone, or even the sun, earth and moon – if it were, it would hardly be worth the trouble of declaring the structure type. Much more likely is that information about the 20 or 100 most massive objects in the solar system is being maintained, perhaps in a program that calculates the times of solar eclipses, or the gravitational forces acting on the space shuttle in orbit. An array is the perfect solution:

```
#define MAXBODIES 100

int nplanets=0;
planet_t planets[MAXBODIES];
```

As always with arrays, a variable is used to count the current number of things stored in the array (integer `nplanets`); and the same care to avoid overflow must be taken when reading in to an array of structures as is taken when reading into an array of simpler variables (Section 7.2 on page 101).

When an array of structures is declared, it becomes even more natural to use structure pointers. For example, the function call `read_planet_ptr(planets+i)` passes a pointer to the `i`'th element of `planets`, and reads values into the five variables that make up `planets[i]`.

The array subscripting operator has the same precedence as the component selection operator, and both are left associative. That means that parentheses to force ordering are usually unnecessary – expressions involving a mix of the "`[]`" subscripting, and "`.`" and "`->`" selection operators, can be read from left to right. For example, `planets[0].orbits` is the `orbits` component of the first object in array `planets`; and `planets[0].orbits[3]` is the fourth `char` variable in that string.

Arrays of structures are an important data organization technique. They represent many real-world situations in which large quantities of data are to be handled.

As with any array, an array of structures needs to be accompanied by a variable that indicates how many entries in the array are currently valid, declared as `nplanets` in the example above. But the two objects `nplanets` and `planets` belong together. So it makes sense for them to be joined in a structure, and a single aggregate type created that includes a description of its own size:

```
typedef struct {
    int nplanets;
    planet_t planets[MAXBODIES];
} solar_system_t;

solar_system_t solar_system;
```

Now a complete solar system can be passed to a function as an argument using a single pointer. This is data abstraction at its best.

Exercises

8.1 Consider the variables `jane` and `bill` declared in Figure 8.5 on page 133. If an `int` occupies four bytes of memory, and a `char` requires one byte, how many bytes each do `jane` and `bill` consume?

How about the array `staff_t allstaff[1000]`?

And `student_t allstudents[10000]`?

(In practice, the compiler will usually pad the various `char` components of a structure so as to obtain word alignment for `int` and `double` variables, but you don't need to worry about that in this question.)

8.2 Define a structure `vector_t` that could be used to store points in two dimensions x and y (such as on a map).

Then write a function `double distance(vector_t p1, vector_t p2)` that returns the Euclidean distance between `p1` and `p2`. If $p1 = (x_1, y_1)$ and $p2 = (x_2, y_2)$, then the Euclidean distance between them is given by

$$\sqrt{(x_1 - x_2)^2 + (y_1 - y_2)^2} \, .$$

8.3 Suppose that a closed polygon is represented as a sequence of points in two dimensions. Give suitable declarations for a type `poly_t` in which it is assumed that no polygon contains more than 100 points. Hint: not all polygons are going to have 100 vertices, so the number of points in use must also be part of your data structure.

Then write a function `double perimeter(poly_t P)` that returns the length of the perimeter of polygon `P` represented in your format.

8.4 (*For a challenge*) Write a second function that calculates the area of a polygon passed using the representation you developed in Exercise 8.3.

8.5 Define a structure type `complex_t` for storing complex numbers (each of which has a real and an imaginary component, both of type `double`).

Then write two functions :

```
complex_t complex_add(complex_t v1, complex_t v2);
complex_t complex_mpy(complex_t v1, complex_t v2);
```

to manipulate them.

8.6 Design constants, data types, and variable declarations to capture the following situation.

A car race consists of as many as 100 laps of a circuit, and involves as many as 30 cars. Each lap takes between 0 and 999.999 seconds. For each car in the race, the time for each completed lap must be recorded, together with a string of at most 40 characters indicating any special notes for that lap (for example, "pit stop for fuel and tires"). In addition, associated with each car is a driver's name (at most 50 characters), an integer serial number, the number of laps completed, the total race time, and the overall position in the race of that car (an integer rank, with -1 used to indicate "did not finish").

8.7 Look again at Exercise 7.5 on page 127. Modify your solution to that problem using the techniques that have been discussed in this chapter.

8.8 Look again at Exercise 7.16 on page 128. Modify your solution to that problem using the techniques that have been discussed in this chapter.

8.9 (*For a challenge*) Look again at the declarations in Figure 8.5 on page 133.

Write a function `sort_staff_by_number` that takes two arguments, an array of type `staff_t`, and an integer `nstaff`, and sorts the first `nstaff` elements in the `staff_t` array into order of ascending `employeenumber`.

Use any of the sorting algorithms introduced in Chapter 7.

Chapter 9

Problem Solving Strategies

If you have absorbed the material presented though until this point, then you have at your disposal the main tools available in almost all programming languages. The exact syntax, and many of the details, change from language to language. But almost all languages offer mechanisms for calculation, for selection, for iteration or recursion, and for abstraction. The majority of languages also support arrays, and those that do not will almost certainly have a "list" mechanism that allows collections of like objects to be manipulated. Most languages also include a facility for grouping dissimilar objects into single entities.

So what is left for you to learn? There are still some aspects of C to be covered before you can claim to be fully C-literate, mechanisms that are specific to C and not common across the broad range of languages. Those topics are covered in Chapters 10 and 11. Before they are introduced, this chapter steps back a little from C, and discusses a more general question: how do we solve problems? It is all very well to know the syntax rules for a language like C, and how to convert an algorithm into a program. But where does the algorithm come from in the first place? And given a new problem, what general approaches are there that might be used as the basis for a successful program?

This chapter discusses several broad techniques for problem solving. Chances are that if you are faced with the need to write a program to solve some problem, one or more of these methods will be applicable. They constitute the "big picture" of programming, in the same way that in house design there are a handful of "big picture" starting points: steel framing; tilt-up concrete slab construction; brick or concrete block; and so on. And as with house construction, none of the details of a program can be considered or finalized until the overall construction method is decided.

9.1 Generate and test

Some problems are best solved by trying out different candidate answers, and stopping when a solution is found. Several programs fitting into this category have been discussed earlier in this book.

In Figure 4.10 on page 55, and in Figure 5.4 on page 68, programs are given that

```
int
nextprime(int n) {
    n = n+1;
    while (!isprime(n)) {
        n = n+1;
    }
    return n;
}
```

Figure 9.1: Using generate and test to search for the next prime number greater than a supplied value. Function `isprime` is shown in Figure 5.4 on page 68.

test whether or not numbers are prime by checking all possible divisors, and accepting a number as prime only if no divisor is found. This is an example of *generate and test*, since a straightforward loop is used to generate candidate divisors, and then an equally straightforward test applied to determine whether each candidate is in fact a divisor. In this instance, if any of the tests succeed, the non-prime status of the tested value has been confirmed.

In the same vein, Exercise 4.9 on page 62 poses the problem of determining the next prime number greater than a given starting value. Figure 9.1 gives a solution to that problem. Again, it seems rather obvious what should be done – the function generates candidates that might be the next prime number, and then tests them using the previous `isprime` function. One slight optimization that might be considered is to only test odd numbers, since, after 2, there are no even prime numbers. Incorporating this optimization would be possible, but then means that 2 has to be handled as a special case. Given that 2 is always the first factor tested in `isprime`, it hardly seems worth the effort – even numbers get rejected quickly anyway.

> The generate and test strategy is appropriate when there is some ordering on candidate answers that allows an exhaustive enumeration, and it is straight forward to test each candidate for correctness.

Another example that includes the generate and test strategy appears in Figure 9.4, towards the end of the next section.

9.2 Divide and conquer

The *divide and conquer* strategy can be summarized in this way: find a subproblem that is related to the main problem but is in some sense easier to solve than the main problem; then solve the subproblem; and then convert the solution to the subproblem into a solution to the main problem.

Several examples of divide and conquer have already been presented in previous chapters without being labeled as such, and will be examined shortly. But as the first example of this paradigm, there is one archetypical example that no programming textbook is ever without – the *towers of Hanoi*. Figure 9.2 illustrates the problem. Three pegs are supplied, and a set of `n` disks of varying diameter. The disks are

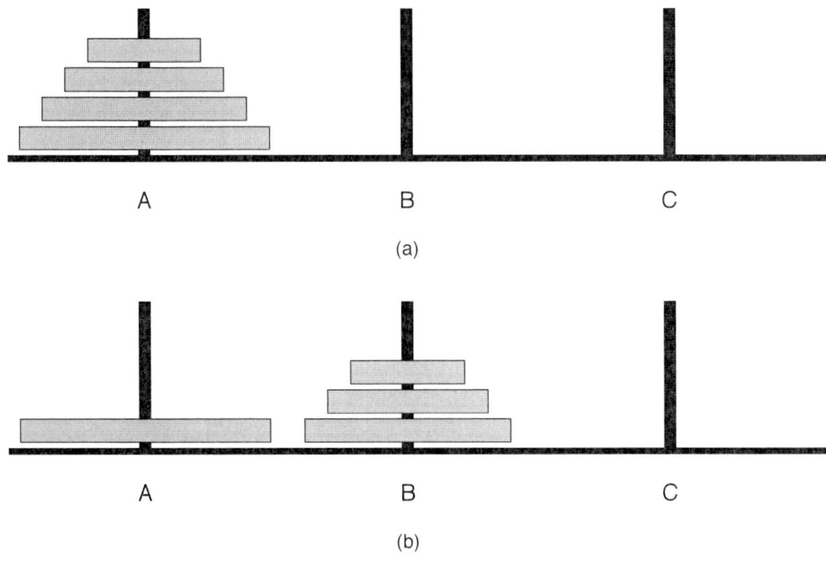

Figure 9.2: The towers of Hanoi problem, with `n` equal to four: (a) before the initial call to `hanoi('A','B','C',4)`; and (b) after the first recursive call to `hanoi(from,to,via,3)`.

initially stacked in order on the leftmost peg, labeled A. The objective is to move all the disks to the peg labeled C, subject to two constraints: that only one disk may be moved at a time; and that no disk may ever be placed on top of a disk of smaller diameter. There are thus only two possible first moves: the smallest disk can move from peg A to peg B, or the smallest disk can move from peg A to peg C.

The divide and conquer strategy for solving this problem hinges upon the observation that if the top `n-1` disks can be moved temporarily from peg A to peg B, then the largest disk can be moved from peg A to peg C. After that, all that remains is to move `n-1` disks from peg B to peg C, and the problem is done. That is, the "divide" involves the identification of two subproblems, each of size `n-1`, which, because they are smaller, must be "easier". Figure 9.3 details the well-known recursive implementation of this strategy.

Like all recursive functions, a base case is required, to deal with the fundamental situation in which the problem is already easy enough. In Figure 9.3, that arises when `n` is zero – in which case there is nothing to be done. When `n` is greater than zero, `n-1` of the disks are moved temporarily from the `from` peg to the `via` peg, so that the `n`'th disk can be transferred from the `from` peg to the `to` peg. Once that is done, the `n-1` disks temporarily sitting on the `via` peg are moved to the `to` peg, to complete the main problem. Note that the loop, and first `printf` statement, are solely to indent the instructions generated by the second `printf` statement. The lower box in Figure 9.3 shows the output produced when `n` is four. The largest disk is always moved just once, while the smallest disk shuttles backwards and forwards amongst the three pegs at a rapid rate.

```
void
hanoi(char from, char via, char to, int n) {
    int i;
    if (n<=0) {
        return;
    }
    hanoi(from, to, via, n-1);
    for (i=1; i<n; i++) {
        printf("    ");
    }
    printf("Move a disk from %c to %c\n", from, to);
    hanoi(via, from, to, n-1);
}
```

```
Move a disk from A to B
    Move a disk from A to C
Move a disk from B to C
        Move a disk from A to B
Move a disk from C to A
    Move a disk from C to B
Move a disk from A to B
            Move a disk from A to C
Move a disk from B to C
    Move a disk from B to A
Move a disk from C to A
        Move a disk from B to C
Move a disk from A to B
    Move a disk from A to C
Move a disk from B to C
```

Figure 9.3: Solving the towers of Hanoi problem using a recursive implementation of a divide and conquer strategy. The lower box shows the output that results from a call `hanoi('A','B','C',4)`.

> The divide and conquer strategy is appropriate when a solution to a subproblem can be readily extended to construct a solution to the original problem.

Several other divide and conquer processes have already been described. Insertion sort can be thought of as consisting of two steps – first, sorting the first $n - 1$ elements in the array, and then inserting the n th one into that list. The selection sort described in Exercise 7.6 on page 127 also uses a divide and conquer strategy. One subproblem is that of finding the largest element in the array, and swapping it into the last position. The other requires the recursive or iterative sorting of an array that contains one less item than the original one.

Figure 9.4 shows a divide and conquer approach to another complex task, known as the *subset sum* problem. The solution also incorporates elements of the generate and test paradigm of the previous section. A subset sum puzzle consists of a set of `n` integers, and a simple question – is there some subset of those integers that adds up to a specified target value `k`? The physical analogy is to a hiker who can carry

```
int
subsetsum(int A[], int n, int k) {
    if (k==0) {
        return 1;
    } else if (n==0) {
        return 0;
    } else {
        return subsetsum(A, n-1, k-A[n-1]) ||
            subsetsum(A, n-1, k);
    }
}
```

Figure 9.4: Using a combination of divide and conquer, and generate and test, to identify whether or not there is a solution to a given subset sum problem.

(say) exactly 50kg in their backpack, and would like to choose food items from their cupboard to add up to exactly that total. These, and similar problems, are sometimes called *knapsack problems*.

Like the towers of Hanoi, the subset sum problem is rather famous in Computer Science. It is a representative of a large class of problems that all share the distinctive attribute of being (it is thought) very hard to solve for non-trivial values of n, but, if a proposed solution is given, very easy to verify. As an example, consider this question – is there a subset of these numbers that adds up to exactly 1,000?

```
 34,  38,  39,  43,  55,  66,  67,  84,  85,  91,
101, 117, 128, 138, 165, 168, 169, 182, 184, 186,
234, 238, 241, 276, 279, 288, 386, 387, 388, 389,
413, 444, 487, 513, 534, 535, 616, 722, 786, 787
```

In this case the answer is "yes", but it may take you quite some time to find a suitable subset of the elements. (There are no subsets just using the first 10 numbers, but there are 1,448 subsets if the first 20 numbers may be used. One solution is given by $38 + 39 + 43 + 55 + 85 + 91 + 101 + 117 + 128 + 138 + 165 = 1000$.)

The function subsetsum in Figure 9.4 determines whether or not a solution exists by exhaustively constructing every possible subset of the n items passed in via array A, and checking to see if that subset sums to the target value k. The function has a non-obvious recursive structure. There are two base cases. The first covers the situation when k is zero. If it is, the values of n and A are irrelevant – a sum of zero can be achieved, simply by taking none of the items in A. The second base case covers the situation when n is zero, and no more objects are available. If the target k is non-zero at this time, then no subset can exist.

In general, when neither n nor k are equal to zero, a decision must be made about the last value in the array: either A[n-1] is part of a solution, or it is not. If it is, then a subset of the first n-1 items in the array must be found, of value k-A[n-1]. If it is not, then a subset of the first n-1 items in the array must be found, of value k. If either of these two sub-problems admits a solution, then a solution for the main problem exists too. The expression in the return statement in Figure 9.4 explores both alternatives, if necessary.

Problem size `n`	Solution time (seconds)
30	5.4
31	10.8
32	21.7
33	43.2
34	87.0
35	173.0

Table 9.1: Time taken by function `subsetsum` (Figure 9.4) for various values of `n`, measured in CPU seconds on a 2.7 GHz Macbook Pro. In each case `k` is chosen so that no subset exists and the value returned is zero.

One problem with generate and test-style algorithms is also brought out in Figure 9.4, and that is the cost of exhaustive enumeration. To assert that no subset with the right sum is possible, every combination of the `n` items must be calculated, and there are an exponentially large number of such combinations. Table 9.1 documents the cost of searching for a subset that does not exist. Each time `n` is increased by one, the time taken to decide the outcome doubles. Unfortunately, this growth rate means that large problems cannot be solved – even though the program exists, and is just a dozen or so lines long. For example, extrapolating from the times in the table, a problem with `n` equal to 40 will require approximately 90 minutes of computation; a problem with `n` equal to 50 will take more than 65 *days* of non-stop calculation; and a problem with `n` equal to 60 will requires more than 183 *years*. As for a problem of size 100, the mind just boggles – it simply can't be done.

In Chapter 1 an analogy was drawn between physics, the science of energy, and computer science, which is the study of information. From physics, we know that perpetual motion is an impossibility; and from chemistry we know that transmutation of lead into gold is an unrealistic aim. So too in computing it appears that there are things that may be impossible to achieve.

Unfortunately, there are a large number of other problems like the subset sum problem, for which the only known algorithms require exponentially growing time. Finding ways to obtain partial or approximate solutions to non-trivial instances of these problems is one of the key challenges in Computer Science.

> There are many problems for which all known algorithms require exponentially growing time. It is also likely that no fast algorithms will ever be found, making the exact solutions to even mid-sized instances of these problems impossible to obtain.

The number of moves required by a towers of Hanoi problem is also exponential, this time in n, the number of disks. Now the high cost arises because there are that many moves necessary to accomplish the transformation, and not because different move sequences have to be explored to find a "right" one. A generate and test approach to the towers of Hanoi problem might never end, as there is no obvious ordering in which to generate possible move sequences, and then evaluate them.

The original setting of the towers of Hanoi problem is said to be in a remote mountainous temple, with generation after generation of dedicated monks manually working with a stack of 60 disks. The lore goes on to say that when the last disk is moved into its final position, it will mark the end of the world. Based upon the estimates made above, and the fact that computers are a hundred million times faster than humans, we are probably safe for a few more years yet.

The situation is not so gloomy with respect to other problems such as sorting. Even the "agricultural" insertion sort is such that arrays containing tens of thousands of items can be sorted in a few seconds, and the sorting algorithms introduced in Chapter 12 are much faster than that, easily handling tens of millions of items. Several of those efficient techniques exploit the divide and conquer strategy.

One particular type of divide and conquer algorithm is worth attention, and that is the *greedy* heuristic. The underlying assumption of the greedy heuristic is that a solution that is good overall can be found by making a sequence of choices at a low level, each of which maximizes some simple definition of progress. For example, selection sort (Exercise 7.6 on page 127) is a greedy process, since at each stage the biggest remaining item is located, and swapped into its correct position. By being greedy at each individual step, a solution is arrived at to the larger problem.

The greedy heuristic seeks a globally good solution to a problem through the use of locally maximal choices.

9.3 Simulation

Consider the following game of chance. To enter the game, contestants pay \$1. They then roll two dice. If the total on the dice is eight or more, they are paid their original stake, plus another \$1; except that if the total is twelve, they are paid back their original stake, plus an additional \$5. On the other hand, if the total is less than eight, they get nothing back.

Suppose a player enters the game with a \$5 initial float, and plays these \$1 games until either all their money is gone, or they have reached a total of \$20, at which time they retire happy. How many turns does it take on average before they leave the gaming table? And what fraction of the time do they leave happy?

It is relatively easy to determine that the casino running this game has a slight edge, and that in the long run, more players should lose than win. Indeed, a mathematician might be able to precisely calculate the average number of games played by each player before one of the two stopping conditions is met. Another way to answer such questions is to make use of a *simulation*. The top box in Figure 9.5 shows a program that tracks the outcome of one player, and their initial \$5.

A key component of Figure 9.5 is use of the functions `srand` and `rand`, described in `stdlib.h`. The first function initializes a pseudo-random number generator by passing in an integer seed; thereafter, each call to `rand` returns a positive integer that for most purposes can be assumed to be quite unrelated to the previous values returned. The actual mechanism involved is beyond the scope of this book. What is worth stressing is that the sequence is not really random at all, and is completely and unambiguously determined by the initial seed. Hence, if you are using such a

```
int
main(int argc, char *argv[]) {
    int cash=START_AT, games=0, dice1, dice2, i;
    printf("seed for this run = %d\n", SEED);
    srand(SEED);
    while (0<cash && cash<STOP_AT) {
        printf("%3d games |", games);
        for (i=0; i<cash-1; i++) {
            printf(" ");
        }
        printf("*\n");
        games += 1;
        cash -= 1;
        dice1 = 1 + rand()%6;
        dice2 = 1 + rand()%6;
        if (dice1+dice2 == 12) {
            cash += 6;
        } else if (dice1+dice2 >= 8) {
            cash += 2;
        }
    }
    printf("%3d games |", games);
    if (cash==0) {
        printf("BUST :-(\n");
    } else {
        printf("EUREKA!\n");
    }
    return 0;
}
```

```
seed for this run = 1234567
0 games |    *
1 games |   *
2 games |  *
3 games | *
4 games |  *
5 games | *
6 games |*
7 games |BUST :-(
```

```
seed for this run = 1234567
winning players:  13620, average length 68.0 games
losing players :  86380, average length 34.7 games
overall        : 100000, average length 39.3 games
```

Figure 9.5: Simulating a game of chance. The middle box shows the output of the program. With this particular seed value for the random number generator, there is only one return in seven games, and the \$5 initial float goes quickly. On the same computer, if `SEED` is 12345678, the game lasts 133 rounds, and the player departs happy with \$20. The third box shows the execution of a modified program that repeats the experiment 100,000 times.

```
    int seed=83449168, i;
    char toss[] = "HT";
    if (argc==2) {
        seed = atoi(argv[1]);
    }
    srand(seed);
    for (i=0; i<5; i++) {
        printf("coin = %c, dice = %d, float = %.6f\n",
            toss[rand()%2], 1+rand()%6,
            rand()/(1.0+RAND_MAX));
    }
```

```
mac: ./random
coin = H, dice = 5, float = 0.236417
coin = H, dice = 3, float = 0.643819
coin = T, dice = 2, float = 0.496856
coin = T, dice = 2, float = 0.336534
coin = H, dice = 3, float = 0.827329
mac: ./random 93481184
coin = H, dice = 6, float = 0.238669
coin = H, dice = 2, float = 0.654376
coin = H, dice = 1, float = 0.980106
coin = T, dice = 2, float = 0.293157
coin = T, dice = 6, float = 0.272191
```

Figure 9.6: Generating pseudo-random numbers using `srand` and `rand`.

program on a regular basis, it is important to use a different initialization value in `srand` each time you execute it, otherwise you will be using the same sequence of values each time the program executes.

Given that `rand` returns an integer, the calculation `1+rand()%6` yields a value between one and six. Similarly, if a random coin toss is required, `rand()%2` can be used. And finally, if a random `float` between 0 and (up to but not including) 1 is required, the value `rand()/(1.0+RAND_MAX)` should be calculated. Figure 9.6 shows a simple program to demonstrate these options. When a different seed value is used, a different sequence of values is generated.

Some versions of `rand` in early C systems were far from random in their low-order bits, and use of, for example, `1+rand()%6`, yielded a stream of integers that had quite distinct correlations between values. Most modern C systems use an improved function that when first written was called `random` (and `srandom`), and might still be available using that name on your system. However, the ANSI C standard specifies `rand` and `srand` as the names, meaning that if your program is to be compliant with the standard (as all the programs in this book are) you must use the older names. If you need your program to be portable, and require the values to be uncorrelated even when compiled with the original `rand` and `srand` functions, you should extract the desired value from high-order bits rather than low-order ones, and use, for example, `1+(int)(6.0*rand()/(1.0+RAND_MAX))` for a random dice roll.

The functions `srand` and `rand` allow programs to generate a stream of apparently uncorrelated integers. The sequence is completely determined by the seed passed to `srand`. Care should be taken that the stream of values generated is indeed suited to the application they are required for.

The simulation carried out by the program in the top box in Figure 9.5 shows how one particular participant gets on in the hypothetical game of chance. However the casino is interested in the long term statistical behavior of the game, not individual players. The third box of the figure shows the output of a modified program, one which, starting with the same seed and then never reinitializing it, commences the process with a \$5 initial stake 100,000 times. A computer-based rent-a-crowd, if you like, only considerably cheaper. Now the reason the casino likes this game is obvious – about $6/7$ of the players eventually lose their stake, and only $1/7$ of players ever make it to \$20.

The ready ability of computers to undertake brute-force computations means that it is also easy to check the stability of such a numerical result, by running the entire program repeatedly, with different seeds each time. For example, when `SEED` is initialized to 12345678, the same program records 13,712 winners and 86,288 losers, and the averages are 67.9 and 34.8 games respectively. Similar results from other seeds suggest that the values in the bottom box of Figure 9.5 are reasonably precise.

The simulation strategy is appropriate when a large amount of randomly generated data can be collated to predict a meaningful overall trend. Multiple runs should be undertaken in order to verify the stability of the answers.

The simulation shown in this example is based upon a single stream of actions. In more general situations each event that is processed may cause some number of future events to be scheduled. For example, in a program modeling the average queue length in a multi-teller bank branch, the arrival of a customer at a teller decreases the length of the queue by one, and requires that a future "customer departs teller" event be scheduled, with the delay between the two events a function of the complexity of the transaction assigned to that customer by the simulation. A queue of pending events is maintained, and processed in simulation-time order.

Discrete event simulations of this kind can become rather complex. One thing worth remembering when using the output of such a program to model real-world behavior is that the projections made by the simulation are valid only if the input assumptions governing the model are realistic. In a simulation of a bank branch, for example, allowing the queue of waiting customers to become arbitrarily long is unrealistic, as real customers entering a real branch will simply turn around and leave again if they see a long queue and their banking business is non-urgent.

Randomness can also be used to help find solutions to other problems. Suppose some complex geometric shape is given, and the internal area of it is required. For example, Figure 9.7 shows an arc-shaped region defined by a unit circle. In this simple example the area can be directly calculated as $\pi/4 - 0.5 = 0.2854$. But suppose that the shape was more complex, and standard geometric formulae could

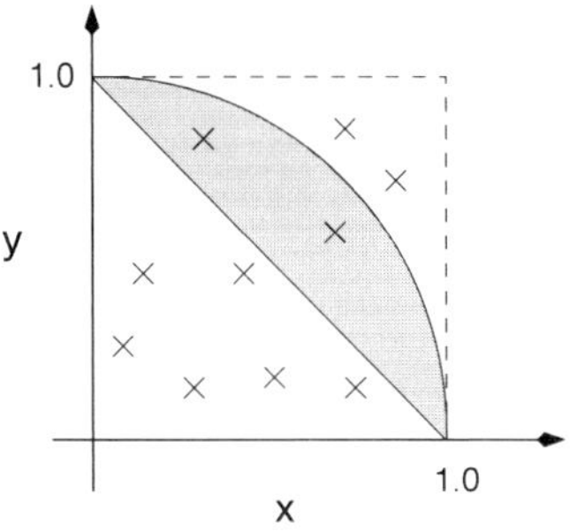

Figure 9.7: Monte Carlo estimation of Figure 9.8 with `steps` equal to ten.

not be used. Suppose also that a mechanism is known for determining if a point lies inside or outside the region of interest. In Figure 9.7, points (x, y) inside the grey region satisfy $(1 - x) \leq y$ and $x^2 + y^2 \leq 1$.

Figure 9.8 shows a program that estimates the area of the shaded region, based purely upon the inside/outside test. Random (x, y) locations are generated using `rand`, and checked against the region. The small "x"s in Figure 9.7 are perhaps the

```
int
inside(double x, double y) {
    return ((1-x)<=y && x*x+y*y<=1.0);
}
```

```
    srand(SEED);
    for (steps=1; steps <= 1000000; steps=steps*10) {
        num_in=0;
        for (i=0; i<steps; i++) {
            x = rand()/(1.0+RAND_MAX);
            y = rand()/(1.0+RAND_MAX);
            num_in = num_in + inside(x,y);
        }
        printf("steps = %7d, num_in = %8d, ratio = %.6f\n",
            steps, num_in, (double)num_in/steps);
    }
```

```
steps =       1, num_in =        0, ratio = 0.000000
steps =      10, num_in =        2, ratio = 0.200000
steps =     100, num_in =       28, ratio = 0.280000
steps =    1000, num_in =      287, ratio = 0.287000
steps =   10000, num_in =     2896, ratio = 0.289600
steps =  100000, num_in =    28514, ratio = 0.285140
steps = 1000000, num_in =   285728, ratio = 0.285728
```

Figure 9.8: Monte Carlo estimation of the area contained in an arc-shaped region of a unit circle. The top box shows a function that returns true if the (x, y) location is inside the region of interest. The third box shows an execution of the program fragment in the middle box.

first 10 random points generated. After a million or so random points have been tested, a reasonably good estimate of the area of the grey region can be obtained, as a fraction of the known area of the enclosing unit square. This kind of technique is sometimes called *Monte Carlo estimation*, with the reference being, of course, to the famous home of gambling.

> Monte Carlo estimation can be used to obtain approximate solutions to computations that it might be impossible to solve analytically.

9.4 Approximation techniques

Consider the function defined by $f(x) = \sin 5x + \cos 10x + x^2/10$, and suppose, for some reason, that the length of this function between $x = 0$ and $x = 10$ is required: perhaps because a wall with this cross-section has to be folded from metal sheeting, and the correct total length of metal sheeting has to be ordered. With the right mathematical techniques and a suitably well-behaved curve, a line integral might be calculated, and an exact answer determined.

If the curve is not well-behaved, or the necessary mathematical techniques are not known, the use of a simple program, and brute-force computation, again allows an approximate answer to be computed. This time, no random number generator is required.

Figure 9.9 illustrates the situation. To estimate the length, the smooth curve is approximated by a sequence of straight line segments. It is easy to calculate the length of a straight line between two points, so if the straight-line distances between a whole lot of points on the curve are summed, an estimate of the overall length of the curve is obtained. The easiest way to generate a set of points on the curve is to make them evenly spaced between the `start` and `stop` values, that is, by dividing that overall x displacement into some number `steps` of equal intervals. Figure 9.10 shows how to do this in C.

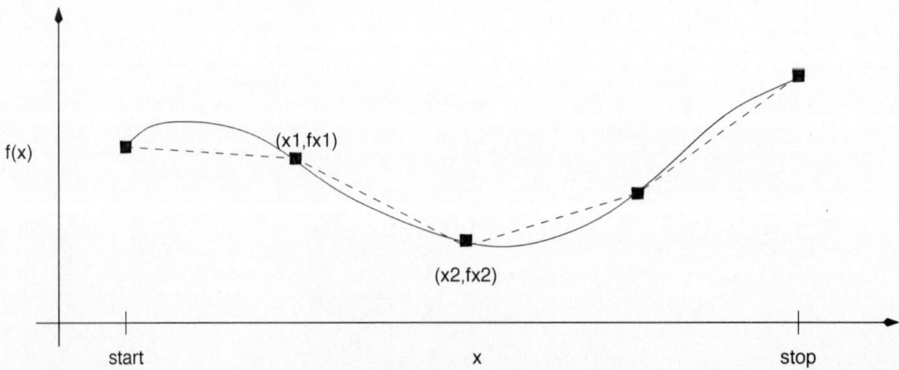

Figure 9.9: Approximating a continuous function by a sequence of straight line segments. In this example, `steps` is four, and the second segment is being evaluated.

```
double
f(double x) {
    return sin(5*x) + cos(10*x) + x*x/10;
}

double
linelength(double start, double stop, int steps) {
    double totlen=0.0, x1, x2, fx1, fx2, dx, dy;
    int i;
    x1 = start;
    fx1 = f(x1);
    for (i=1; i<=steps; i++) {
        x2 = start + (double)i*(stop-start)/steps;
        fx2 = f(x2);
        dx = x2-x1;
        dy = fx2-fx1;
        totlen = totlen + sqrt(dx*dx + dy*dy);
        x1 = x2;
        fx1 = fx2;
    }
    return totlen;
}
```

```
steps =        1, line length = 13.862140
steps =       10, line length = 21.444593
steps =      100, line length = 67.042603
steps =     1000, line length = 69.509999
steps =    10000, line length = 69.534930
steps =   100000, line length = 69.535179
steps =  1000000, line length = 69.535182
steps = 10000000, line length = 69.535182
```

Figure 9.10: Function to calculate the length of the function `f` between `start` and `stop`. The main program (not shown) varies the number of `steps` used, and prints the length returned by `linelength`. The lower box shows an execution, with `start` taking on the value 0.0 and `stop` the value 10.0.

In the figure, function `linelength` calculates the length of the external function described by `f` between the `start` and `stop` values, using `steps` points that are regularly spaced in the horizontal direction. As `steps` is made larger, the computation becomes more accurate, but only within limits – here is a clear case where the inaccuracies associated with floating point arithmetic can really cause problems, and use of a too-large value for `steps` can be detrimental. It is also important in this function that the local variables are declared as `double` rather than `float`. If `float` variables are used, when `steps` is 10,000,000, the value 70.1454 is returned, and it is clear that the computation has drifted from the true answer.

> Numerical approximation methods can be used to compute useful values on functions and curves that may not yield to mathematical analysis. Care needs to be taken to ensure that the computed answers are not adversely affected by calculation rounding errors.

A variant of this problem is that of *numerical integration*. If the area under the curve is required rather than the length of the curve, a set of points on the curve is used as the basis of a collection of trapezoidal regions reaching down to the horizontal axis, and the areas of those regions summed using (in terms of the variables in Figure 9.10) the assignment `totarea = totarea + (x2-x1)*(fx1+fx2)/2`. This mechanism is called the *trapezoidal rule*.

> The trapezoidal rule approximates a curve by a set of line segments, and allows integrals to be computed numerically.

Another problem that can be rather neatly solved by an approximation-based technique is that of *root finding*. Consider the function $f(x) = \sin 5x + \cos 10x + x^2/10$ again. At $x = 0.0$, the value of $f(x)$ is 1.0. At $x = 1.0$, the value of $f(x)$ is -1.698. So somewhere between $x = 0.0$ and $x = 1.0$, the function f crosses the x axis. Suppose we want to find that crossing point – the value of x such that $f(x) = 0$, which is a root of the equation. (This function has several more roots, including a second between $x = 1.0$ and $x = 2.0$.) How can we do it?

One way would be to step along the curve using a program similar to that of Figure 9.10, and stop as soon as the sign of `f(x)` changes. But this approach has the potential to be quite expensive to evaluate. If the value of the root was required to an accuracy of (say) ten decimal places, then `steps` would need to be set to 10^{10}, and the loop would potentially iterate 10,000,000,000 times. That will take several minutes.

A better approach relies on the observation that the curve is continuous, and if the midpoint of the current region is tested at each iteration, either the left half of the region or the right half of the region can be discarded. This *bisection method* is rather like the binary search algorithm that was mentioned in passing in Section 7.3 on page 103, and is considered in detail in Section 12.2 on page 205. Figure 9.11

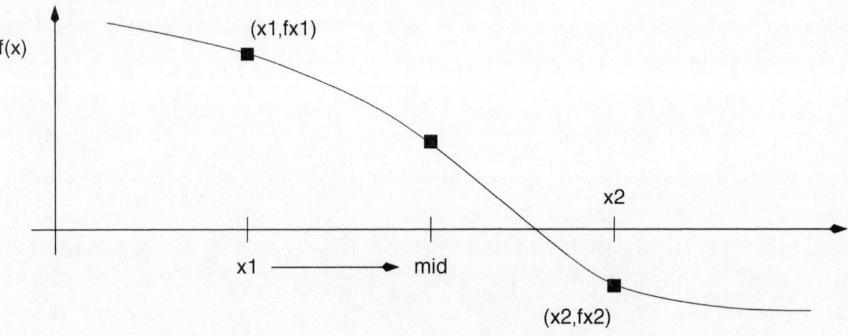

Figure 9.11: One step in the bisection method.

```
double
bisection(double x1, double x2, double eps, int limit) {
    double fx1, fx2, mid, fmid;
    int iterations=0;
    fx1 = f(x1);
    fx2 = f(x2);
    while (x2-x1 > eps) {
        iterations = iterations+1;
        if (iterations==limit) {
            exit(NOT_CONVERGING);
        }
        mid = (x1+x2)/2;
        fmid = f(mid);
        if (fx1*fmid < 0) {
            /* root is to left of middle */
            x2 = mid;
            fx2 = fmid;
        } else {
            /* root is to right */
            x1 = mid;
            fx1 = fmid;
        }
    }
    printf("(bisection) eps=%.1e, iterations=%d\n",
            eps, iterations);
    return (x1+x2)/2;
}
```

```
(bisection) eps=1.0e-08, iterations=27
(main) x = 0.7371977754, f(x) = 0.0000000445
(bisection) eps=1.0e-10, iterations=34
(main) x = 0.7371977788, f(x) = 0.0000000002
(bisection) eps=1.0e-12, iterations=40
(main) x = 0.7371977788, f(x) = 0.0000000000
```

Figure 9.12: Function to calculate a root of the function `f`, presuming that one or more roots exist between the initial values `x1` and `x2`. The lower box shows several executions of function `bisection`. The main program (not shown) passes in `x1` equal to 0.0, `x2` equal to 1.0, and varies the tolerance value `eps`. It then prints (shown by the output lines starting `(main)`) the value returned by `bisection`, and the value of `f` at that point. In a production implementation of function `bisection`, the `printf` statement would not be present. The function `f` is shown in Figure 9.10.

shows one step of this process, and Figure 9.12 gives a function that uses the bisection method to determine the root of an external function `f`.

There are several points to note in function `bisection`. The first is the termination criterion. To test if a value `x` is a good approximation to the root, it is not sensible to use a statement like `f(x)==0.0`, as floating point rounding effects make it unlikely that this condition could ever be met. Instead, the function stops the refinement process when `x1` and `x2` get sufficiently close together – in the examples, when they differ by less than 10^{-8}, or 10^{-10}, or 10^{-12}. Another possible stopping condition would be to test `fabs(f(mid))` and terminate the loop when it is suitably small. The difference between doing that and what is shown in Figure 9.12 is small.

A second point to note is that there is a safety-net termination condition that is also checked at every iteration. If an over-aggressive tolerance `eps` is specified, the floating point arithmetic might be such that the value of `x2-x1` never meets the primary stopping criterion – when `x1` and `x2` are very close together, the value computed for `mid` will be one or the other of `x1` or `x2`, and once this situation is arrived at, it is possible that there will be no further convergence, and an infinite loop. To prevent this (remember, you have to assume that the person using your software is guaranteed to use it in ways you didn't expect or allow for), the function terminates the whole program if it is clear that convergence to the required accuracy cannot be achieved. The constant `NOT_CONVERGING` needs to be declared at a point where the function has it within scope.

The third point that requires discussion is the guard on the `if` statement. To keep the root "trapped" within a shrinking region, values of `x1` and `x2` must be maintained such that the signs of `fx1` and `fx2` are opposite. The guard tests for this, without worrying about which is positive and which is negative.

Finally, note how quickly the function arrives at accurate answers. Just a few dozen iterations are required, which means that root finding using this technique is extremely fast. In effect, one bit of accuracy in the binary representation of the answer is determined at each iteration. One decimal digit corresponds to about 3.2 bits of binary precision, so when 10 decimal digits of accuracy are required, around 30–35 bisection iterations are necessary, with the exact number depending on the width of the initial interval too.

> The bisection method uses a binary search mechanism to find roots of non-linear equations. Care should be taken to guard against over-ambitious termination conditions.

9.5 Physical simulations

As a blend between discrete-event simulations based on randomness, and the approximation techniques described in the previous section, there is a range of numeric problems that can be computed by simulating the passage of fixed amounts of *time*. As example of these techniques, consider a simple arrangement in which an object of mass m is suspended from a vertical spring. Hooke's law for springs says that (within its operating range) the force exerted by a stressed spring is given by $F_s = -kx$, where k is the spring constant, in units of Newtons per meter; x is the current displacement from the rest position, in meters; and F_s is in Newtons. In the case of a suspended weight, the resting point for which $x = 0$ is when gravity is balanced by the tension in the spring.

In the absence of friction, an object displaced from its rest point oscillates back and forth without end, as sketched in Figure 9.13. But when there is friction from the surrounding fluid (air, or water, or the oil in a car's shock absorber), it opposes the object's motion, and slows it down in proportion to the object's current *velocity*. That

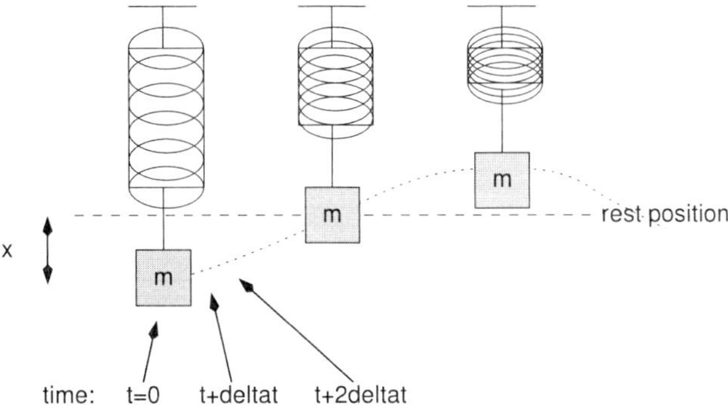

Figure 9.13: Three snapshots at different times of a mass m suspended by a spring, starting from an initial displacement of x at time $t = 0$.

is, there is a damping force F_d that is also acting on the object, given by

$$F_d = -cv = -c\frac{dx}{dt}$$

where v is the velocity, in meters per second, and c is related to the viscosity of the fluid in question. The two forces combine to act on the object, meaning that the acceleration on the object, a, in meters per second squared, is given by

$$a = \frac{1}{m}(F_s + F_d) .$$

Putting all these parts together means that the object's motion is completely described by the *differential equation*

$$\frac{d^2x}{dt^2} = \frac{1}{m}\left(-kx - c\frac{dx}{dt}\right) .$$

Now for the critical question – if $k = 10$, $c = 2$, and at time $t = 0$ an object of mass $m = 4$ kilograms is released at a displacement of $x = -1.0$ meters, what happens?

Figure 9.14 shows how this can be simulated. The heart of the computation involves a relatively simple loop: if at some moment in time t the displacement and velocity are given by x and v respectively, then the forces that apply at that instant can be calculated, and used to estimate values for x' and v' a tiny time-step Δt into the future. In the program, the size of each time-step is given by the variable `deltat`, and in the sample execution it has the value 0.0001. The output that is shown in the bottom of the figure involves more than 70,000 loop iteration, but still only takes just fractions of a second of computer time to simulate 7 seconds of "real" time.

As with the examples in the previous section, there is numerical tension between the desire to make `deltat` small, and the desire to minimize the problems caused by accumulated rounding errors. If `deltat` is too small, then the small changes in velocity and displacement will be swamped, and fidelity will be lost. But if `deltat` is too big, the computation might veer away from the reality of the system it is simulating. Indeed, in the end, all such computations will drift off track, and no such

```
    x = atof(argv[1]);
    m = atof(argv[2]);
    deltat = atof(argv[3]);
    v = 0.0;
    t = 0.0;
    while (fabs(x)>EPS || fabs(v)>EPS) {
        if (t > next_output_time) {
            graph(t, x);
            next_output_time += INTERV;
        }
        a = (1/m)*(-K*x - C*v);
        x += deltat * v;
        v += deltat * a;
        t += deltat;
    }
```

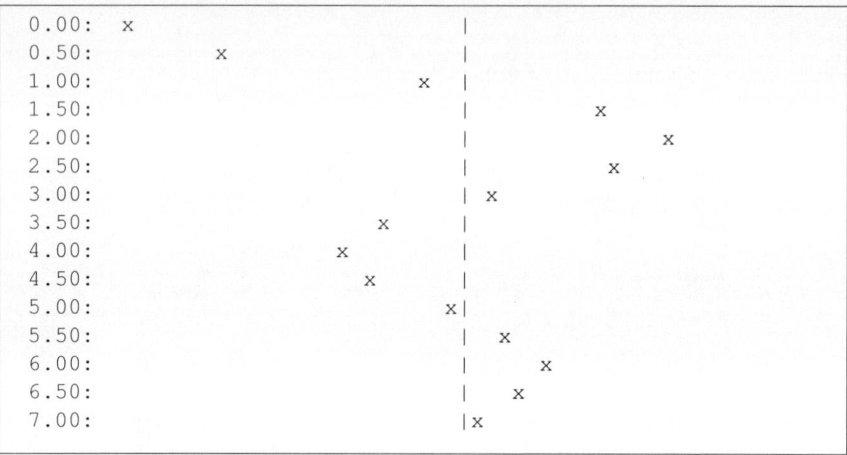

Figure 9.14: Simulating the behavior of an object suspended on a damped spring. The lower box shows the first 7 simulated seconds (printed every `INTERV` seconds) when started with $k = 10.0$ (constant `K` in the program), $c = 2.0$ (constant `C` in the program), $x = -1.0$ meters at time $t = 0$, $m = 4$ kilograms, and $\Delta t = 0.0001$ seconds. All of x, m, and Δt are command-line arguments. Function `graph` is not shown.

computation can be exact. In the case of the spring, this effect is easy to demonstrate by setting $c = 0$. The oscillations should continue indefinitely with exactly the same amplitude. But after approximately fifteen minutes of simulated time (using the same value of $\Delta t = 0.0001$), the amplitude of the simulated oscillation has grown to 1.1 meters. Similar effects arise even if c is not changed, if $\Delta t > 0.1$ seconds and hence is large relative to the anticipated length of the simulation.

> Time-stepped simulation of physical systems is a useful programming technique. But it is relatively easy for simple methods to be numerically unstable, and generate erroneous answers.

The approach shown in Figure 9.14 is an *Euler forward difference* technique. In these methods, the forces are evaluated at the start of each time interval, and then assumed to be constant throughout the interval. The inappropriateness of that assumption is one of the factors that causes these techniques to be unstable, and in reality the forces might be quite different by the end of the interval than they were at the start, because the object has both moved and changed its speed during the interval.

A wide range of enhanced predictive methods have been developed with reduced divergence rates compared to the Euler forward difference method. For example, one such improved method first of all uses the Euler method to make a crude prediction of where the object will be at time $t + \Delta t/2$, and how fast it will be moving; then uses that prediction to work out the forces that would be applying if that were the interval midpoint; and then goes back to the start of the interval, and applies those modified forces to the original x and v to predict the new location x' and velocity v' at the end of the interval. The idea behind this approach is to estimate an "average" force by looking at the middle of the time interval, and then apply the average force to the whole interval. More sophisticated linear combinations of predictors can also be formed. Members of one particular family – the *Runge-Kutta* methods – are usually implemented when physical simulations are being relied upon to yield precise answers. They compute a weighted average of multiple predictors of the form just sketched, and can be applied to simulations as diverse as weather forecasting, fluid flows in pipes and over aircraft wings, and analysis of electrical circuits.

9.6 Solution by evolution

The last of the problem solving techniques described in this chapter is rather obvious, but still worth mentioning explicitly, and is loosely called *solution by evolution*.

Many of the problems you encounter in your professional life will be similar to ones that you have already handled in alternative guises. For example, instead of sorting an array of integers, you might need to sort an array of structures, where the sort key is one of the components in the structure. Clearly, the starting point for the function you seek is a function for sorting an array of integers, and there are several sorting techniques illustrated in this book. It would thus be crazy to start completely afresh, and design a new function, since much of the control structure is the same, and only the details of the swapping process and item comparison process will differ. So, when faced with a new problem that is slightly different to a previous one, but also a lot the same, take your solution to that previous problem, and see if you can modify it to fit the new one. That is much more sensible than getting out a blank sheet of paper and saying "right, now where do we start".

> The best place to look for a solution to a problem is in a program that solves a related problem. If that program can be evolved to cope with the new situation, a great deal of design time will be saved.

Exercises

9.1 Modify the subset sum calculation in Figure 9.4 so that if a subset adding to the target value exists, the possible ways of making that target are printed.

9.2 Write the program that produced the output shown in the bottom box of Figure 9.5 on page 148.

9.3 Write a program that deals four random five-card poker hand from a standard 52-card deck. You need to implement a suitable "shuffling" mechanism, and ensure that the same card does not get dealt twice. For example:

```
mac: ./poker
player 1:   3-S, Ac-C, Qu-D, 4-H, Qu-H
player 2:   10-C, 2-H, 5-H, 10-H, Ki-H
player 3:   2-C, 6-D, 10-D, Ki-D, 9-H
player 4:   8-S, 9-S, 10-S, Qu-S, 4-D
```

Then modify your program to allow you to estimate the probability that a player in a four-person poker game obtains a simple pair (two cards with the same face value in different suits) in their initial hand. Compute your estimate using 40,000 hands dealt from 10,000 shuffled decks.

How about three of a kind (three cards of the same face value)?

And a full house (three of a kind, plus a pair with the other two cards)?

9.4 The playing surface at the Melbourne Cricket Ground is an ellipse with major axis $a = 86.45$ meters and minor axis $b = 73.65$ meters. The equation for an semi-ellipse with major axis a and minor axis b is given by $f(x) = b\sqrt{1 - x^2/a^2}$.

Use the function illustrated in Figure 9.10 on page 153 to verify that the circumference of the MCG playing area is approximately 503.8 meters.

Then convert your function to evaluate the trapezoidal rule, to work out (in square meters) the area of the playing surface.

9.5 The square root of the number z is the root of the equation $f(x) = x^2 - z$.

Evaluate the bisection rule by hand (using a calculator or computer if you wish, but not a program) and calculate the square root of the number 3, starting with `x1` equal to 0 and `x2` equal to 3, and stopping when `x2-x1<0.1`. Count the number of iterations required.

9.6 An alternative iterative rule for determining square roots is based upon the Newton-Raphson approximation – if x is an approximate square root of z, then $(x + z/x)/2$ is a better approximation.

Starting with $x = 3$, hand-calculate the sequence of approximations generated when searching for the square root of $z = 3$. Stop when two consecutive values differ by less than 0.05.

How many iterations are required?

9.7 Devise a mechanism for determining the set of adjacent elements in an array of n that has the largest sum.

For example, when all the elements in the array are positive, the correct answer is "take all of them, from 0 to $n - 1$".

When there are negative elements, they may or may not be part of the solution. In the array $\{+5, -6, +5, +3, -2, +3, -1, +4\}$ the correct answer is "take elements 2 to 7, which give the sum $5 + 3 - 2 + 3 - 1 + 4 = 12$".

Which of the problem solving techniques discussed in this chapter might yield algorithms for this problem?

9.8 Suppose you have to write a function to return the kth largest value in an array of n integers. What problem solving techniques might be used?

Sketch, for each of the possible techniques, an algorithm for determining an answer to the problem.

9.9 (*For a challenge*) Write an iterative function for the towers of Hanoi problem.

9.10 (*For a challenge*) Write an iterative function for the subset sum problem.

9.11 A toy rocket has a dry (with no fuel) weight of 10.0 kg, and is loaded with 8.0 kg of fuel, to have a total takeoff weight of 18.0 kg. When the rocket motor is burning, it consumes 0.8 kg of fuel per second, and generates a thrust (that is, force) of 500.0 Newtons.

At time $t = 0$ on a windless day the rocket engine is ignited. The rocket travels straight upwards until the fuel burns out, then falls back to earth.

The forces that act on the rocket while it is in flight are gravity, acting in the negative y direction, with a force given by $m \cdot G$, where m is the current mass of the rocket in kilograms, and $G = 9.81$ m/sec^2; the rocket's thrust while it is still burning, acting in the positive y direction; and air resistance, which opposes the velocity v, and at the speeds in question is given by $k \cdot A \cdot |v|^2$, where k is a constant proportional to the density of air and should be assumed to have the value $k = 0.6$ kg/m^3, and where A is the cross-sectional area of the rocket and should be assumed to be 0.1 m^2.

Write a program that computes the maximum altitude reached by the rocket, in meters; and the duration of the rocket's flight, in seconds. Explore the effect of the time-step Δt on the estimates that are generated.

9.12 Implement a second solution to the same rocket problem using the "midpoint estimation" technique described at the end of Section 9.5.

Chapter 10

Dynamic Structures

In the programs discussed prior to this chapter, arrays have been declared and dimensioned at the time the program is compiled, and have been of fixed sizes. To change them has involved recompilation.

For example, in Figure 7.14 on page 122 the maximum number of distinct words that can be handled is declared in advance, and the program fails if an input text containing more than this limit is supplied. If very large documents are to be catered for, the constant `MAXWORDS` could be set to (say) 1,000,000 rather than 1,000. Similarly, if there is a requirement that words longer than 10 characters are to be handled properly, the constant `MAXCHARS` could be set to (say) 50. But this combination of changes then means that the array `all_words` in Figure 7.14 requires 50 MB of memory – plausible if very large texts are to be processed, but probably excessive if just a few kilobytes of input are expected. Nor is it sensible to have two different compiled versions of the same program, one for small inputs and one for large – when a program commences operation, it may not be known whether the input is large or not.

That is, there is tension between the desire to cope with large inputs, and the desire to not allocate memory wastefully. The only way around this dilemma is to have a mechanism that allows the array in question to be given a relatively modest initial size, and then grown as required each time it becomes full.

Exactly that facility is introduced in this chapter – the ability for a program to request the allocation of fresh regions of memory *after* it has commenced execution. Section 10.1 introduces the relevant functions from the `stdlib.h` library, and shows how they are used to achieve dynamic arrays. Sections 10.2 and 10.3 then add a further twist, and consider the possibility of inserting pointers into part of the newly allocated space, with those pointers in turn used as a basis for further memory allocation. Finally, Section 10.4 considers another way in which pointers can be used in C, this time to allow functions to be selected at the time the program executes, rather than fixed at the time it is compiled.

10.1 Run-time arrays

Table 10.1 lists a set of functions that are used to request, manage, and eventually relinquish, sections of memory at run-time.

Function	Purpose
`size_t sizeof(`*thing*`)`	
	Returns the number of bytes required to store the type or variable supplied as argument *thing*. Not really a function.
`void *malloc(size_t size)`	
	Allocates a fresh segment of memory containing `size` bytes.
`void *calloc(size_t nmemb, size_t size)`	
	Allocates a fresh segment of memory that contains the number of bytes required to store an array of `nmemb` items each of `size` bytes. Once allocated, the memory segment is set to byte zeros.
`void *realloc(void *ptr, size_t size)`	
	Allocates a fresh segment of memory that contains `size` bytes; then copies into it the contents of the memory segment indicated by `ptr`; and then calls `free(ptr)`.
`void free(void *ptr)`	
	Deallocates the segment of memory indicated by `ptr` and returns it to the pool of available memory.

Table 10.1: A subset of the memory management functions provided in C. Functions `malloc`, `calloc`, and `realloc` return a pointer to the first byte of the memory allocated, or `NULL` if no allocation was possible. All of these functions are described by the header file `stdlib.h`.

The first component in this suite of functions is `sizeof`. The program fragment in Figure 10.1 shows the effect of applying `sizeof` to a range of types and variables. On this particular machine `double` and pointer variables occupy eight bytes, while `float` and `int` variables occupy four bytes. Note that `sizeof` distinguishes between arrays (the ten-element array `A` is reported to occupy 80 bytes) and pointers (the pointer `p` occupies eight bytes).

The pseudo-function `sizeof` returns the number of bytes used to store the indicated type or variable.

The values returned by `sizeof` are implementation dependent, and for program portability it is critical that `sizeof` be used rather than hard-coded constants such as eight for the size of a `double`, or four for the size of an `int`. Note also that the facility provided by `sizeof` is not a true function, as it is implemented within the compiler and operates on both variables and types. Indeed, `sizeof` is sufficiently important in C that it is a reserved word, and may not be used as an identifier.

The value returned by `sizeof` is of type `size_t`. This type is essentially an unsigned integer, but has the specialized interpretation of applying to memory sizes measured in bytes of storage, and is utilized in a range of functions to do with storage allocation. For example, in Table 7.2 on page 119 the function `strlen` was listed as returning a value of type `int`. But strictly speaking, `strlen` returns a value of type `size_t`, as it is a measure to do with memory consumption.

```
double A[10]; char *p="mary mary quite contrary";
printf("sizeof(char)    = %2lu\n", sizeof(char));
printf("sizeof(int)     = %2lu\n", sizeof(int));
printf("sizeof(float)   = %2lu\n", sizeof(float));
printf("sizeof(double) = %2lu\n", sizeof(double));
printf("sizeof(A)       = %2lu\n", sizeof(A));
printf("sizeof(*A)      = %2lu\n", sizeof(*A));
printf("sizeof(p)       = %2lu\n", sizeof(p));
printf("sizeof(*p)      = %2lu\n", sizeof(*p));
```

```
sizeof(char)   =  1
sizeof(int)    =  4
sizeof(float)  =  4
sizeof(double) =  8
sizeof(A)      = 80
sizeof(*A)     =  8
sizeof(p)      =  8
sizeof(*p)     =  1
```

Figure 10.1: Using `sizeof` to determine the number of bytes required to store an object. The lower box shows an execution of the program fragment in the upper box.

Table 10.1 also introduces another type that has not been used in previous chapters: `void*`. In functions the reserved word `void` is used indicate that the function has no arguments, or no result. The type `void*` describes a pointer of no particular type, but one that can be cast to become of *any* type. That is, a pointer of type `void*` is a raw byte address in memory, and has no associated type. In particular, if `p` is of type `void*`, it makes no sense to interrogate the value of `*p`, since there is no associated type that would allow a value to be formed. Instead, pointers of type `void*` must always be cast to become pointers of an actual defined type prior to being dereferenced. For example, if `void*` pointer `p` is known to point at an `int`, then the expression `*((int*)p)` is used to access that variable.

The allocation routines in Table 10.1 all manipulate memory using `void*` pointers. Doing so makes a great deal of sense, as the allocation routines have no need to know the purpose for which the memory is being requested. As will be clear by the end of the chapter, use of the types `void*` and `size_of` also makes it possible to write functions that operate on objects without any regard for their type, by referring to them using the combination of a pointer of type `void*` that indicates the byte address at which they begin, and a `size_t` value that indicates their length in bytes.

Figure 10.2 illustrates the use of two of the allocation functions in Table 10.1. Function `malloc` is passed a single `size_t` value, representing a request for that many bytes of memory. If the memory management routines that underly `malloc` are able to satisfy the request, a `void*` pointer to that space is returned. The returned pointer is usually immediately assigned, and thus automatically cast, to a typed pointer variable. The program may then use that segment of memory for whatever purpose it wishes – typically, but not always, to form an array. On the other hand, if the available memory is less than what is requested, or if there is no single section of

```
#include <stdlib.h>
#define PTRS 5

    char *p[PTRS];
    size_t nbytes=10;
    int i;
    /* try to allocate an array of pointers */
    for (i=0; i<PTRS; i++) {
        printf("malloc of %10lu bytes ", nbytes);
        if ((p[i] = (char *)malloc(nbytes)) == NULL) {
            printf("failed\n");
        } else {
            printf("succeeded\n");
        }
        nbytes *= 100;
    }
    /* now free all the memory that did get allocated */
    for (i=0; i<PTRS; i++) {
        if (p[i]) {
            free(p[i]);
            p[i] = NULL;
        }
    }
```

```
malloc of         10 bytes succeeded
malloc of       1000 bytes succeeded
malloc of     100000 bytes succeeded
malloc of   10000000 bytes succeeded
malloc of 1000000000 bytes succeeded
```

Figure 10.2: Using `malloc` and `free`. The lower box shows an execution of the program fragment in the upper box.

contiguous memory available that can satisfy the request, a `NULL` pointer is returned, and the program must react accordingly.

> Function `malloc` returns a pointer to a segment of memory of the requested size in bytes, or `NULL` if no such segment can be allocated.

All allocated memory is automatically returned to the system when a program terminates. But it might also happen that segments of memory become surplus to requirements even while the program is still executing. Such regions can be relinquished through the use of the function `free`. It takes a pointer argument that was previously generated by a call to `malloc` (or `calloc`, or `realloc`), and informs the memory management system that it may reclaim that space, and coalesce it back with other adjacent free segments if possible. The pointer passed as an argument to `free` should then not be used to access memory again – the best policy is to immediately assign `NULL` to it to prevent this happening. That pointer should now only be used if a valid value is assigned to it again – for example, by a subsequent call to `malloc`.

Programs that `malloc` fresh data storage space for each phase of their operation must be careful to `free` that space again when it is no longer required. That is, unless all allocated memory is required until the moment that a program terminates, it is important for the programmer to carefully track calls to `malloc`, and match them with corresponding calls to `free`. If this balancing is not done – if there is memory that is not freed when no longer required – then the amount of memory allocated to the program will inexorably grow, and eventually a call to `malloc` is going to fail. Programs that do not scrupulously match each `malloc` with a subsequent `free` are said to have a *memory leak*, and can be very frustrating to debug. Memory management is an important topic in computing, and if you progress beyond the study of programming, you are almost certain to learn some of the techniques used to make it an efficient and effective process.

> The function `free` releases a previously allocated segment of memory back to the memory management system. Unless a program requires all allocated memory through to termination, each call to `malloc` should be matched by a later call to `free`.

In Figure 10.2, a total of five segments of memory are allocated, and then freed again without even being used – the program is purely an example, and accomplishes no useful computation. On this hardware – a Macbook Pro – it was possible to accommodate requests for more than 1 GB from within a simple C program.

Figure 10.3 shows the use of `malloc` and `realloc` in a more interesting example. The program in Figure 10.3 has the same functionality as the one shown in Figure 7.14 on page 122, but without the conservative limit on the maximum length of each distinct word, and with no restriction on the number of distinct words that can be handled. To achieve this flexibility, function `malloc` is used to create a first array of `INITIAL` string pointers; thereafter, each time the array pointed at by `all_words` gets full, it is doubled in size using `realloc`, and processing continued.

It may seem excessive to keep on doubling the size of the `all_words` array. An alternative would be to add (say) 100 locations to `all_words` via the altered assignment `current_size+=INITIAL` prior to the call to `realloc`. Doing so may reduce the average amount of space wasted as the array repeatedly fills and is extended, but it also makes the program slower to execute. This is an important point – for large inputs the byte copying required by `realloc` can dominate the execution time if an arithmetic (rather than geometric) sequences of array sizes is used. Doubling `all_words` at each stage guarantees that at least half of the allocated storage is always being put to use, and means that on average each array item is copied into a new location just twice – a good compromise between speed and space.

> The function `realloc` is used to manage arrays that must expand to accept more data. The first array must be created with `malloc`, thereafter array sizes should grow as a geometric sequence.

Note the type of variable `all_words`. It is a pointer to a pointer to a character – with that character being the first one in an array of characters, and its pointer being

```
#define MAXCHARS 1000     /* max chars per word */
#define INITIAL   100     /* initial size of word array */

typedef char word_t[MAXCHARS+1];
int getword(word_t W, int limit);
void exit_if_null(void *ptr, char *msg);

int
main(int argc, char *argv[]) {
    word_t one_word;
    char **all_words;
    size_t current_size=INITIAL;
    int numdistinct=0, totwords=0, i, found;
    all_words = (char**)malloc(INITIAL*sizeof(*all_words));
    exit_if_null(all_words, "initial allocation");
    while (getword(one_word, MAXCHARS) != EOF) {
        totwords = totwords+1;
        /* linear search in array of previous words... */
        found = 0;
        for (i=0; i<numdistinct && !found; i++) {
            found = (strcmp(one_word, all_words[i]) == 0);
        }
        if (!found) {
            /* a new word exists, but is there space? */
            if (numdistinct == current_size) {
                current_size *= 2;
                all_words = realloc(all_words,
                    current_size*sizeof(*all_words));
                exit_if_null(all_words, "reallocation");
            }
            /* ok, there is definitely space in array */
            all_words[numdistinct] =
                (char*)malloc(1+strlen(one_word));
            exit_if_null(all_words[numdistinct],
                "string malloc");
            /* and there is also a space for the new word */
            strcpy(all_words[numdistinct], one_word);
            numdistinct += 1;
        }
    }
    printf("%d words read\n", totwords);
    for (i=0; i<numdistinct; i++) {
        printf("word #%d is \"%s\"\n", i, all_words[i]);
        free(all_words[i]);
        all_words[i] = NULL;
    }
    free(all_words);
    all_words = NULL;
    return 0;
}
```

Figure 10.3: Using `realloc` so that an array can grow as large as is required. Function `getword` is defined in Figure 7.13 on page 121.

the first one in an array of pointers to characters. Hence the declared type: `char**`, the same as the `(char*) []` that is used to describe the program argument `argv`.

Figure 10.3 also shows a second common operation in C – that of using `malloc` to obtain exactly enough space for some particular string to be stored, using `strlen` to determine the length of it. The "`1+`" in that call is to allow for the null byte at the end of the string. Apart from the null, there is no waste space at all in the strings being stored. In this framework, the memory waste caused by over-sizing `all_words` by as much as a factor of two might be more than compensated for by not wasting any space in the stored strings.

When using `malloc` to create an array to store a string, one extra character must be requested, to hold the terminating null byte.

A third point is illustrated by Figure 10.3: the use of a function `exit_if_null` to test each pointer after any of the memory allocation routines has been used. If the allocation fails, the pointer is `NULL`, and program execution should be aborted. The second argument passed to `exit_if_null` is a message to be printed prior to program exit. The flexibility associated with `void*` pointers means that a possible implementation of the function is thus:

```
void
exit_if_null(void *ptr, char *msg) {
    if (!ptr) {
        printf("unexpected null pointer: %s\n", msg);
        exit(EXIT_FAILURE);
    }
}
```

The minimalist guard is possible because `NULL` is equivalent to integer zero, meaning that `!ptr` is one (true) exactly whenever the pointer `ptr` is `NULL`.

A more general way of achieving a similar result is to use the `assert` function specified in the header file `assert.h`:

```
    assert(all_words[numdistinct] != NULL);
```

If the argument expression is false, program execution is halted and a diagnostic message printed indicating the line number and the assertion that has been violated. It is also perfectly reasonable to write:

```
    assert(0 <= numdistinct && numdistinct < current_size);
```

This one checks that two variables are maintaining an expected relationship, and could be used to guard an array access.

The `assert` function is used in the remainder of this book to indicate a property that should always be true at that point in a program, and that if violated, represents a serious problem. You are encouraged to use `assert` in the same way in your programming. On the other hand, a less abrupt handling of `NULL` pointers is sometimes required, in which case a dedicated test should be written. Whichever route is used, the value returned from `malloc` should always be tested before the pointer is used.

> The `assert` function is used to punctuate programs with checks that, if violated, indicate that program execution should be halted.

Like the program in Figure 7.14 on page 122, the version in Figure 10.3 uses a linear search, and words are assigned to positions in `all_words` in order of first appearance. On the example text shown in the middle box of Figure 7.14, the program in Figure 10.3 produces this output:

```
14 words read
word #0 is "Mary"
word #1 is "had"
word #2 is "a"
word #3 is "little"
word #4 is "lamb"
word #5 is "fourleggedwhitefluffything"
```

The calls to `free` and subsequent `NULL` assignments are not strictly necessary in Figure 10.3, as all memory is held through to program termination. Nevertheless, it is good discipline to include them as shown.

> Dynamic arrays allow runtime memory to be efficiently used, as programs can adjust their memory consumption to the scale of the input data without needing to be recompiled.

10.2 Linked structures

In the previous section `malloc` was used to create space for an array. But it is also possible to `malloc` space for a single variable, or for a structure. Provided that a pointer variable is declared in the usual way to serve as a handle through which the structure can be reached, the structure variable need not be allocated until it is required. For example, using the structure types described in Figure 8.5 on page 133, the following is perfectly sensible:

```
subject_t *maths, *compsci;
staff_t *sara;
sara = (staff_t*)malloc(sizeof(*sara));
maths = (subject_t*)malloc(sizeof(*maths));
compsci = (subject_t*)malloc(sizeof(*compsci));
assert(sara!=NULL && maths!=NULL && compsci!=NULL);
```

The three variables `*sara`, `*maths`, and `*compsci` can then be used in the program. When no longer needed, they are returned to the pool of available memory:

```
free(sara);
free(maths);
free(compsci);
sara = maths = compsci = NULL;
```

What is gained? In this example, relatively little, and the underlying variables could equally well have been declared without any use of `malloc` being required. But now consider the type `node_t`, defined by:

```
typedef struct node node_t;

struct node {
    data_t data;
    node_t *next;
};
```

This relatively innocuous definition represents one of the harder things you will be asked to absorb in this book – `node_t` is a structure in which one of the components is a pointer to an object of type `node_t`, which means that one of the components of that second structure is a pointer to a third, and so on. The other component in each `node_t` variable is some type `data_t`, and represents the information that is to be stored in each node. For simplicity, in this section `data_t` is be assumed to be an `int`, but it might be any type – a `staff_t` variable, for example.

Recursive functions were discussed earlier in this book. The type `node_t` is a *recursive data structure*. Just as a recursive function must have a base case to be sensible, so too must a recursive data structure. In the case of `node_t`, the base case is a `next` pointer that has the value `NULL`. Using these `node_t` variables, it is possible to build a chain, or *linked list*, with each `node_t` in the chain using its `next` pointer to indicate the next element. The first pointer in the chain needs to be a variable in the program. But thereafter, the nodes in the chain can all be created through the use of `malloc`.

Earlier it was remarked that the array was a data structuring device with strong links to the control structure provided by the `for` statement. Similarly, a linked list is a data structuring device that has parallels in both the `while` statement, and, as was already noted, in recursion.

> A linked list is a one-dimensional data structure in which objects are threaded together using a pointer in each node.

The `typedef` and functions in Figure 10.4 build upon the basic idea of a linked list. A type `list_t` is defined, with two components: a pointer `head`, which indicates the first item in a linked list of nodes; and a pointer `foot` that indicates the last item in the list. If the list is empty, both pointers are `NULL`. Function `make_empty_list` creates a new empty list, and returns a pointer to it. That pointer is then retained in the calling program as the handle that allows access to the list as it grows and shrinks. The last operation performed on a list is to free every node in the list, and then the list variable itself. A function for that is also shown in Figure 10.4. Note the form of the loop: `while(p){...;p=p->next;}` is to linked lists what the loop `for(i=0;i<n;i++)` is to arrays.

Figure 10.5 shows further elements of this list management module. There are two quite different ways in which new objects (which are of type `data_t`) can be added to an existing list: at the head of the list, to become the new first item; or as a new last item in the list, by appending it after the current foot. Functions are provided in Figure 10.5 for both of these options. In either case, insertion when the list is currently empty must be handled with extra care. An example showing the use of these two functions appears shortly.

```
typedef struct {
    node_t *head;
    node_t *foot;
} list_t;

list_t
*make_empty_list(void) {
    list_t *list;
    list = (list_t*)malloc(sizeof(*list));
    assert(list!=NULL);
    list->head = list->foot = NULL;
    return list;
}

int
is_empty_list(list_t *list) {
    assert(list!=NULL);
    return list->head==NULL;
}

void
free_list(list_t *list) {
    node_t *curr, *prev;
    assert(list!=NULL);
    curr = list->head;
    while (curr) {
        prev = curr;
        curr = curr->next;
        free(prev);
    }
    free(list);
}
```

Figure 10.4: Declaration, initialization, and freeing of a general `list_t` data type.

The other two functions shown in Figure 10.5 allow a list to be interrogated, and values extracted from it. Function `get_head` returns the `data_t` value that is currently at the front of the list, without altering the list in any way. To actually consume that value, and remove it from the list, function `get_tail` is used. It unlinks the node at the head of the list, and adjusts the `head` pointer to step past it. Variable `oldhead` is used to temporarily retain the location of that first node, so that it can be freed once it is no longer part of the list. This is a situation where a memory leak results if the `free` is not carried out, as there is no suggestion that the program might be about to terminate when this operation is performed. The possibility of the list becoming empty must also be handled properly.

> The four main operations performed on a linked list are to insert prior to the first item; append after the last item; fetch the contents of the first item; and delete the first item.

Specialized structures result if only a subset of the available operations are used. For example, if all insertions are at the foot of the list, then it is called a *queue* (or

```
list_t
*insert_at_head(list_t *list, data_t value) {
    node_t *new;
    new = (node_t*)malloc(sizeof(*new));
    assert(list!=NULL && new!=NULL);
    new->data = value;
    new->next = list->head;
    list->head = new;
    if (list->foot==NULL) {
        /* this is the first insertion into the list */
        list->foot = new;
    }
    return list;
}

list_t
*insert_at_foot(list_t *list, data_t value) {
    node_t *new;
    new = (node_t*)malloc(sizeof(*new));
    assert(list!=NULL && new!=NULL);
    new->data = value;
    new->next = NULL;
    if (list->foot==NULL) {
        /* this is the first insertion into the list */
        list->head = list->foot = new;
    } else {
        list->foot->next = new;
        list->foot = new;
    }
    return list;
}

data_t
get_head(list_t *list) {
    assert(list!=NULL && list->head!=NULL);
    return list->head->data;
}

list_t
*get_tail(list_t *list) {
    node_t *oldhead;
    assert(list!=NULL && list->head!=NULL);
    oldhead = list->head;
    list->head = list->head->next;
    if (list->head==NULL) {
        /* the only list node just got deleted */
        list->foot = NULL;
    }
    free(oldhead);
    return list;
}
```

Figure 10.5: Some functions that manipulate a linked list of objects.

sometimes a FIFO queue, standing for "first in, first out"). On the other hand, if all insertions take place at the front of the list, it is a *stack*, or LIFO ("last in, first out") queue. Stacks and queues are fundamental data structures that are used in more complex algorithms, and while the linked list implementation shown here is a good basis for them, there are also other ways of implementing them. Exercise 10.3 on page 190 explores one alternative.

A stack is a data structure in which the most recently inserted item is returned next. A queue is a data structure in which the least recently inserted item is returned next.

Figure 10.6 shows a simple program that makes use of this suite of functions. There are two further points to be noted in this example.

First is that the functions must be compiled as part of the main program, as the way they are written requires that the type `data_t` be known. They cannot be compiled separately from the main program, as it is the main program that determines the type of object being stored in each list node. In the example, type `data_t` is a single `int`. To achieve the compilation, but still allow the list operations to be maintained in a separate source file, a `#include` directive is used to inform the compiler that it must read another file, with the use of quotes rather than angle brackets indicating a file in the current directory, rather than a file in the central directory of C header files. The list operations form a distinctive collection of functions, but cannot be compiled and used as a library. A mechanism for bypassing this restriction appears in Section 10.5.

The second point to note is that the main program refers to the list object purely by the `list_t` handle, and manipulates the list entirely through function calls. At no stage does the main program in Figure 10.6 look at the internal implementation of the list – for example, there are no accesses to `list->head` in it. This separation of concerns is important for flexibility and robustness. To the calling program, it is the operations that are important, and not the details of how they are achieved. Making the interface between the data structure and the process using it a set of function calls means that the choice of implementation mechanism need not be made until the program is compiled. In a sense, there is another level of abstraction taking place here – *representational abstraction*, to match the functional abstraction that was introduced in Chapter 5, and the data abstraction that was introduced in Chapter 8. An abstract data structure is provided by the library of list functions shown in Figures 10.4 and 10.5, and all that the program in Figure 10.6 needs is to use those functions to manipulate the data structure.

Representational abstraction allows programs to be independent of the underlying implementation of the data structures that they manipulate.

To ensure brevity on the printed page, the functions in Figures 10.4 and 10.5 have been presented with almost no comments. It was suggested in Chapter 1 that you need to be rather more generous with comments in your programs than the formatting of this book permits, and now that the programs are getting more complex, it is timely to remind you of that advice. In your programs each function should be preceded by a

```
/* Example program to illustrate linked list operations.
*/
#include <stdio.h>
#include <stdlib.h>
#include <assert.h>

typedef int data_t;
#include "listops.c"

int
main(int argc, char *argv[]) {
    list_t *list;
    int i;
    list = make_empty_list();
    while (scanf("%d", &i) == 1) {
        list = insert_at_head(list, i);
        list = insert_at_head(list, i+1);
        list = insert_at_foot(list, i+2);
    }
    while (!is_empty_list(list)) {
        i = get_head(list);
        printf("%d ", i);
        list = get_tail(list);
    }
    printf("\n");
    free_list(list);
    list = NULL;
    return 0;
}
```

```
mac: ./listeg
10 20 30 40
^D
41 40 31 30 21 20 11 10 12 22 32 42
```

Figure 10.6: A simple main program making use of the list operations. Notice how the list functions must be brought in as source text using the `#include` facility, so that the definition for `data_t` is available as they are compiled. The lower box shows the program being executed.

description of its arguments and return values – the same information as is presented in the prose of this book. In a professional programming environment, the comments describing each function get written *before* the function, as part of the overall design.

Figure 10.7 shows pictorially the first three insertions into the list during the execution shown in the lower box of Figure 10.6. The `list_t` variable initially consists of two `NULL` pointers. Then, after the node for the `data_t` value 10 is created and inserted, both pointers point at it. Insertion of 11 at the head then follows, and a new node is threaded in prior to the node for 10, by adjusting the appropriate pointers. The `foot` pointer is unchanged during this second insertion. The third insertion adds the node for `data_t` value 12 at the foot of the queue, and leaves the `head` pointer

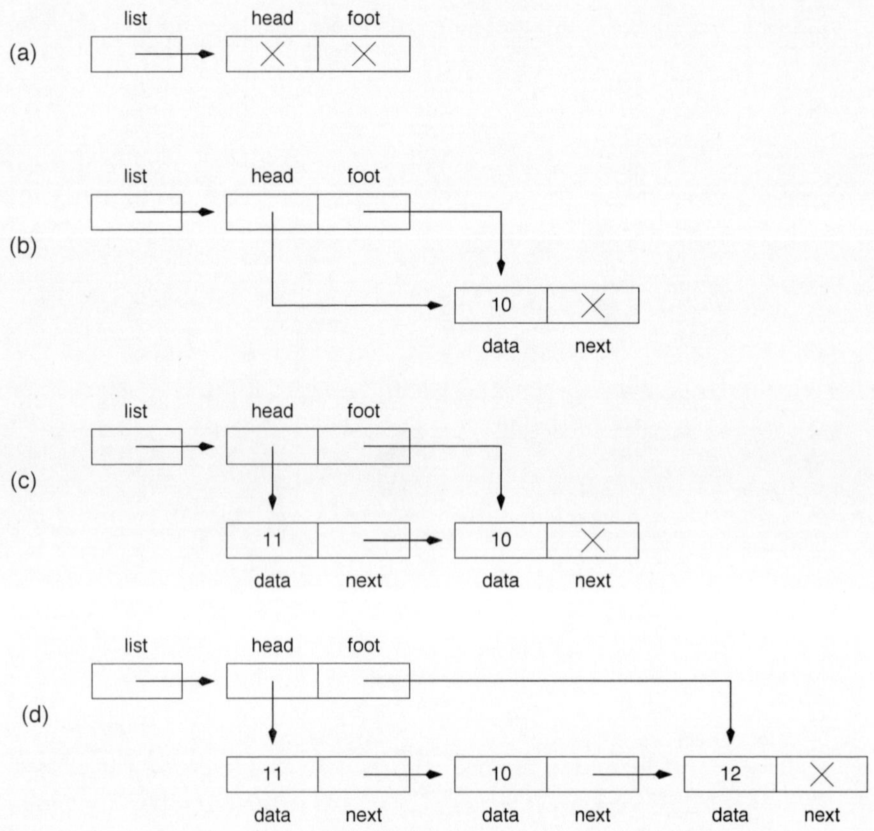

Figure 10.7: Declaring and using a variable of type `list_t`: (a) after the initial call in Figure 10.6 to `make_empty_list`, which creates the variable `list`; (b) after then performing `insert_at_head(list,10)`; (c) after performing `insert_at_head(list,11)`; and (d) after performing `insert_at_foot(list,12)`. In this example the type `data_t` is an `int`.

unchanged. The three values remain together in the list when it is finally printed, shown in the lower box in Figure 10.6.

The interface presented in this list example has a number of drawbacks, not the least of which is that in any single program lists can only be of one type. What if we need both a list of `staff_t` and a list of `student_t` in the same program? Mechanisms to cope with this need – to provide *polymorphic* data structures – are introduced shortly. But first, the next section describes an even more powerful linked data structure.

10.3 Binary search trees

In a linked list, each data node has one pointer. In a *binary tree* each data node has *two* pointers. When both pointers of some node are non-`NULL`, there are two successors, or *children*, of that node. Those two children might then provide a total of four grand-children, eight great grand-children, and so on. The explosive growth in numbers that comes from an exponential series like this means that a million items can be stored in a binary tree in which the longest path from the original ancestor node – the *root* of the tree – to any child need be no longer than twenty steps. Wow!

A binary tree is a two-dimensional data structure in which objects are threaded together using two pointers in each node.

Before examining the implementation details of such a structure, the overall operations that are required need to be considered. As with a linked list, we wish to be able to insert objects, and later on retrieve them. For linked lists, two insertion options were described – insertion at the front of the list, and insertion at the end of the list. And in Exercise 10.5 on page 190, a third option is explored, that maintains the list in sorted order at all times.

In a binary tree, there is usually only one insertion option considered, corresponding most closely to the third insertion option in a linked list. Use of this "ordered" insertion option results in a particular tree structure called a *binary search tree*, sometimes abbreviated to BST.

In a binary search tree, the data value stored at each node directs the flow of values into the two subtrees. Data values that are less than the one stored at this node must always be placed in one of the two subtrees, usually called the "left" subtree because of the way that trees are drawn with the root of the tree at the top, and the two subtrees suspended below. Similarly, data values that are greater than the one stored at this node must always be placed in the other, or "right" subtree.

A binary search tree is a binary tree in which the objects are ordered from left to right across the tree.

For example, consider the arrangement shown in Figure 10.8. String `Mercury` is the first inserted into the tree, and because the tree is initially empty, becomes the root of the tree. All subsequent insertions follow the left/right convention. Hence, when `Venus` is inserted, it goes in the right subtree of `Mercury`, since `Mercury < Venus`. That right subtree is empty, and so `Venus` becomes the right child of `Mercury`.

In the same manner, when `Earth` is inserted, it is as the left child of `Mercury`. String `Mars` is next. It must go to the left of `Mercury` (because `Ma < Me`), so attention turns to the subtree of which `Earth` is the root. But `Mars` comes alphabetically after `Earth`, and so the search for the insertion point moves to the right subtree of `Earth`. That subtree is empty, and `Mars` is inserted.

The tree of Figure 10.8 results when the remaining planets are inserted in order – `Jupiter`, `Saturn`, `Uranus`, `Neptune`, and `Pluto`. You should trace those insertions now, to be sure you understand the process involved. Note that the tree is unambiguously determined by the sequence of keys, and the order they are presented – a different tree may result if the keys are inserted in a different order. (Try building the tree by inserting in the reverse order, starting with `Pluto`.) Note also that the objects in the tree uniquely partition the universe of possible objects – each null leaf, represented by a dotted line in Figure 10.8, corresponds to a range of values. For example, the empty left subtree of `Neptune` corresponds to all values that are

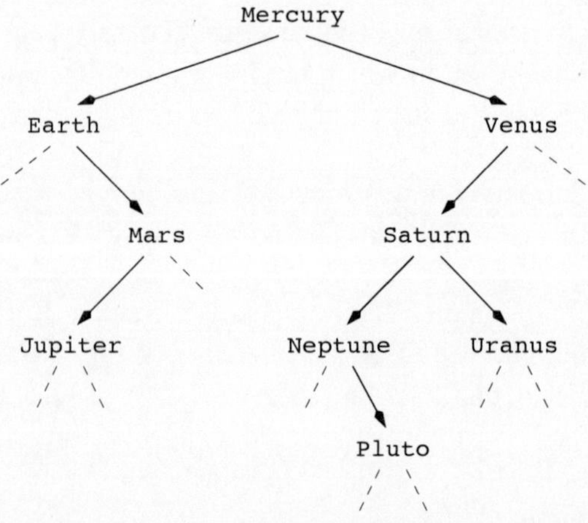

Figure 10.8: Binary search tree created by inserting the names of the planets in order of distance from the sun. The dashed lines represent `NULL` pointers.

greater than `Mercury` and smaller than `Neptune`, and the right subtree of `Venus` corresponds to all values greater than `Venus`.

Why are binary search trees so special? Suppose now that we want to use Figure 10.8 to find out if `Charon` is a planet. First, the root of the whole tree is checked – it is the handle through which all accesses must come. But `Charon` is not equal to `Mercury`. More importantly, `Charon < Mercury`, and so if it is in the tree anywhere, it is in the left subtree of `Mercury`. Attention is thus switched to the tree that has `Earth` at its root. Now, if `Charon` is to exist anywhere in the tree, it must be in the left subtree of `Earth`. But the left subtree of `Earth` is empty, and it can be concluded – after just two of the tree nodes are inspected – that `Charon` is not in the tree. (Charon, discovered in 1978 by I.W. Christie, is the moon of Pluto.)

Did you see what just happened? A search in a tree with nine objects in it was completed after only two objects were inspected. More generally, a search in a binary search tree inspects exactly the nodes that lie on the path from the root to the location of that item, and as has already been discussed, that path can be very short relative to the number of items stored. If we are lucky, that is.

If we are unlucky, and the keys are presented in sorted or reverse sorted order, then the tree is not a tree at all, it is a *stick*. Even so, the worst that can happen is the same as would happen if a linked list was used to store the objects. Fortunately, on average, the depth of the tree is small. If a set of n items is randomly shuffled, and then inserted one after the other in that shuffled order, the average depth in the tree (taken over all of the n items, and over all possible initial permutations of n items) is about $1.4 \log_2 n$. To give a numeric example, when $n = 1{,}000{,}000$, the average node depth in a random tree is a fraction under 28. So one item in a million can be located after inspecting fewer than 30 objects.

Searching in a binary search tree is rather like looking up a word in a paper dictionary. To find "gullible", for example, we open the dictionary up somewhere near the middle, and look at a word. If that middle word is "mousetrap", we know to go left, because "gullible" cannot possibly be to the right. Similarly, if that middle word is "fanfare", we go right. The only difference is that in a BST the sequence of nodes examined is exactly determined by the tree structure, whereas when we search a dictionary the sequence of words examined involves an element of randomness, because we don't always open at the same first page. There are also strong links between binary search and BSTs. In binary search, the exactly middle item in the range is checked each time; in a BST we hope that the item checked at each iteration is somewhere near the middle, so as to get the same logarithmic performance.

A randomly ordered set of objects placed into BST can be searched extremely quickly. If the insertion order is not random, there is a risk that the searching behavior will become significantly slower.

In order to give a completely flexible implementation of binary search trees, some more C programming knowledge is required. The next section describes that new technique; and then Section 10.5 returns to binary search trees.

10.4 Function pointers

Consider the program fragment shown in Figure 10.9, in which the declaration of variable `F` is different from anything previously shown. It says that `F` is a pointer to a function that when called with a `double` argument, returns a `double` result.

If a program can declare a function variable, then what can be assigned to it? As is shown in Figure 10.9, any function constant that has a matching type can. So all of `sqrt`, `sin`, and `log` (plus many more) can be assigned to variable `F`. And, once the pointer has been assigned, it can be used exactly as a function constant would be – to call the function. Indeed, calling it is the only operation that can be applied to a function pointer. So C provides a shortcut to do this: if `F` is a function pointer, then `*F` is the function, and to call it, `(*F)` `(`*argument list*`)` should properly be used, with the

```
double (*F)(double), x=2.0;
F = sqrt;
printf("x=%.4f, F(x)=%.4f\n", x, F(x));
F = sin;
printf("x=%.4f, F(x)=%.4f\n", x, F(x));
F = log;
printf("x=%.4f, F(x)=%.4f\n", x, F(x));
printf("x=%.4f, (*F)(x)=%.4f\n", x, (*F)(x));
```

```
x=2.0000, F(x)=1.4142
x=2.0000, F(x)=0.9093
x=2.0000, F(x)=0.6931
x=2.0000, (*F)(x)=0.6931
```

Figure 10.9: A simple program showing the declaration and use of a function pointer variable. The lower box shows an execution of the fragment in the upper box.

parentheses necessary. Instead, C allows the obvious abbreviation, and `F(`*argument list*`)` has exactly the same effect.

An analogy to bear in mind when digesting Figure 10.9 is that of arrays and array pointers. An array is a pointer constant, in the same way that `sin` is a function constant. Just as a pointer variable can be assigned the base address of an array and then used to access the elements in the array, so too a function pointer can be assigned the value of a function, and thereafter used to call the function.

If that were all there was to function pointers, they would perhaps be rather uninteresting. But they can also be passed as arguments into other functions, and this is where it starts to become fun. Figures 10.10 and 10.11 give a more compelling example that shows the tremendous flexibility that is achieved with function pointers.

In Figure 10.10, functions `double_ascending` and `string_descending` are defined. They seem to operate on different types, but the use of `void*` arguments means that in fact they have the same type – both are `int (void*, void*)`, functions that take two `void*` arguments and return an `int` value.

```
int is_sorted(void *A, size_t nelem, size_t size,
              int (*cmp)(void*,void*));

int
double_ascending(void *v1, void *v2) {
    double *d1=v1, *d2=v2;
    if (*d1<*d2) return -1;
    if (*d1>*d2) return +1;
    return 0;
}

int
string_descending(void *v1, void *v2) {
    char **s1=v1, **s2=v2;
    return -strcmp(*s1,*s2);
}

int
main(int argc, char *argv[]) {
    double X[] = {1.87, 3.43, 7.64, 7.68, 8.16, 9.86};
    char *S[] = {"wombat", "wallaby", "quoll", "quokka",
        "koala", "kangaroo", "goanna", "bilby"};
    if (is_sorted(X, sizeof(X)/sizeof(*X), sizeof(*X),
              double_ascending)) {
        printf("Array X is ascending\n");
    }
    if (is_sorted(S, sizeof(S)/sizeof(*S), sizeof(*S),
              string_descending)) {
        printf("Array S is descending\n");
    }
    return 0;
}
```

Figure 10.10: Passing arguments to a polymorphic function.

```
int
is_sorted(void *A, size_t nelem, size_t size,
        int (*cmp)(void*,void*)) {
    char *Ap=(char *)A;
    while (nelem>1) {
        if (cmp(Ap, Ap+size) > 0) {
            /* these two are out of order */
            return 0;
        }
        Ap += size;
        nelem -= 1;
    }
    /* all elements have been checked, and are ok */
    return 1;
}
```

```
Array X is ascending
Array S is descending
```

Figure 10.11: Receiving and using a function argument in a polymorphic function. The lower box shows an execution of the main program depicted in Figure 10.10, making use of function `is_sorted`.

To use their arguments, the two functions cast the incoming `void*` pointers into local variables that are typed, and then use the local variables to access the final arguments. In the case of `double_ascending` the function returns a negative value if the first argument should precede the second; zero if the two arguments are equal; and a positive value if the second argument should precede the first. In this function the arguments are interpreted as pointers to `double`s.

Function `string_descending` similarly returns an integer value to indicate the relative ordering of its two arguments, but this time the arguments are interpreted as pointers to strings, and "precedes" means "is alphabetically greater than". Other generic functions of this type could also easily be written: `double_descending`, `int_ascending`, `staff_ascending_by_name`, `staff_ascending_by_dob`, and so on – once the framework is established, the possibilities are endless.

The main program in Figure 10.10 declares two arrays, one of type `double`, and one of strings. The function `is_sorted` is then called twice, once to check if array `X` is in ascending order (which it is), and then again to check that array `S` is in descending order (which it also is). Both calls both make use of a single `is_sorted` function, an abstraction that is possible because the actual ordering test to be applied is passed in as a function pointer.

The description of the argument array is also passed to `is_sorted` in a type-anonymous manner, via the use of three arguments that describe the base address of the array (a `void*` pointer), the number of elements in the array (type `size_t`), and the size in bytes of each element of the array (also type `size_t`). Note how `sizeof` can be used to determine the number of entries that are present in an array. Doing it this way saves the trouble of counting them, and making a symbolic constant.

Figure 10.11 shows the other half of this carefully-engineered partnership. Function `is_sorted` manipulates its arguments purely as type-anonymous values, since it doesn't have any idea what type of object got passed – it could be an array of doubles, an array of string pointers, or an array of `staff_t` records. What it does know is that each pair of adjacent entries is to be compared using the function that is supplied as the final argument to the call. So it steps through the array of things `size` elements at a time, counting off the objects, and passing adjacent `void*` pointers to the function `cmp` it was given. That function needs to know the types of its arguments, but `is_sorted` does not. An initial assignment and cast to a `char*` pointer is to ensure that the address arithmetic is performed on bytes, and to prevent the compiler warning of arithmetic being performed on `void*` pointers.

> Function pointer arguments and `void*` pointers allow polymorphic functions to be written.

The result is that `is_sorted` is polymorphic – it can operate on any array. And while testing whether an array is sorted is perhaps somewhat trivial, getting an array into sorted order certainly isn't. Figure 10.12 shows how to achieve this rather more challenging task using a polymorphic function called `qsort` – a library function described by the `stdlib.h` header file. There is only one detail in this example that has

```
int
string_ascending(const void *v1, const void *v2) {
    return strcmp(*(char**)v1,*(char**)v2);
}

int
main(int argc, char *argv[]) {
    int i;
    char *S[] = {"koala", "kangaroo", "quoll", "quokka",
        "wombat", "goanna", "wallaby", "bilby"};
    qsort(S, sizeof(S)/sizeof(*S), sizeof(*S),
            string_ascending);
    for (i=0; i<sizeof(S)/sizeof(*S); i++) {
        printf("%s\n", S[i]);
    }
    return 0;
}
```

```
bilby
goanna
kangaroo
koala
quokka
quoll
wallaby
wombat
```

Figure 10.12: Calling the library `qsort` function.

not already been explained: the storage class `const`. Arguments are tagged as `const` if they do not change at all while the function is executing, allowing the compiler to handle them efficiently. The definition of `qsort` (see `man qsort`) includes `const` arguments, so the calling sequence must likewise specify a comparison function that takes `const` arguments if compiler warning messages are to be avoided.

The algorithm embedded in `qsort` is discussed in detail Chapter 12, and is not important here. What is important is for you to know that `qsort` is enormously better than the sorting methods that were introduced in Section 7.3 on page 103, and can be used to sort arrays containing tens of millions of items. And that means that you must know how to call the `qsort` function, passing in a type-anonymous array, and a pointer to a suitable comparison function.

> The `qsort` library function is a highly efficient sorting mechanism. It is polymorphic, and can be used to sort any array, provided a suitable comparison function is written.

10.5 Case study: A polymorphic tree library

Now for the most complex program in this entire book. Binary search trees were discussed in Section 10.3, without an implementation being given. The remainder of this chapter rectifies that omission, and provides a library of polymorphic BST routines that can be separately compiled, and used to maintain multiple trees over multiple data types. This final program is not for the faint-hearted, but if you need any encouragement, be sure that if you can master this program, you are well on the way to becoming a C expert. Here is the design specification:

> Write a program that reads a text file, and parses it into words. For each of the distinct words in the file, the number of occurrences of that word is to be reported. The output listing should be sorted in alphabetic order.

Figure 10.13 starts the presentation of a solution. It declares a `node_t` type that is used to manage the tree, including the two pointers required by the tree structure, and a third data pointer of type `void*` that is used to indicate the type-anonymous record stored at this node of the tree. Figure 10.13 also defines a `tree_t` type that includes a pointer to the root of a whole tree, and a function pointer `cmp` that is used to store the comparison function in use in this particular instance of a tree. These declarations are in a header file `treeops.h` to facilitate their use as a separately compiled module.

Figure 10.14 is the first of three figures that show the tree library functions. A new tree is created using `make_empty_tree`, which must be passed a pointer to the comparison function to be used in all subsequent operations on this tree. The handle passed back to the calling program is a pointer to the `tree_t` structure created by `make_empty_tree`, and all subsequent access to the tree is via that handle.

Figure 10.15 adds two further operations to the library: searching a tree for an object, using the comparison function to determine the search path at each node; and then an insertion routine that adds a new object to an existing tree. As always, the

```
typedef struct node node_t;

struct node {
    void *data;                     /* ptr to stored structure */
    node_t *left;                   /* left subtree of node */
    node_t *rght;                   /* right subtree of node */
};

typedef struct {
    node_t *root;                   /* root node of the tree */
    int (*cmp)(void*,void*);        /* function pointer */
} tree_t;

/* prototypes for the functions in this library */
tree_t *make_empty_tree(int func(void*,void*));
int is_empty_tree(tree_t *tree);
void *search_tree(tree_t *tree, void *key);
tree_t *insert_in_order(tree_t *tree, void *value);
void traverse_tree(tree_t *tree, void action(void*));
void free_tree(tree_t *tree);
```

Figure 10.13: Header file `treeops.h` describing data structures and functions for a library of tree manipulation routines.

```
#include <stdio.h>
#include <stdlib.h>
#include <assert.h>
#include "treeops.h"

tree_t
*make_empty_tree(int func(void*,void*)) {
    tree_t *tree;
    tree = malloc(sizeof(*tree));
    assert(tree!=NULL);
    /* initialize tree to empty */
    tree->root = NULL;
    /* and save the supplied function pointer */
    tree->cmp = func;
    return tree;
}

int
is_empty_tree(tree_t *tree) {
    assert(tree!=NULL);
    return tree->root==NULL;
}
```

Figure 10.14: A library of functions for binary search tree manipulation: part one.

```
static void
*recursive_search_tree(node_t *root,
        void *key, int cmp(void*,void*)) {
    int outcome;
    if (!root) {
        return NULL;
    }
    if ((outcome=cmp(key, root->data)) < 0) {
        return recursive_search_tree(root->left, key, cmp);
    } else if (outcome > 0) {
        return recursive_search_tree(root->rght, key, cmp);
    } else {
        /* hey, must have found it! */
        return root->data;
    }
}

/* Returns a pointer to the tree node storing object "key",
   if it exists, otherwise returns a NULL pointer. */
void
*search_tree(tree_t *tree, void *key) {
    assert(tree!=NULL);
    return recursive_search_tree(tree->root, key, tree->cmp);
}

static node_t
*recursive_insert(node_t *root, node_t *new,
        int cmp(void*,void*)) {
    if (root==NULL) {
        return new;
    } else if (cmp(new->data, root->data) < 0) {
        root->left = recursive_insert(root->left, new, cmp);
    } else {
        root->rght = recursive_insert(root->rght, new, cmp);
    }
    return root;
}

/* Returns a pointer to an altered tree that now includes
   the object "value" in its correct location. */
tree_t
*insert_in_order(tree_t *tree, void *value) {
    node_t *new;
    /* make the new node */
    new = malloc(sizeof(*new));
    assert(tree!=NULL && new!=NULL);
    new->data = value;
    new->left = new->rght = NULL;
    /* and insert it into the tree */
    tree->root = recursive_insert(tree->root, new,
        tree->cmp);
    return tree;
}
```

Figure 10.15: A library of functions for binary search tree manipulation: part two.

```
static void
recursive_traverse(node_t *root, void action(void*)) {
    if (root) {
        recursive_traverse(root->left, action);
        action(root->data);
        recursive_traverse(root->rght, action);
    }
}

/* Applies the "action" at every node in the tree, in
   the order determined by the cmp function. */
void
traverse_tree(tree_t *tree, void action(void*)) {
    assert(tree!=NULL);
    recursive_traverse(tree->root, action);
}

static void
recursive_free_tree(node_t *root) {
    if (root) {
        recursive_free_tree(root->left);
        recursive_free_tree(root->rght);
        free(root);
    }
}

/* Release all memory space associated with the tree
   structure. */
void
free_tree(tree_t *tree) {
    assert(tree!=NULL);
    recursive_free_tree(tree->root);
    free(tree);
}
```

Figure 10.16: A library of functions for binary search tree manipulation: part three.

comparison function returns a negative value if the first argument is smaller; zero if the two arguments are equal; and positive if second argument is smaller.

Both the searching and insertion functions work with a pointer of type `void*` to the data object involved, rather than the data object itself. This change (compared to the earlier routines for list manipulation) is necessary if the structure is to be polymorphic. Exercise 10.6 asks for the same alteration to be made to the list routines.

Searching and insertion both make use of an auxiliary recursive functions that step down the levels of the tree. This is a common structure for tree functions – a public routine presents an interface to the calling program, and sets up some initial values, and then a private recursive function is used to trace the linked data structure. The argument to the public routines is a pointer to a `tree_t`, while the argument to each of the corresponding private routines is a pointer to a `node_t`, a type not used by the main program. To ensure that the private routines are only accessible from within this module, their declarations are prefaced with the storage class `static`, which restricts their scope to the current C source file.

Functions search_tree and insert_in_order both return pointers. Function search_tree returns a pointer to the stored object, if it exists in the tree, thereby allowing the calling program to re-access a record it had earlier inserted. Function insert_in_order returns a pointer to an altered tree_t, which must be assigned in the calling function if the changes made to the tree are to be properly recorded. Both make use of the comparison function cmp that was passed to make_empty_tree.

Figure 10.16 adds another routine to this repertoire. In a *traversal*, every node in the tree is visited and some transformation applied, or output generated. In the case of a binary search tree, a traversal is again best accomplished recursively, first of all traversing the left subtree; then processing the data item associated with this node; then traversing the right subtree. This *in-order* visitation sequence means that the stored data items are processed in sorted order according to the cmp function used to build the tree. For example, if each data object is printed as it is visited, then the output is in sorted order, a fact that is exploited shortly.

Figure 10.16 also includes a free_tree function that traverses the tree and releases all of the space associated with it. This time the nodes are visited in a *post-order* traversal rather than in-order, since both subtrees must be deallocated before

```
/* Use a binary search tree to count words, and print
   a sorted list of words and their frequencies.
*/
#include <stdio.h>
#include <stdlib.h>
#include <assert.h>
#include <string.h>
#include "treeops.h"
#include "getword.h"

typedef struct {
    char *word;         /* pointer to a word */
    int  freq;          /* frequency of that word */
} data_t;

int
compare_string_parts(void *x1, void *x2) {
    data_t *p1=x1, *p2=x2;
    return strcmp(p1->word, p2->word);
}

void
print_then_free(void *x) {
    data_t *p=x;
    printf("%4d  %s\n", p->freq, p->word);
    free(p->word);
    free(p);
}
```

Figure 10.17: A main program using the binary search tree library: part one. The header file treeops.h is described in Figure 10.13 on page 184.

```
int
main(int argc, char *argv[]) {
    data_t *new, *locn;
    tree_t *tree;
    word_t oneword;
    tree = make_empty_tree(compare_string_parts);
    while (getword(oneword, MAXCHARS) != EOF) {
        new = malloc(sizeof(*new));
        assert(new!=NULL);
        new->word = oneword;
        new->freq = 1;
        locn = search_tree(tree, new);
        if (!locn) {
            /* not in tree, so create a new string */
            new->word = malloc(1+strlen(oneword));
            assert(new->word!=NULL);
            strcpy(new->word, oneword);
            /* and insert into tree */
            tree = insert_in_order(tree, new);
        } else {
            /* already in tree, so increment count */
            locn->freq += 1;
            /* and release the temporary node */
            free(new);
        }
    }
    /* now print all the words, freeing on the way */
    traverse_tree(tree, print_then_free);
    /* and release the tree itself */
    free_tree(tree);
    tree = NULL;
    /* ta daaa! */
    return 0;
}
```

```
   2  Mary
   2  a
   1  fourleggedwhitefluffything
   2  had
   3  lamb
   4  little
```

Figure 10.18: A main program using the binary search tree library: part two. Function `getword` is described in Figure 7.14 on page 122, with the type `word_t` and the constant `MAXWORD` assumed to have been declared in a matching header file `getword.h`. The other functions appear in Figure 10.14, Figure 10.15, and Figure 10.16. The lower box shows an execution on the input file shown in Figure 7.14 on page 122.

this root node can be relinquished. Note that the `free_tree` function does not (and should not) release the space consumed by the data items themselves, since the tree library did not allocate that space in the first instance. For example, the data items that were threaded into the tree might not have been created with separate calls to `malloc`, and instead might all have been allocated in a single large array. The mechanism used to create them is known only to the calling program, so the calling program must take responsibility for freeing the data items when they are no longer required.

Figures 10.17 and 10.18 present a main program that makes use of the tree library to perform the required processing. Two auxiliary functions are required. The first compares the `word` components of the two records it is passed. The second auxiliary function, `print_then_free`, is used when the end of input is reached, at which time the contents of each of the data items is printed. Once a word and its frequency have been printed, that data item is no longer required, so the space used by it can be released. The `word` at each node is freed first, then the node itself.

As before, the body of the program consists of a loop based on function `getword`. Once each word is read, it is searched for in the tree. To facilitate the search, a complete `data_t` is constructed in `new`, so that a pointer to it can be passed to `search_tree`. If the search yields a `NULL` result, the object is not in the tree, and must be inserted. If so, a permanent array for the string is created using `malloc`, a pointer to that space placed into the `new` record, and the string copied in to it. On the other hand, if the search returns a pointer to the `struct` describing the object, then the `freq` field for that word is incremented using the pointer, and the space used by `new` can be freed.

To compile the overall program, the three modules main, `getword`, and `treeops` need to be combined into a single executable:

```
gcc -ansi -Wall -o treeeg treeeg.c treeops.c getword.c
```

The techniques mentioned in Figure 5.5 on page 69 can also be employed if desired. Constructing a `makefile` will save typing out that long compilation line multiple times, and ensure that the right set of files is compiled each time you make changes.

Finally, after all the programming, the lower box in Figure 10.18 shows what happens when the word counting program is executed on the input file shown in Figure 7.14 on page 122. Isn't it absolutely stunning!

> Polymorphic libraries allow software modules to be abstracted and reused. The additional design effort in writing them is recouped in their enhanced versatility.

Of course, polymorphism does come at a price – the functions given in this section are hard to debug, and given the absence of helpful type information, potentially hard to use. A direct and simple implementation of a binary search tree using a named structure type is sufficient for many needs, and if a program is only manipulating one such tree type, monomorphic functions are all that is required. But if your program is manipulating more than one type, or if you want to write these functions once and never have to write them again in future, then polymorphism is required.

Exercises

10.1 Execute the program in Figure 10.1 on page 165 on your computer, and note the number of bytes required to store objects of different kinds.

Are there any differences to what is shown in Figure 10.1?

Then try executing the program shown in Figure 10.2. How much memory can be accessed by a C program on your computer?

10.2 Trace the action of function `insert_at_foot` (Figure 10.5 on page 173), by drawing two sequences of pictures, one covering the case when the argument list is non-empty, and the other sequence covering the case when it is. Verify that the new node is correctly linked into the list, and that all pointers are updated appropriately.

10.3 Describe (without undertaking all of the details of an implementation) how the stack and queue operations listed in Section 10.2 on page 170 could also be supported using an array of type `data_t`, together with some bookkeeping variables.

10.4 Using the type `list_t` defined in Section 10.2 on page 170, write a function `int is_list_element(list_t *list, data_t value)` that returns true if `value` appears in `list`, and false if it does not (including the case if the list is empty).

You will need to call a comparison function `cmp` to compare two objects of type `data_t`. You may either pass an appropriate function as a third argument to your function, or call a global function of the appropriate type. The function should return a value less than zero if its first argument is smaller; zero if the two arguments are equal; and a value greater than zero if the second argument should come first.

10.5 Using the type `list_t` defined in Section 10.2, write a function `list_t *insert_in_order(list_t *list, data_t value)` that inserts `value` into the `list` so that the list is always sorted from head to tail in non-decreasing order. The modified list should be returned. Use the same comparison function `cmp` as for the previous question.

Then modify the program in Figure 10.6 on page 175 so that it reads integers and inserts them one by one into a list that is maintained in sorted order. At the end of the input, the list is printed.

This is another version of *insertion sort*.

10.6 Modify the list manipulation routines so that they operate using a `void*` pointer to each data object, rather than embedding a `data_t` type into each list node.

To make your routines polymorphic, all other references to `data_t` will also need to be replaced using pointers of type `void*` and variables of type `size_t`.

A pointer to a comparison function will also need to be passed and stored.

10.7 Verify that an in-order traversal of the binary search tree shown in Figure 10.8 on page 178 visits the tree nodes in sorted order.

10.8 Construct a binary search tree by inserting the signs of the Zodiac in their sequence order into a tree that is initially empty: Aquarius, Pisces, Aries, Taurus, Gemini, Cancer, Leo, Virgo, Libra, Scorpio, Sagittarius, Capricorn.

Then add in the twelve animals of the Chinese zodiac (don't worry about the fact that these are years, not months): Rat, Ox, Tiger, Rabbit, Dragon, Snake, Horse, Goat, Monkey, Rooster, Dog, Boar.

Then add in your name and the names of some friends.

Finally, calculate the average depth of the items in the tree, with the root node of the tree at depth 1, its children at depth 2, and so on.

Verify that for "typical" input sequences like this one, the average depth of items in the tree is much smaller than the number of objects in the tree.

10.9 Write the function `staff_ascending_by_name` that is suggested in connection with Figure 10.10 on page 180. Use the definitions in Figure 8.5 on page 133.

10.10 Write a program that reads an unknown number of `double` values into an array in memory, then uses `qsort` to sort them into ascending order, and then writes them out again.

10.11 Modify the function `linelength` shown in Figure 9.10 on page 153 so that the function `f` whose length is being computed is passed in as an argument.

10.12 Write a function `int tree_size(tree_t *tree)` that calculates and returns the number of objects in the tree passed as an argument.

Hint: you will need to write a public starter function, and then a corresponding private recursive function. Model both upon the traversal functions given in Figure 10.16 on page 186.

10.13 Write a function `int avg_depth(tree_t *tree)` that calculates and returns the average depth of the objects in the tree passed as an argument.

10.14 Write a function `int is_bst(tree_t *tree)` that returns true if the tree passed as an argument is a BST (that is, is ordered from left to right), and false otherwise.

10.15 Using an `int` as a `data_t`, and the functions presented in Figure 10.14, Figure 10.15, and Figure 10.16, write a program that reads integers and inserts them into a binary search tree, then uses a traversal to retrieve them in sorted order. This variant of insertion sort is sometimes known as *tree sort*.

10.16 If all of the n items to be installed in a BST are available in advance, a *balanced* tree can be constructed, in which no object has a depth greater than $\lceil \log_2(n+1) \rceil$. In such a tree, searching is guaranteed to be fast.

Write a function that accepts as arguments an array of n objects assumed to be in sorted order, and constructs and returns a balanced binary search tree.

Hint: which item in the array should be the root of the tree? Then what happens to the rest of the items?

10.17 The smallest item in a binary search tree is the first element on the leftmost edge of the tree that does not itself have a left subtree.

Write a function `void *get_tree_head(tree_t*)` that returns a pointer to the smallest item in a BST.

Then write the companion function `tree_t *get_tree_tail(tree_t*)` that returns a modified tree, with the smallest item removed.

Hint: is there a subtree that can always be used to replace the item that is being pruned out of the tree?

10.18 (*For a challenge*) More generally, it might also be desirable to delete an arbitrary object from a binary search tree, given its key. Develop an algorithm for doing this.

10.19 (*For a challenge*) One drawback of the implementation of binary search trees that was given in this chapter is that when the tree is deep, a non-trivial amount of memory space may be required by the stack frames associated with the recursive function calls.

Implement a library in which the private functions associated with BST searching and insertion are iterative rather than recursive.

10.20 (*For a challenge*) Another kind of tree allows multiple children (without any upper limit) at each node. How could such a data structure be implemented? What might it be used for?

Chapter 11

File Operations

All of the input and output that has been done in the previous chapters has involved reading text from the keyboard or from a file through the use of Unix-level redirection; and writing output to the terminal screen.

C offers a wide range of other input and output options, and they are the topic of this chapter. Broadly, there are two types of files that can be manipulated in C: text files, and binary files. They are handled using largely the same suite of functions, and the only real difference is the type of data that gets written to them. The two sections in this chapter consider these two types of file.

11.1 Text files

Three files, or *streams*, are always opened when a C program starts running. So far you have seen two of them, without them being mentioned by name:

- `stdin` is the standard input file. It is usually associated with the keyboard, but can take input from a file using Unix input redirection. Functions `scanf` and `getchar` take their input from `stdin`.

- `stdout` is the standard output file. It is usually associated with the terminal screen, but can write to a file using Unix output redirection. Functions `printf` and `putchar` send their output to `stdout`.

The third file is another output file:

- `stderr` is the standard error output file. It is usually associated with the terminal screen, but can be directed to a file using a more complex Unix output redirection.

To write to `stderr`, a variant of `printf` is used in which a filename argument is also supplied: `fprintf(stderr,"error: null pointer\n")`, for example. Indeed, the function `printf` is implemented as a call to `fprintf` with `stdout` specified as the first argument. The convention in C is that all error messages, or other non-standard outputs, are written to `stderr`, in the expectation that the user of the program will see the `stderr` stream even if `stdout` is being directed to a file.

Function	Purpose
`FILE *fopen(char *fname, char *mode)`	Returns a pointer to a file that has been made ready for the specified operation. Argument `fname` is the name of the file to be opened; `mode` describes the operations that are required, `"r"` for reading, `"w"` for writing, or `"a"` for appending. In mode `"w"`, if the file already exists it is truncated to zero bytes. In mode `"a"`, if the file already exists the current location is set to the end of the file.
`FILE *freopen(char *fname, char *mode, FILE *stream)`	Closes the file specified by `stream`, and then attempts to re-open it using the first two arguments.
`int fclose(FILE *stream)`	Flushes all pending output to file `stream`, and then closes it.
`int getc(FILE *stream)`	Reads a single character from `stream`, as for `getchar`. Returns `EOF` if end of file is detected.
`int putc(int ch, FILE *stream)`	Writes character `ch` to file `stream`, as for `putchar`. Returns `EOF` if the output operation fails.
`int fscanf(FILE *stream, const char *format, ...)`	Input from file `stream`, controlled by `format`, as for `scanf`. Returns the number of values read.
`int fprintf(FILE *stream, const char *format, ...)`	Output to file `stream`, controlled by `format`, as for `printf`. Returns the number of bytes written.
`size_t fread(const void *A, size_t size, size_t nelem, FILE *stream)`	Reads binary data from `stream` to address `A`. A total of `nelem` objects each of `size` bytes are sought; the number of such objects actually read is returned.
`size_t fwrite(const void *A, size_t size, size_t nelem, FILE *stream)`	Writes binary data from `A` to the file `stream`, A total of `nelem` objects each of `size` bytes is to be output; the number of such objects actually written is returned.
`size_t fseek(FILE *stream, long offset, int whence)`	Moves the current location within file `stream` by `offset` bytes relative to the starting point specified by `whence`. See Section 11.2 for details.

Table 11.1: A subset of the file management functions provided in C. Functions `fopen` and `freopen` return a pointer to a `FILE` structure, or `NULL` if the file does not exist or for some other reason (such as access permissions) the specified operation is not possible. All of these functions are described by the header file `stdio.h`.

What about other files? Is it possible to open other files and use them? And is it possible to write to and read from named files on disk, without using Unix redirection? The answer to all of these questions is yes. Table 11.1 lists the common file operations supported in the library described by the `stdio.h` header file.

Fundamental to all of these operations is the notion of a *stream*, which is a sequence of bytes moving to or from a file. To track information about the state of a stream, a `FILE` variable is created by the file opening routine `fopen`, and all subsequent operations make use of the pointer handle of type `FILE*` that is passed back from `fopen`. That is, the `FILE*` pointer serves the same purpose as the `list_t*` and `tree_t*` structure handles that were used in Chapter 10.

Function `fopen` takes two arguments. The first is a string that indicates the name of the file. On most systems the string can be a file name in the current directory, or can specify a full pathname such as `/usr/share/dict/words`. The string can also be taken from a command-line argument.

The second argument to `fopen` indicates the way in which the file is to be used. Opening with an `"r"` string indicates that the file is to be read, and so an error arises if the file is not already present, or cannot be opened for some other reason such as restrictive access permissions. A mode of `"w"` indicates that a new file is to be created and written to. If a file already exists with that name, then it is truncated to zero bytes by the `fopen` call. The third access mode is `"a"`, which indicates that the file is to be appended to. In this case it is opened for writing, but is not truncated if it already exists, and the output operations commence at the end of the file.

Once a file has been successfully opened, the appropriate subset of the file operations can be used. Figure 11.1 shows an example program that uses `fopen` and `fread` to process a sequence of named files. To deal with each file, a call to `fopen` is attempted, to connect a stream variable with the file, and obtain a handle. If it can be opened, function `getc` is used to read the file, and the first two lines are echoed to `stdout`. The file is then closed, and processing of the next one commenced.

Figure 11.2 shows an execution of the program in Figure 11.1, in the directory of C programs associated with this book. The Unix wildcard expansion `two*.c` is expanded by the shell before the program is called, so the program is passed two command-line arguments.

> In a text file, information is stored as a sequence of ASCII printable characters.

11.2 Binary files

The functions `fscanf` and `fprintf` are used to convert between internal representations and sequences of printable ASCII characters. The advantage of using ASCII representations is that there is a wide variety of tools for editing, viewing, and printing files that contain them. This is why all of the programs in this book have used ASCII output, generated by `putchar` and `printf`. But the format conversion functions take time, and ASCII-mode storage can be expensive compared to the internal representation. For example, a four-byte `int` variable can store the number $-2{,}000{,}000{,}000$, but as the ASCII string `"-2000000000"` the same value requires eleven bytes.

```
/* Print the first few lines of a set of files.
*/
#include <stdio.h>
#include <stdlib.h>

#define LINE_LIMIT 2
#define SEPARATOR "=========================================="

void first_lines(FILE *fp, int n);

int
main(int argc, char *argv[]) {
    int fnum;
    FILE *fp;
    /* process the list of command line arguments */
    for (fnum=1; fnum<argc; fnum++) {
        fprintf(stderr, "Opening %s: ", argv[fnum]);
        if ((fp = fopen(argv[fnum], "r")) == NULL) {
            fprintf(stderr, "...........failed\n");
        } else {
            fprintf(stderr, "\n");
            printf("%s %s\n", SEPARATOR, argv[fnum]);
            first_lines(fp, LINE_LIMIT);
            fclose(fp);
        }
    }
    return 0;
}

/* Copy the first few lines of the file fp to stdout.
   Follow them with a count of the lines in the file.
*/
void
first_lines(FILE *fp, int n) {
    int c;
    int lines=0;
    while ((c = getc(fp)) != EOF) {
        if (lines < n) {
            putchar(c);
        }
        lines += (c=='\n');
    }
    printf("[%d lines in total]\n", lines);
    return;
}
```

Figure 11.1: Using `fopen` to access a named file for reading. The first two lines of each file listed on the command-line are to be displayed.

```
mac: ./twolines two*.c > tt.txt
Opening twodarray.c:
Opening twolines.c:
mac: more tt.txt
======================================= twodarray.c
/* Manipulate a two-dimensional array.
*/
[38 lines in total]
======================================= twolines.c
/* Print the first few lines of a set of files.
*/
[45 lines in total]
```

Figure 11.2: An execution of the program shown in Figure 11.1 in a directory of C programs. Note how the `stderr` output still comes to the screen, even when output is redirected to a file. The program in file `twodarray.c` appears in Figure 7.6 on page 110.

To allow the space and time overheads of ASCII files to be eliminated, C offers two further functions, in which no format conversions take place, and which operate on *binary* files in which data is stored using its internal representation. Table 11.1 lists the two relevant functions: `fread` and `fwrite`, and Figure 11.3 shows a simple program that uses `fwrite` to create a binary file of type `double` from an array `A`, and then uses `fread` to read the file back into the array.

One of the unfortunate inconsistencies in C is that the ordering of three values describing the type-anonymous parameter in `qsort` and in `fread`/`fwrite` is different: in `qsort`, the sequence is pointer, then the number of elements, then the size in bytes of each element; whereas in `fread` and `fwrite` it is pointer, then the size in bytes of each element, and then the number of elements. Be careful when using these functions, and check the manual pages if in doubt.

The program in Figure 11.3 creates a binary file in the current directory. Because each `double` on this machine occupies eight bytes, and there are seven numbers written, the file created is exactly 56 bytes long. It is just a sequence of bytes, with no suggestion as to how it should be interpreted. This means that it could also be read back as 56 variables of type `char`, or as 14 variables of type `int`, or as any mixture of `char`, `int`, and `double` variables. It could also be read as a single lump of 56 bytes into a suitably defined structure variable. However, if the data in a file is to be interpreted sensibly, it must be read using exactly the same type, or sequence of types, as was used to create it. For example, an array of `int` variables could be written after the seven doubles, provided that when the file is read back, seven doubles are read before any integers are accessed.

> In a binary file the stored form of information is exactly the same as the internal representation used in program variables. Functions `fread` and `fwrite` allow variables and arrays to be written to and from files without any format conversions taking place.

When working with binary files in which all of the objects are the same type, the option of both reading from and writing to the same file is possible – using the file a

```
/* Show use of the functions fopen, fwrite, and fread.
*/
#include <stdio.h>
#include <assert.h>

#define SIZE 7
#define FILENAME "temp.dat"

void print_doubles(double *A, int n);

int
main(int argc, char *argv[]) {
    double A[SIZE];
    FILE *fp;
    int i;
    /* initialize the array with some values */
    for (i=0; i<SIZE; i++) {
        A[i] = 1.2345*i + 0.6789;
    }
    print_doubles(A, SIZE);
    /* open the file for writing */
    fp = fopen(FILENAME, "w");
    assert(fp != NULL);
    /* write the whole array in one operation */
    i = fwrite(A, sizeof(*A), SIZE, fp);
    assert(i == SIZE);
    /* clear the array */
    for (i=0; i<SIZE; i++) {
        A[i] = 0.0;
    }
    print_doubles(A, SIZE);
    /* open the file for  reading */
    fp = freopen(FILENAME, "r", fp);
    assert(fp != NULL);
    /* read the array  back*/
    i = fread(A, sizeof(*A), SIZE, fp);
    assert(i == SIZE);
    print_doubles(A, SIZE);
    fclose(fp);
    return 0;
}
```

```
  0.679  1.913  3.148  4.382  5.617  6.851  8.086
  0.000  0.000  0.000  0.000  0.000  0.000  0.000
  0.679  1.913  3.148  4.382  5.617  6.851  8.086
```

Figure 11.3: Using `fopen`, `fwrite`, `freopen`, and `fread` to manipulate a binary file. The lower box shows an execution of the program in the upper box. Function `print_doubles` uses a `printf` inside a loop to write the array contents as text to `stdout`.

little like an array is used in memory. To allow *random access*, all of the "r", "w", and "a" mode options can be modified by the addition of a "+", to make "r+", "w+", and "a+". This flag indicates a file that will be used for both input and output. For example a file opened as "w+" is truncated to zero bytes, if it already exists, and any fprintf or fwrite operations extend the file from there. But fscanf and fread operations can also be performed on the file, intermixed with the output operations. The only requirement is that an fseek operation be performed when there is a change from input to output operations, or vice versa, so that the next record to be processed is unambiguously identified.

Function fseek shifts the current location in a stream. The first argument is a stream pointer, and the second an integer offset to specify the size of the move. The third argument is one of three symbolic constants defined in stdio.h: SEEK_SET, which indicates positive locations relative to the start of the file; SEEK_CUR, which indicates positive and negative locations relative to the current location in the file; or SEEK_END, which indicates positive or negative locations relative to the current end of the file. For example, the call fseek(fp,-sizeof(staff_t),SEEK_CUR) shifts the current location back by exactly the size of one staff_t structure. So if a staff_t record had just been read using fread, it can be modified in memory, and then written back to the file, overwriting the old record that was in its place. Another fseek should then be executed prior to the next fread operation.

Files can be opened for interleaved input and output operations. Function fseek is used to move the current location within the file. This mode of operation usually only makes sense if all objects in the file are of the same type.

11.3 Case study: Merging multiple files

Now for a more complex example involving files. Consider this next specification:

> Write a program that reads a set of text files, with the lines in each file presumed to be in sorted order; and writes a single sorted file to the standard output. Lines may be assumed to be at most 1024 characters long. As many as ten input files must be allowed for, specified as command-line arguments.

Figure 11.4 shows an example of the desired behavior. In the example, four text files f1.txt, f2.txt, f3.txt, f4.txt are each in sorted order. The program mergefiles is then executed, with those four filenames passed as command-line arguments. The output of mergefiles, written to stdout, is the sorted combination of all of the lines in the four input files. In this application the sorting is based purely upon the alphabetic characters in each line, so that "dolphins eat" precedes "dolphins live". A more sophisticated merging program would allow the user to specify where in each file the sort key was located, and would also offer the option of handling files that were in descending order, or keys that were numeric values, or where secondary keys are also specified to handle the case of equal primary keys.

```
mac: more f1.txt
apples are green
bananas are yellow
oranges are orange
pears are green
mac: more f2.txt
clothing comes in different sizes
wine comes in bottles and casks
mac: more f3.txt
dolphins live in the ocean
gorillas live in the forest
nothing lives on the moon
mac: more f4.txt
dolphins eat fish
mac: ./mergefiles f1.txt f2.txt f3.txt f4.txt
apples are green
bananas are yellow
clothing comes in different sizes
dolphins eat fish
dolphins live in the ocean
gorillas live in the forest
nothing lives on the moon
oranges are orange
pears are green
wine comes in bottles and casks
```

Figure 11.4: Executing the program shown in Figure 11.5.

Figure 11.5 shows how the required output is achieved. The most notable point in this process is that multiple files are open simultaneously, and an array of file pointers is used to access them. At any given time only one line of each file is held in memory, as a best current candidate for the corresponding file. Only when that line is written to `stdout` is the next line from the file fetched.

Figure 11.5 also introduces a new function from the `stdio` library: `fgets` reads bytes from the named file until a newline character is encountered. It stores the byte sequence, including both the newline and a terminating null byte, into the specified character array. The character array must thus allocate two more bytes than the maximum string that is to be allowed for. There is also a corresponding function `gets` that reads from `stdin`, but places no upper limit on the string size – which makes it dangerous to use, and best avoided. In a further small inconsistency, the function `gets` again reads through until a newline character "`\n`" is encountered, but does *not* store the newline into the string.

Finally, note that for brevity (to fit the figure onto one page) there are no `fclose` calls in Figure 11.5. All open files are automatically closed when a program terminates, in the same way that all allocated memory is reclaimed when a program terminates. But, as with `malloc` and `free`, a careful programmer marries up every call to `fopen` with an explicit matching call to `fclose`.

```
/* Merge multiple files, all assumed to be sorted.
*/
#include <stdio.h>
#include <stdlib.h>
#include <string.h>

#define MAXLINE 1024
#define MAXFILE 10

int
main(int argc, char *argv[]) {
    FILE *fp[MAXFILE];
    char line[MAXFILE][MAXLINE+2];
    int valid[MAXFILE], numvalid=0;
    int i, first, next=0;
    /* open each of the files */
    for (i=1; i<argc; i++) {
        fp[i] = fopen(argv[i], "r");
        if (fp[i] == NULL) {
            fprintf(stderr, "Cannot open %s\n", argv[i]);
            exit(EXIT_FAILURE);
        }
        valid[i] = 1;
        numvalid += 1;
    }
    /* read the first line of each file */
    for (i=1; i<argc; i++) {
        if (fgets(line[i], MAXLINE, fp[i]) == NULL) {
            valid[i] = 0;
            numvalid -= 1;
        }
    }
    while (numvalid) {
        /* find smallest current line */
        first = 1;
        for (i=1; i<argc; i++) {
            if (valid[i]) {
                if (first) {
                    next = i;
                    first = 0;
                } else if (strcmp(line[i],line[next]) < 0) {
                    next = i;
                }
            }
        }
        /* print out line[next], and try to replace it */
        printf("%s", line[next]);
        if (fgets(line[next], MAXLINE, fp[next]) == NULL) {
            valid[next] = 0;
            numvalid -= 1;
        }
    }
    return 0;
}
```

Figure 11.5: Merging multiple text files.

Exercises

11.1 If you are working on a Unix machine and running a `csh`-like shell such as `tcsh`, try the following sequence of executions, where `prog` is a program that writes `"message 1"` to `stdout` using `printf`, and then writes `"message 2"` to `stderr` using `fprintf`:

```
mac: ./prog
mac: ./prog > file1.txt
mac: ./prog >> file1.txt
mac: ./prog >& file1.txt
mac: ./prog >>& file1.txt
mac: (./prog > file1.txt)
mac: (./prog > file1.txt) >& file2.txt
```

Different redirection commands may be needed for the shell on your computer. If the one shown give error messages, consult a manual or a local expert.

11.2 Write a program `append` that duplicates one file (the first command-line argument) at the end of a second (the other command-line argument).

11.3 The Unix `tee` command writes its `stdin` through to `stdout` in the same way that the `cat` command does. But it also creates an additional copy of the file into each of the filenames listed on the command-line when it is executed.

Implement a simple version of this command.

Hint: you will need an array of files all opened for writing.

11.4 Write a simple program that opens a file for output, does an `fseek` to byte number 100,000 in the file, writes a single newline character, and then closes the file.

Measure the size of the file using the Unix `ls -lg` command, the Unix `wc` command, and then the Unix `du` (disk utilization) command, which lists the amount of disk consumed by a file, measured in kilobytes. What do you notice? Can you explain the discrepancy?

Finally, write a program that reads the file using `getc`. What value do the first 100,000 bytes have?

Chapter 12

Algorithms

Chapter 1 opened with the assertion that computer science was the study of information, and of ways of transforming information. When immersed in the nitty-gritty of learning programming it is easy to lose sight of that objective. This chapter is intended to kindle an excitement for the big picture, in which programming is just a tool and information manipulation is the true goal. It is devoted to algorithms, and presents some of the very good ones that have been developed during the study of computer science. They epitomize the intellectual richness of computing as a discipline, and they are probably quite unlike anything you have encountered until now.

The focus is on two fundamental tasks that permeate almost all data processing applications – searching, and sorting. The techniques employed to efficiently tackle these two problems are also used in many other algorithms, and you are certain to study the associated problems in more detail if you take your interest in computing beyond the level considered in this book.

12.1 Measuring performance

Some algorithmic tools are required to get started. The most important of these is a way of comparing algorithms. Cars are measured by their acceleration and fuel economy; and digital cameras by their zoom ratio and the number of pixels they record. Algorithms are measured with reference to their time and space consumption. The amount of *space* some technique requires has a direct impact on its usefulness, since computers have finite memory. And the *time* taken is also critical – why would algorithm X be used if it takes 100 times longer than algorithm Y, and runs in the same amount of memory?

> The two resources consumed by an executing program are memory space and computation time.

With cars, acceleration is in part a function of the number of passengers in the car, and of their weight. But measurements are usually based upon a single "average" driver, meaning that zero to 100 km/h acceleration is regarded as being a fixed value, measured in seconds. In contrast to this, the time taken to run a computer program depends directly upon the number of objects being processed. For example, in Section 7.3 on page 103 it was argued that to sort n objects, the insertion sort algorithm performs as many as $n^2/2$ comparisons. As a consequence, if the number of objects doubles, the sorting time quadruples.

Suppose that another sorting algorithm requires $n(n-4)/4$ comparisons to sort n items. It might or might not be faster than insertion sort in a direct speed comparison, since the running time of both methods depends in part on factors other than the number of element-to-element comparisons. But in a sense the second algorithm is the same as insertion sort, because if the size of the input array is doubled, the running time again quadruples. The relativity between this algorithm and insertion sort is independent of problem size.

To capture this kind of broad-brush relationship, a special notation is used, and an algorithm is said to be $O(n^2)$ ("big-Oh of n squared", or "order n squared") if its running time grows quadratically in n, the size of its input. Similarly, an algorithm is $O(n)$ if its execution cost grows as a linear function of the input size.

The formal definition of $O()$ goes like this. Suppose that $f(n)$ and $g(n)$ are two functions defined over the positive integers. Then function $f(n)$ is $O(g(n))$ if some threshold value n_0 and some constant value c can be found such that, for all values of n greater than n_0, the inequality $f(n) \leq c \cdot g(n)$ holds. That is, the notation $O(g(n))$ describes the set of all functions that, for large enough values of n, grow at a rate that is less than or equal to the rate at which $g(n)$ grows. Mathematically,

$$f(n) \in O(g(n)) \Leftrightarrow \exists n_0, c : \forall n > n_0, f(n) \leq c \cdot g(n) .$$

Normally the $g(n)$ function is taken to be a standard representative of a class of functions: n, or n^2, or n^3, and so on. For example, both $n^2/2$ and $n(n-4)/4$ are members of the set $O(n^2)$. Both are also members of the set $O(5n^2 - n + 3)$, but $O(n^2)$ is a more succinct description, and is preferred. According to the definition, the function $15n - 6$ is also a member of $O(n^2)$, but is most precisely described as being $O(n)$.

In advanced study you will need to manipulate functional relationships with greater precision than is permitted by $O()$ alone. However, $O()$ is the only functional comparator that is introduced in this book, and is abused slightly: if an algorithm is described here as being $O(g(n))$, it may be assumed that the time taken by the algorithm is, for large enough values of n, proportional to $g(n)$. Function $g(n)$ is also referred to as the *asymptotic cost* of the algorithm in question.

> The big-Oh notation allows the growth rate of functions to be compared in a way that is independent of their numeric values.

What does all this mean? Suppose that algorithm X requires $O(n^2)$ time, and algorithm Y requires $O(n \log n)$ time, where n describes the "size" of an instance of the problem addressed by X and Y. Suppose further that both X and Y can process problem instances of size $n = 10{,}000$ in one second. This is a reasonable assumption – $10{,}000^2$ is one hundred million, and computers execute around that many instructions per second.

Size of problem	Time taken by algorithm	
	X	Y
n	$O(n^2)$	$O(n \log n)$
10,000	1 second	1 second
100,000	1.7 minutes	13 seconds
1,000,000	2.7 hours	2.8 minutes
10,000,000	11.6 days	33 minutes
100,000,000	3.2 years	6.5 hours
1,000,000,000	3.2 centuries	3.1 days

Table 12.1: The effect of asymptotic growth rate on the cost of solving large problems. Algorithms X and Y are assumed to require the same time to solve a problem of size n = 1,000, but to have different asymptotic costs.

Table 12.1 shows what happens when the asymptotic cost of the two algorithms is used to estimate the time taken for larger values of n. By assumption, there is no difference between $O(n^2)$ and $O(n \log n)$ when $n = 10{,}000$; but there most certainly is a difference when n is large. As a concrete example, imagine trying to sort the list of ten million names to prepare the phone book for a large city such as New York. Using insertion sort, which is a quadratic-time algorithm, there is a good chance that it will take several days to do the sorting – assuming that the computer doesn't need rebooting during that time. On the other hand, an $O(n \log n)$-time sorting algorithm allows the same task to be carried out in just a few minutes. You don't know any sub-quadratic sorting algorithms yet, but they are only a few pages away now.

The choice of algorithm is critically important to the usefulness of a computing application.

This difference in performance is one of the things that makes computing so fascinating – a factor of 1,000 or more between one technology and another is impossible to imagine in other engineering disciplines. A Ferrari might be ten times faster than a tractor, but no cars (and very few planes!) are one hundred times faster than a tractor, let alone one thousand times faster. Yet in computing such differences in performance are commonplace.

The space required by an algorithm can also be assessed as a function of n, the problem size. Fortunately, a wide range of useful algorithms operate in $O(n)$ space. Hence, unless n is extremely large, memory limits are unlikely to be an impediment. Another observation worth making is that the space used cannot grow asymptotically faster than the time used, since it takes at least one unit of time merely to initialize each unit of space. This observation means that if the time taken by an algorithm is acceptable, the space requirement of it is also likely to be acceptable.

12.2 Dictionaries and searching

Exercise 10.16 on page 192 posed the problem of constructing a balanced binary search tree from a sorted list of data values. In the resultant tree, the middle item of the sorted list is always the one tested first, as it is at the root of the search tree. The search then recursively enters either the left subtree or the right subtree. These two subtrees correspond respectively to the first and second halves of the sorted list.

The same searching process can be carried out directly in a sorted array, without building the tree at all. When executed in an array this "either discard the left half or discard the right half" process is called *binary search*. Figure 12.1 shows a recursive function that implements binary search. At each recursive call, the two arguments `lo` and `hi` respectively specify the lowest location in the array `A` at which the `key` (of type `data_t`) can possibly appear, and the first location greater than `lo` at which it cannot appear. The mid-point between these bounds is calculated, and the data item at that location tested against the key, using a standard comparison function `cmp`.

If `lo>=hi` entering any call, the range of possible locations is empty, and the item cannot appear in the array at all. In this case the function returns immediately.

If the range is non-empty, and the key is smaller than the middle item in the array, the search recursively focuses on the left half of the current array section, from `lo` through to, but not including, `mid`. Conversely, if the key is larger than the middle item, the search recursively focuses on the right half of the current array section, from `mid+1` through to, but still not including, `hi`. If neither of these two conditions occurs, the key has been found. In this third case, pointer `locn` is used to record the array position at which the key was located, and the search returns the success flag.

How long does binary search take? Each recursive test eliminates almost exactly half of the objects. So searching a sorted array of n data objects takes just one comparison more than searching an array of $n/2$ objects, and the complete cost of

```
int
binary_search(data_t A[], int lo, int hi,
        data_t *key, int *locn) {
    int mid, outcome;
    /* if key is in A, it is between A[lo] and A[hi-1] */
    if (lo>=hi) {
        return BS_NOT_FOUND;
    }
    mid = (lo+hi)/2;
    if ((outcome = cmp(key, A+mid)) < 0) {
        return binary_search(A, lo, mid, key, locn);
    } else if (outcome > 0) {
        return binary_search(A, mid+1, hi, key, locn);
    } else {
        *locn = mid;
        return BS_FOUND;
    }
}
```

Figure 12.1: An implementation of the binary search algorithm. Function `cmp` returns a negative value if the first argument is less than the second; zero if they are equal; and positive if the first argument is greater than the second. To start the search on an array `stuff` containing `n` items, the initial call `binary_search(stuff,0,n,&key,&result)` is made. The values `BS_FOUND` and `BS_NOT_FOUND` are symbolic constants.

executing a search among n items is given by

$$C(n) = \begin{cases} 1\,, & \text{when } n = 1 \\ 1 + C(\lceil n/2 \rceil)\,, & \text{when } n > 1\,. \end{cases}$$

The solution to this recurrence is $C(n) = \lceil \log_2 n \rceil$, which means that the asymptotic cost of binary search is $O(\log n)$. Compare this to the $O(n)$ cost of a linear search, and it is clear why binary search is such an important technique.

> Binary search in a sorted list is an extremely fast process. When a search tree is balanced, or approximately balanced, the same excellent performance can be obtained.

Binary search trees, linked lists, and arrays all provide a way of supporting another abstract data type: the *dictionary*. In a dictionary, the required operations include insertion, deletion, and search, and there are several implementation options. Which structure is the most appropriate for a given application depends on the relative number of such operations required by the algorithm being supported. For example, if search operations are the most frequent, and only a small number of insertions or deletions are anticipated, then binary search in a sorted array is the most sensible option. Or, if search operations are rare, then a linked list might suffice, with linear search used when searching is required. If all three operations must be efficient, then a binary search tree may be a good compromise. It has the additional advantage that an in-order traversal allows the data objects to be visited in sorted order. Table 12.2 summarizes these considerations.

> Dictionary data structures support the operations of insertion, searching, and deletion. There are a range of implementation options, and the choice depends on the mix of operations to be performed.

12.3 Hashing

There are other data structures that also provide the three dictionary operations. The one considered in this section is *hashing*. It has the disadvantage of not allowing the

Data structure	Insert	Search
Unsorted array	$O(1)$	$O(n)$
Sorted array	$O(n)$	$O(1)$
Unsorted linked list	$O(1)$	$O(n)$
Sorted linked list	$O(n)$	$O(n)$
Binary search tree	$O(\log n)$ average case	$O(\log n)$ average case
	$O(n)$ worst case	$O(n)$ worst case
Hash table	$O(1)$ average case	$O(1)$ average case
	$O(n)$ worst case	$O(n)$ worst case

Table 12.2: Per-operation costs of different implementations of the dictionary data type.

objects to be processed in sorted order, but in many ways that is not a handicap, since they can always be sorted directly if the presentation order matters.

If the keys being used to access the stored items are known to be small integers, an array can be directly indexed using the key. For example, if the keys are staff ID numbers, and all are in the range 1,000 to 9,999, then an array of 10,000 `staff_t` pointers can be declared, and the ID number used to directly index the array. In this example, the first 1,000 pointers in the array would definitely never be used, and there would also be other pointers that were left `NULL`. Even so, the apparent waste might be worthwhile, as the resultant search structure allows searching in $O(1)$ time – that is, searching in time that is constant and independent of the number n of items stored in the dictionary. But what if the domain of key values is not so conveniently compact? What if staff ID numbers are eight digits long, or if character strings are being used as the keys?

The fundamental idea in hashing is to create a compact set of integers from *any* set of keys, and then use those integers to directly index a table of pointers. For example, suppose that staff ID numbers are eight-digit values in the range 10,000,000 to 99,999,999. If there are only 5,000 different staff at any given time, then declaring an array of 100 million pointers is enormously wasteful, and cannot be contemplated.

But an array of 10,000 pointers is not unreasonable. If the last four digits of the ID number – or any other four digit combination derived mathematically from it – were used to index such a table, there might only be a relatively small number of *collisions* occur, in which different objects seek to use the same slot in the table of pointers. So instead of an array of 10,000 pointers, each of which can only store a single record, an array of 10,000 linked lists is used. Each secondary list stores the set of objects that share the same four-digit extracted value; and each search operation performs a linear search in just one of the secondary lists. With 10,000 possible lists, and only 5,000 keys to be stored, the number of long lists should be relatively small, and hence most search operations should be fast.

> A hash function converts a value drawn from a large or indeterminate range into a seemingly random integer over a constrained range.

Taking the last four digits of each staff ID as the index is a simple and obvious transformation to reduce a large number into a more compact integer range, but has a serious drawback – it doesn't involve all of the digits of the original number, and should not be used in practice. For example, both 86,864,007 and 92,184,007 "hash" to the same location. If the staff ID values are genuinely random, this doesn't really matter. But real-life values are rarely random – for example, in a staff number like this, there might be a two-digit code to indicate year of commencement, then a three-digit code to indicate the cost center for salary payments, and then a three digit sequence number assigned starting at 000 for each cost center, each year. There will thus be far more ID codes ending with "x000" than with "x999", meaning that the randomness assumption is out the window, and with it the good "on average" behavior of the hash table.

Getting a good distribution of values from the hash function is critically important, even when the input values are correlated, or non-uniformly distributed. In particular, all components of the input value should affect the eventual constrained-range output value. So rather than extracting the last four digits, which is the same as taking the remainder mod 10,000, it is better to treat the staff ID number as if it were a character string, and seek a more general approach to hashing that applies to any string. A good hashing technique for strings can also be applied to numeric data.

> Hash functions should be constructed so that all parts of the key contribute to the calculated hash value.

Figures 12.2 and 12.3 show one way of constructing a hash function for character strings. In Figure 12.2, the function `hash_func_create` adopts the usual pattern of allocating space for a structure, and then returning a pointer to it. It takes just one argument, the size of the table that the calling program will be using. Note that this code constructs a hash function; not a hash table. It is assumed that the calling program manages the hash table.

Each time `hash_func_create` is called a different set of prime number `values` is generated in the array associated with the `hash_t` structure. The consequence of this arrangement is that even if two strings happen to collide in one hash function of a given size, in another hash function, even if of the same table size, they are no more likely collide than any other pair of randomly chosen strings. That is, these functions describe a *family* of hash functions, since more than one hash function can

```
#define NVALUES 20

typedef struct {
    unsigned nvalues;
    unsigned *values;
    unsigned tabsize;
} hashfunc_t;

hashfunc_t
*hash_func_create(unsigned tabsize) {
    int i;
    hashfunc_t *h;
    /* allocate the required memory space */
    h = malloc(sizeof(*h));
    assert(h != NULL);
    h->values = malloc(NVALUES*sizeof(*(h->values)));
    assert(h->values != NULL);
    h->nvalues = NVALUES;
    /* then create a sequence of prime numbers from it */
    for (i=0; i<NVALUES; i++) {
        /* assumes that srand() has already been called */
        h->values[i] = nextprime(tabsize + rand()%tabsize);
    }
    h->tabsize = tabsize;
    return h;
}
```

Figure 12.2: Initializing a hash function for use on character strings.

```
unsigned
hash_func_calculate(hashfunc_t *h, char *key) {
    unsigned i, k=0, hval=0;
    /* first, process every character in the string */
    for (i=0; key[i]!='\0'; i++) {
        hval += key[i] * h->values[k];
        k += 1;
        if (k==NVALUES) {
            k = 0;
        }
    }
    /* then reduce into the desired range */
    return hval % h->tabsize;
}
```

Figure 12.3: Calculating a hash value for a character string.

be employed in a program using these routines, with each incorporating a different hash mapping.

Figure 12.3 gives details of the hash computation recommended for character strings. So that the hash table can be any size (including round numbers such as 10,000 and 65,536), great care is taken to engage all characters equally and fully. Each ASCII value in the string is multiplied by one of the prime numbers established when the hash function was seeded, and is added to a running total. When all characters have been processed the final sum is reduced into the range zero through to `tabsize-1` using the "`%`" mod operator.

Integer overflow might occur during the various computations in the loop in function `hash_func_calculate`. The numeric type `unsigned` is used to avoid the difficulties that might be caused if this happens. Only positive values can be represented in an `unsigned` integers, and overflow still gives positive values. Furthermore, overflow drops only high order bits, which does not affect the randomness of the hash value, as the "information" about the characters in the string is smeared across all of the bits of `hval` through the use of prime multipliers that are roughly of the same magnitude as the table size.

Figure 12.4 validates of the approach shown in Figures 12.2 and 12.3. To create the graph, a dictionary file containing 235,884 distinct strings was hashed with different table sizes, with each string searched for before it was inserted. During the processing, the number of `strcmp` calls required was counted. As the table size is changed in the range from 10,000 buckets through to 100,000 buckets, the average number of string comparisons required to insert each new string decreases by a factor of 10 from 11.8 to 1.18, pretty much exactly as expected if the hash values are uniformly distributed.

The computation shown in Figure 12.3 is moderately costly – two array accesses and a multiplication, plus a few other operations, for each character in the string. As a contrast, consider the simpler hash function shown in Figure 12.5, which involves (slightly) fewer per-character operations. Unfortunately, now everything goes wrong, and the strings are not uniformly distributed across the buckets – so much so that

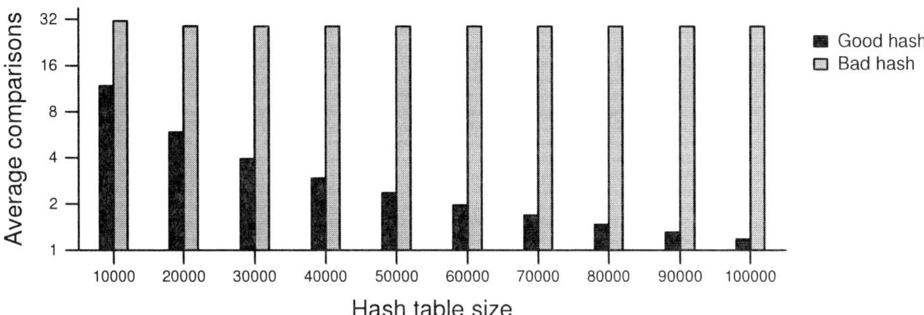

Figure 12.4: The average number of comparisons performed during each search-then-insert cycle as 235,884 distinct strings are added into a hash table using the mechanisms shown in Figures 12.2 and 12.3 (dark bars) and Figure 12.5 (light bars).

as the size of the table increases, the average cost of inserting each string remains stubbornly high, shown by the grey bars in Figure 12.4. With a little thought, it is easy to see what has happened – because ASCII values are all less than around 120, a typical word of eight characters or less generates a hash value of at most $120 \times 8 \times 8 \approx 8{,}000$, making the distribution hopelessly skewed towards the bottom end of the table. Using the bad function, with a table of 50,000 buckets, the biggest bucket is at location 3,812, and has 140 entries, every single one of them an eight character word: "accumber", "aluminic", and so on, through to "zirconic". On the other hand, the good hash function gives rise to a biggest bucket of just 18 words when 50,000 buckets are used. There is an important lesson to be learned from this.

> A hash function should always be checked on realistic data, to ensure it is distributing input values randomly, and to verify that the majority of buckets are getting used. Don't try to economize.

The easiest way to handle collisions in a hash table is to collect the colliding objects together into a either a linked list, or in a dynamic array managed using `realloc`. Doing so is called *separate chaining* in the computing literature. Separate chaining has the advantage of providing a graceful degradation in performance

```
/* BEWARE: Dangerous code. Don't do this! */
unsigned
hash_func_calculate(hashfunc_t *h, char *key) {
    unsigned i, hval=0;
    for (i=0; key[i]!='\0'; i++) {
        hval = hval + (i+1)*key[i];
    }
    return hval % h->tabsize;
}
```

Figure 12.5: A risky hash function.

as the number of objects gets larger. It also allows (as was the case in the example shown in Figure 12.4) the number of objects stored to exceed the allocated table size.

There are several other methods for collision handling that have also been studied, and you may see these described in other texts. But separate chaining is the first mechanism you should always consider using, and the shift to a different approach should only be undertaken if you are sure you have a reason to do it, you and fully understand the implementation and operational risks as well.

Hashing n objects into a table of size t allows searching in average time $O(1 + n/t)$ if the hash function is appropriate for the data. Provided t is maintained as a fixed fraction of n, the time is $O(1)$ per operation.

12.4 Quick sort

This section describes an elegant sorting mechanism known as quick sort, described in 1961 by the computer science pioneer C.A.R. Hoare. Hoare developed quick sort as a direct consequence of his exploration of Algol 60, one of the first programming languages to support recursive functions.

Quick sort uses a divide and conquer strategy to split an array into three sections, in a manner not dissimilar to the way a binary search tree is constructed. All of the objects in one section (the "left" partition) are less than some *pivot* object; all of the objects in the "right" partition are greater than the pivot value; and all objects equal to the pivot are retained together in the center. The central group are in their correct positions in the sorted array, and need not be moved any further. Recursion on the left partition and on the right partition is thus sufficient to sort the array.

Figure 12.6 shows one way of doing the partitioning process, and Figure 12.7 illustrates the arrangement part way through an execution of function `partition`. At first, all of the array items are in the "unknown" section, and there are no elements in the three sections delineated by the variables `fe`, standing for "first equal", and `fg`, standing for "first greater".

At each iteration, the counter `next` indicates the item that is to be considered and possibly moved. If `A[next]` is less than the pivot value, it is exchanged with the array element indicated by `fe`, and then both `fe` and `next` are incremented to re-establish the arrangement shown in Figure 12.7. The net effect is that the item at `A[next]` at the beginning of this iteration joins the "less than" group, and the "equal" group moves one slot to the right, but remains the same size.

If the item at `A[next]` is greater than the pivot, it is exchanged with the last of the "unknown" objects, and `fg` decremented to include that item in the "greater than" section. In this case `next` cannot be incremented. But the difference between `fg` and `next` decreases by one, and progress is again made towards the loop termination criterion.

Finally, if the object at `next` is equal to the pivot, then `next` is incremented, thereby increasing the size of the equal group by one. Eventually `next` and `fg` become equal, meaning there are no elements left in the "unknown" category, and that all elements are in their correct group, as required.

```
void
partition(data_t A[], int n, data_t *pivot,
        int *first_eq, int *first_gt) {
    int next=0, fe=0, fg=n, outcome;
    while (next<fg) {
        if ((outcome = cmp(A+next, pivot)) < 0) {
            swap_data(A+fe, A+next);
            fe += 1;
            next += 1;
        } else if (outcome > 0) {
            fg -= 1;
            swap_data(A+next, A+fg);
        } else {
            next += 1;
        }
    }
    assert(0<=fe && fe<fg && fg<=n);
    *first_eq = fe;
    *first_gt = fg;
    return;
}
```

Figure 12.6: Partitioning an array into three sections: less than the partition value; equal to the partition value; and greater than the partition value. Function `cmp` returns a negative value if the first argument is less than the second; zero if they are equal; and positive if the first argument is greater than the second.

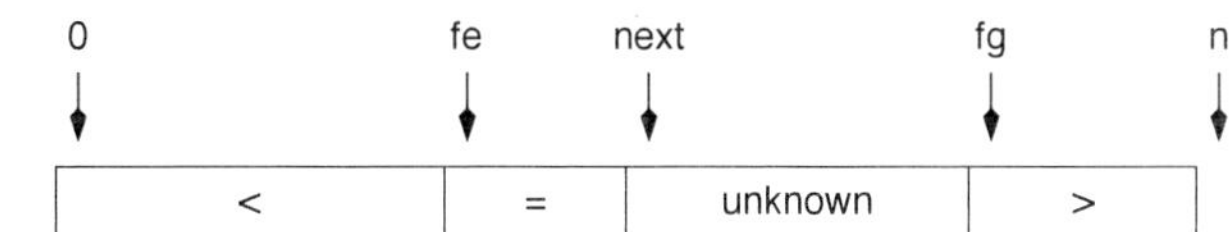

Figure 12.7: Partitioning an array into three sections.

The approach to partitioning shown in Figures 12.6 and 12.7 is sometimes called the *Dutch national flag* mechanism, after a problem considered by another influential computer scientist, E.W. Dijkstra. There are several other ways that partitioning can be implemented, explored in the exercises at the end of the chapter.

Figure 12.8 fills in more of the details of quick sort. Because function `quick_sort` is recursive, the first test checks for the base case. Arrays of length one or less are sorted, and the function makes an immediate `return`. To process an array that is longer, a pivot value is drawn from the array. The operation of function `choose_pivot` will be discussed shortly. That pivot value is then used to partition the array of items into the necessary three sections.

Figure 12.9 illustrates the steps that take place during a call to `quick_sort`. In Figure 12.9(a), the initial array is unsorted. The partitioning process results in the arrangement shown in Figure 12.9(b), with the variables `first_eq` (represented by `fe` in the figure) and `first_gt` (represented by `fg` in the figure) marking the boundaries of the three sections. Figure 12.9(c) shows the two array sections that

```
void
quick_sort(data_t A[], int n) {
    data_t pivot;
    int first_eq, first_gt;
    if (n<=1) {
        return;
    }
    /* array section is non-trivial */
    pivot = choose_pivot(A, n);
    partition(A, n, &pivot, &first_eq, &first_gt);
    quick_sort(A, first_eq);
    quick_sort(A+first_gt, n-first_gt);
}
```

Figure 12.8: The recursive part of the quick sort process.

are the inputs to the two recursive calls to `quick_sort`, from zero through to, but not including, `fe`; and from `fg` (which has pointer address `A+fg`) through to, but not including, `n`. The latter is a section containing `n-fg` items. Figure 12.9(d) shows the arrangement at the completion of the two recursive calls. Without any further action being required, the arrangement shown in Figure 12.9(e) has thus been computed, in which the whole of the original array is now sorted. Perhaps now you can understand why Hoare felt empowered to invent quick sort when a recursive language became available to him.

Quick sort splits the input array into three sections by partitioning the elements relative to a pivot value; and then recursively sorts two of the partitions.

There is one small detail that has not yet been described, but is of vital importance: how to choose the pivot element. What is also critical is that you know how *not* to choose the pivot value. To understand why there are good and bad choices, it is helpful to first look at the execution cost of quick sort. As for insertion sort, it is appropriate to count the number of element-to-element comparisons that are required.

When an array section of n items is being sorted, there are n comparisons required by the partitioning process, and then two recursive calls. Suppose that all of the items in the array are distinct, and the "equal" group contains just one item. The best that can happen is that the other two groups share the remaining items evenly, and that each of the two recursive calls is required to sort $(n-1)/2 \approx n/2$ items. If equal partitions are achieved, the total number of comparisons is given by

$$C(n) = \begin{cases} 0\,, & \text{when } n \le 1 \\ n + 2 \cdot C(n/2)\,, & \text{when } n > 1\,. \end{cases}$$

The solution to this recurrence is $C(n) = n \log_2 n$, which is $O(n \log n)$. But the assumption that the partitions are balanced is very brave.

Suppose instead that by bad luck the pivot item is always such that one item ends up in the "equal" section, none in the "less than" section, and $n-1$ items in the

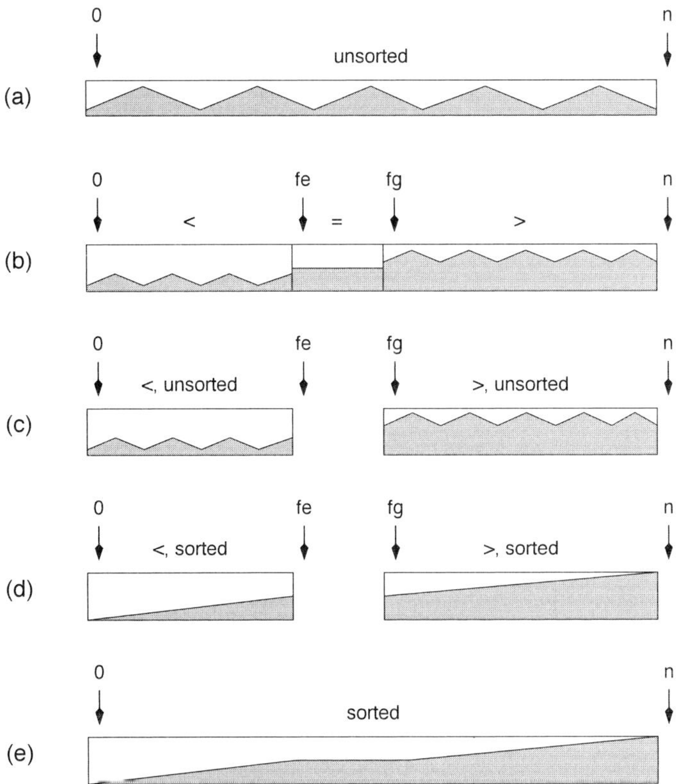

Figure 12.9: Tracing the behavior of the quick sort algorithm: (a) the initial unsorted array; (b) after the partitioning process splits it into three parts; (c) the array sections passed to the two recursive calls; (d) the sorted array sections returned from those calls; and (e) the original array is now sorted.

"greater than" section. Now the number of comparisons is given by

$$C(n) = \begin{cases} 0\,, & \text{when } n \le 1 \\ n + C(n-1)\,, & \text{when } n > 1\,, \end{cases}$$

which has the closed form $C(n) = n(n+1)/2 - 1$, and is quadratic. When things go wrong, they go very wrong indeed.

On *average*, if it can be assumed that the pivot element is equally likely to end up in any position in the array, the cost is given by the rather complex expression

$$C(n) = \begin{cases} 0\,, & \text{when } n \le 1 \\ n + (1/n) \cdot \sum_{k=0}^{n-1}(C(k) + C(n-k-1))\,, & \text{when } n > 1\,. \end{cases}$$

This is equivalent to assuming that the "less than" group is equally likely to contain any number of items between 0 and $n - 1$. Using techniques not discussed here, this third recurrence can be shown to have the closed form $C(n) \approx 1.4n \log_2 n$.

If the partitions in quick sort are equally likely to be of any size, then the average execution time is $O(n \log n)$.

Now, back to the question of choosing a pivot element. It would be nice to choose the median element in the array as the pivot, to guarantee that the two recursive calls are balanced; but finding the median of a set of numbers is quite a complex task. Instead, we can at least ensure that each of the two recursive calls are on array sections that are equally likely to be of any size, by randomly choosing the pivot:

```
data_t
choose_pivot(data_t A[], int n) {
    return A[rand()%n];
}
```

If this function is used we can be confident that on *any* input array, even ones that are already sorted or reverse sorted, the expected execution time required by quick sort is $O(n \log n)$. Using `rand` ensures that the randomness required for the "average" analysis above is automatically generated by the program, and is not required to be in the input data. In contrast, in a binary search tree the average cost of searching is $O(\log n)$ (indeed, it is pretty much the same analysis), but the input data must be truly random for that analysis to hold.

There are two kinds of average case analysis: ones where the randomness is assumed to be present in the input data; and ones where the necessary randomness is supplied by the program itself.

If the cost of evaluating the random number generator is deemed to be too high, then another possibility is to make use of this alternative:

```
    return A[n/2];
```

Now a particular location is always used as the pivot, but because it is drawn from the middle of the array, it is actually rather hard to construct pathological sequences that force quick sort to its worst-case behavior, and on sorted and reverse-sorted lists, the number of comparisons is $O(n \log n)$. A variant of this method is to take the median of the three values `A[0]`, `A[n/2]`, and `A[n-1]`, which ensures that the "less than" and "greater than" sections are also likely to be non-empty. The median of three pivot selection strategy is rather more complex to implement than the two methods suggested here, because if full use is to be made of the initial median-finding calculations, the three selected elements must be placed into their correct places in the array before function `partition` is called.

What you must *never* do is take the easy route offered by this pivot selection mechanism:

```
    return A[0];
```

Table 12.3 shows why. To construct the table, four different types of arrays were sorted using three different pivot selection mechanisms, and a static counter incremented each time the `cmp` comparison function was called. In each experiment, the total number of comparisons required to sort the array was divided by the corresponding value of n, so that the growth in the number of comparisons per item could be identified. For a good sorting algorithm, the per-item comparison count should grow

Array size	Initial array data			
Pivot selection	ascending	descending	uniform	random
$n = 1{,}000$				
`A[rand()%n]`	11.5	11.9	1.0	11.6
`A[n/2]`	9.5	9.3	1.0	11.9
`A[0]`	36.2	500.5	1.0	11.9
$n = 10{,}000$				
`A[rand()%n]`	16.2	16.1	1.0	16.5
`A[n/2]`	13.0	12.9	1.0	16.4
`A[0]`	106.4	5000.5	1.0	16.3
$n = 100{,}000$				
`A[rand()%n]`	20.9	20.8	1.0	20.8
`A[n/2]`	16.6	16.5	1.0	20.7
`A[0]`	318.8	—	1.0	21.1

Table 12.3: Comparisons per item required to sort $n = 1{,}000$, $n = 10{,}000$, and $n = 100{,}000$ items using three different pivot selection strategies, and four different types of input array. The `A[0]` pivot selection method gives rise to quadratic behavior on descending lists, and was not tested for $n = 100{,}000$.

slowly in proportion to the logarithm of the array size. If the ratio grows in proportion to n, the cost is quadratic.

The table shows that all of the three pivot selection methods yield $O(n \log n)$ behavior when the input data is random. As expected, the randomized pivot selection method also gives this same level of performance on sorted and reverse sorted lists; and the `A[n/2]` method appears to perform well too on the special cases. But look how bad the `A[0]` method is when the array is already sorted. From the evidence in the table, it appears that the reverse sorted sequence requires $O(n^2)$ time to sort, and the sorted sequence perhaps as much as $O(n^{1.5})$ time. That is, two input arrangements that might be considered to be relatively likely are both handled very poorly – behavior that cannot be tolerated.

Having an algorithm deliver its worst behavior on likely inputs is extremely risky.

Finally, note the excellent behavior of all three alternatives when the elements in the array are all the same. Equal elements is also a situation that must be regarded as a likely input to quick sort, since whenever there are duplicate items in the initial array, the bottom levels of the recursion deal with many small array segments containing those uniform values. Unfortunately, as recently as 1990 there were C systems in which the `qsort` provided as part of the `stdlib` library degenerated to quadratic behavior when the array consisted of identical elements. The good performance of the implementation described in Figures 12.6 and 12.8 is a consequence of the three-way partitioning process. You will also find textbooks that use a two-way split, into "less than or equal to" and "greater than or equal to" sections. These run a real risk of behaving poorly when duplicate items are present, and should be treated with scepticism until evidence to the contrary is accumulated. Always remember that, despite the fundamental idea of quick sort being simple and elegant, there are several subtleties in its implementation that can trap the unwary.

Sorting algorithms should be stress-tested on a range of inputs, and their asymptotic cost verified through experimental analysis.

12.5 Merge sort

A question that you might by now be asking yourself is this: if it is impossible to completely eliminate the pathological input sequences that drive quick sort to $O(n^2)$ behavior, is there another sorting algorithm that never takes more than $O(n \log n)$ comparisons? Is there a mechanism that is $O(n \log n)$ time in the *worst* case? The answer to that question is an emphatic "yes", and the next excitement in this chapter is *merge sort*. Merge sort requires more temporary space to execute than does quick sort, but makes up for that deficiency by operating in $O(n \log n)$ time in the worst case, and also requiring fewer comparisons on average.

Merge sort has a strong resemblance to quick sort. There are two recursive calls, to sort two sublists. In quick sort those two sublists are created by partitioning the original array section. In merge sort they are created by simply breaking the initial array section into two equal halves.

In quick sort, when the two parts are sorted, the whole is sorted. In merge sort, after the two halves have been sorted, they must be *merged* to create a sorted whole. So one way of categorizing these two methods is to say that quick sort is "hard split, easy join", whereas merge sort is "easy split, hard join".

Figure 12.10 gives details of two functions, `merge`, and `merge_sort`. A private recursive function is also specified – it is called from `merge_sort` after a temporary array `T` has been created. Rather than call `malloc` in every merging step to get the necessary workspace, `T` is created once, used in all of the merging steps, and released.

To merge, the first of the two regions is copied into the temporary array `T`. Elements are peeled off the front of array `T` and the front of the second segment in array `A` in sorted order, filling up `A` again, starting at `A[0]`. Once either of the segments is exhausted, the remaining items (if any) from `T` are copied into the last vacant locations in `A`. If `T` is exhausted first, the remaining items in the second segment in `A` are already in their correct locations, and no further action is required. Figure 12.11 shows the arrangement of items at two different stages of the merge.

Given that merge sort requires that $O(n)$ extra memory be allocated, why is it of interest? Consider the number of comparisons required. The call to `merge` that completes each recursive call never requires more that $n-1$ comparisons when two $n/2$-item lists are being merged. That means that the number of comparisons to sort n items is never greater than

$$C(n) = \begin{cases} 0\,, & \text{when } n \le 1 \\ n - 1 + 2 \cdot C(n/2)\,, & \text{when } n > 1\,. \end{cases}$$

```
static void
merge(data_t A[], int mid, int n, data_t T[]) {
    /* merge array sections A[0..mid-1] and A[mid..n-1] */
    int i, s1, s2;
    /* copy first section into temporary array T */
    for (i=0; i<mid; i++) {
        copy_data(T+i, A+i);
    }
    i = 0;
    s1 = 0; s2 = mid;
    /* merge second section at A[mid] with T, putting output
        back into section starting at A[0] */
    while (s1<mid && s2<n) {
        if (cmp(T+s1,A+s2) < 0) {
            /* element from T goes next */
            copy_data(A+i, T+s1);
            s1 += 1;
        } else {
            /* element from A goes next */
            copy_data(A+i, A+s2);
            s2 += 1;
        }
        i += 1;
    }
    while (s1<mid) {
        /* copy over any remaining elements in T */
        copy_data(A+i, T+s1);
        s1 += 1;
        i += 1;
    }
    /* all elements are now in their final positions */
}

static void
recursive_merge_sort(data_t A[], int n, data_t T[]) {
    int mid;
    if (n<=1) {
        return;
    }
    mid = n/2;
    recursive_merge_sort(A, mid, T);
    recursive_merge_sort(A+mid, n-mid, T);
    merge(A, mid, n, T);
}

void
merge_sort(data_t A[], int n) {
    data_t *T;
    T = malloc((n/2)*sizeof(*T));
    assert(T != NULL);
    recursive_merge_sort(A, n, T);
    free(T);
}
```

Figure 12.10: Merge sort.

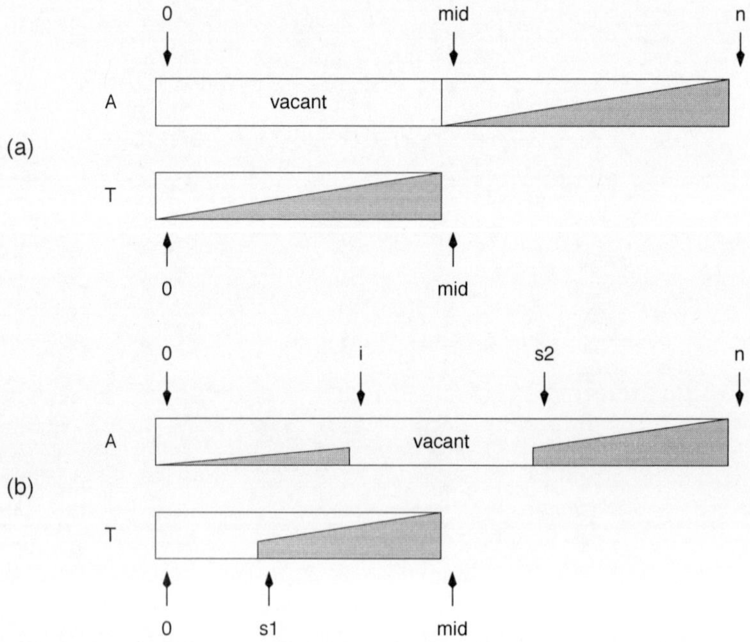

Figure 12.11: The merging process: (a) after the first sorted section of `A` has been copied into the temporary array `T`; and (b) part way through the merge of `T` and the second section of `A`.

which has the solution $C(n) = n \log n - n + 1$. That is, merge sort requires around 70% of the number of element-to-element comparisons required by quick sort. Indeed, in terms of comparisons, merge sort is so good that it is very hard to beat it – it is close to being *optimal*. When comparisons are expensive – for example, if the keys involved are long character strings, or complex combinations of fields drawn from a large structure – merge sort comes into its own.

> Merge sort requires $n \log_2 n$ comparisons in the worst case, but has the drawback of requiring $O(n)$ temporary memory while it executes.

12.6 Heap sort

Comparing quick sort and merge sort, it seems there is still a compromise required – quick sort has the advantage of being an *in situ* mechanism, but cannot guarantee execution time; whereas merge sort guarantees the worst case execution time, but requires extra temporary space. So the next question has to be: is there an in-situ sorting algorithm that requires $O(n \log n)$ time in the worst case? Of course, the answer is again "yes". So brace yourself, here it comes.

Figure 12.12 gives a C function for the *heap sort* algorithm, first described by J.W.J. Williams in 1964. Heap sort uses an abstract data type called a *priority queue*. The operations required in a priority queue are *insert*, to add a new data item; *get_maximum*, to return the data item with the largest key value; and *delete_maximum*, which removes that same data item from the structure. Given these three operations, it is easy to see how a sorting algorithm can be devised: all of the items are inserted into an initially empty queue, and then a sequence of *get_maximum* and *delete_maximum* operations are performed to empty the queue one item at a time.

A priority queue allows items to be extracted in key order.

One obvious way of constructing a priority queue is to use a linked list, with items reverse-ordered according to their key. Each *insert* operation requires $O(n)$ time, performing a linear search to find the correct position in the decreasing order; and thereafter the maximum is always available at the head of the list. The total cost of sorting (see Exercise 10.5 on page 190) is $O(n^2)$.

An unsorted array can also be used as a priority queue structure (Exercise 7.6 on page 127). Now insertion is cheap, but *get_maximum* and *delete_maximum* operations are expensive, and the overall cost of sorting is again $O(n^2)$. A third option is to use a binary search tree as a priority queue, since an in-order traversal accomplishes the same end result as a sequence of *get_maximum* operations (Exercise 10.15 on page 191). But a search tree implementation can also require as much as $O(n^2)$ time – and worse, that quadratic behavior arises exactly when it seems most unnecessary, on a sorted input list. Nor does use of a BST meet the current goal of performing the sort in-situ – it requires significant extra space, more so even than merge sort.

An ingenious structure called a *heap* provides a compromise between these various extremes, and allows the three priority queue operations to be carried out in $O(\log n)$ time each when there are n objects in the queue. A heap is an implicit binary tree, laid out in an array without any actual pointer variables being required. The root of the tree is in location zero in the array. Thereafter, if `A[i]` is an item in the tree, its two children are stored at locations `A[2*i+1]` and `A[2*i+2]`. So the children of the root are in `A[1]` and `A[2]`; their four children are in `A[3]`, `A[4]`, `A[5]`, and `A[6]`; and so on. Conversely, the parent of `A[i]` is in `A[(i-1)/2]`.

Within the tree, there is a partial ordering requirement that restricts the relationship between a node and its children: for an array to be a heap, each item must be not smaller in value than either of its two children, if they exist. That is, `A[0]` can be no smaller than either of `A[1]` and `A[2]`; the object in `A[1]` can be no smaller than either of `A[3]` and `A[4]`; the item `A[2]` can be no smaller than either of `A[5]` and `A[6]`; and so on, down every path in the tree until the leaves are reached.

In an array that is heap-ordered, the maximum item is at the root, in location `A[0]`. It can thus be extracted, and swapped with the object in the last position in the array, `A[n-1]`. If the number of active items in the heap is decreased by one, and the heap property restored by sifting the displaced item down the tree, a variant of the selection sort process can be supported.

Function `heap_sort` in Figure 12.12 gives details of the heap sort process. Once a heap has been built by function `build_heap`, the root item is repeatedly swapped with the last active item in the heap, and the heap property restored. At each cycle, the number of active items decreases by one, until in the end all items are in their correct sorted position in the array. Figure 12.13 shows the arrangement in the array at some intermediate point in the process. The items to the left of `active` are partially

```
void
sift_down(data_t A[], int parent, int n) {
    int child;
    if ((child = 2*parent+1) < n) {
        /* there is at least one child to be checked */
        if (child+1<n && cmp(A+child, A+child+1)<0) {
            /* the right child exists, and is larger */
            child += 1;
        }
        if (cmp(A+parent, A+child)<0) {
            /* parent is smaller than larger child */
            swap_data(A+parent, A+child);
            sift_down(A, child, n);
        }
    }
}

void
build_heap(data_t A[], int n) {
    int i;
    for (i=n/2-1; i>=0; i--) {
        sift_down(A, i, n);
    }
}

void
heap_sort(data_t A[], int n) {
    int active;
    build_heap(A, n);
    for (active=n-1; active>0; active--) {
        swap_data(A+0, A+active);
        sift_down(A, 0, active);
    }
}
```

Figure 12.12: Heap sort.

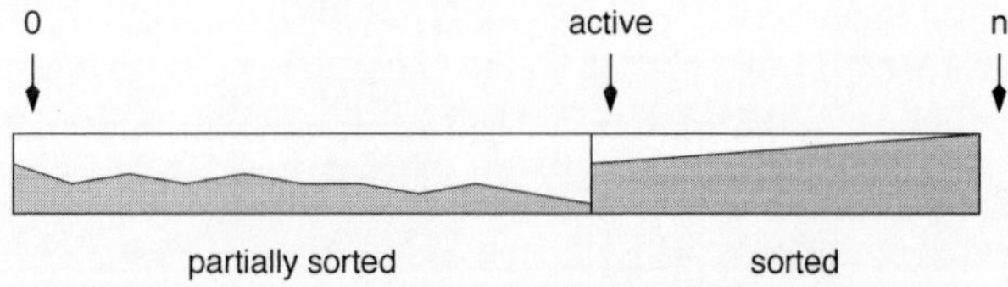

Figure 12.13: The two sections in the array while it is being sorted by heap sort.

ordered according to the heap property, with the largest at the root. The objects to the right of `active` are all greater than any of the objects to the left, and are fully sorted.

Most of the work is carried out in the recursive function `sift_down`. It checks whether the heap property is valid at the node `parent`, by first of all checking whether or not `parent` has any children at all; then whether it has a second child; then (if it does), whether the second child is larger than the first child; and then fi-

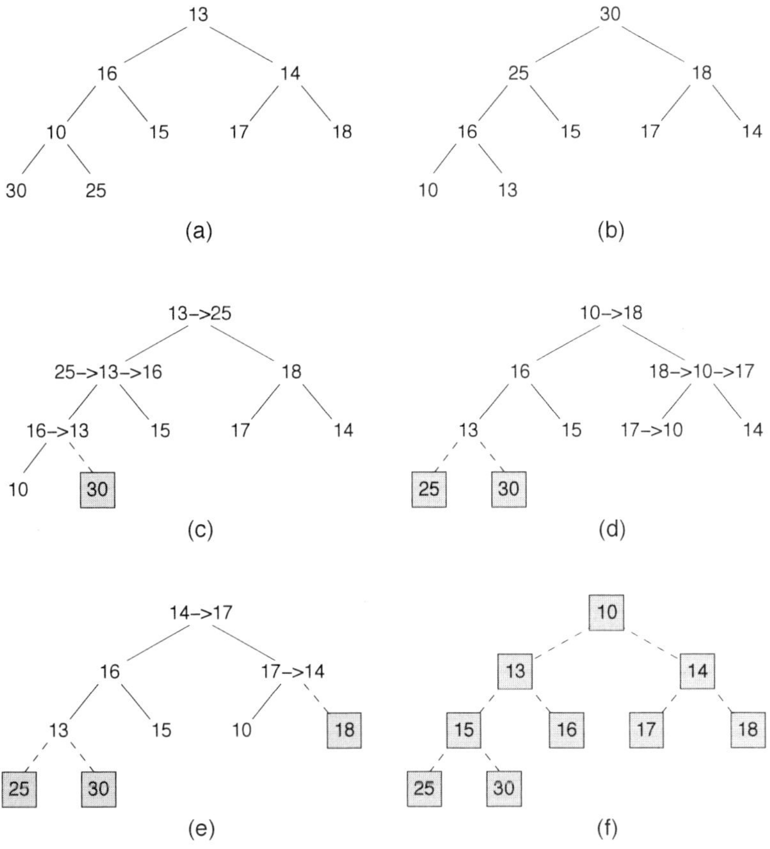

Figure 12.14: Example of heap sort applied to the array $\{13, 16, 14, 10, 15, 17, 18, 30, 25\}$: (a) the initial values in the array, drawn to show the implicit tree structure; (b) the same values after being formed into a heap by function `build_heap`; (c) after the largest item 30 has been swapped out of the root position, and the `sift_down` process applied to the value 13 that replaced it at the root; (d) after the second largest item 25 has been swapped out of the root position, and the `sift_down` process applied to the value 10 that replaced it at the root; (e) after the third largest item 18 has been swapped out of the root position, and the `sift_down` process applied to the value 14 that replaced it at the root; and (e) after all items have been swapped out of the root position, and the number of active items has been reduced to zero.

nally, whether `A[parent]` is greater than the larger of the valid children. If it is not, a swap is performed, and the function is recursively called on `child` to check the heap property in the subtree corresponding to the larger of the two children.

The implicit tree in the array `A` has at most $\log_2 n$ levels, since it is balanced. Each call to `sift_down(A,0,active)` thus costs at most $O(\log n)$ time, since two comparisons and a constant amount of time are required per recursive call, and each recursive call operates one level deeper in the tree. That is, the loop in function `heap_sort` requires at most $O(n \log n)$ time and at most $2n \log_2 n$ comparisons.

The only detail not yet specified is the process of building the initial heap out of the unsorted input array `A`. It could be constructed by repeated application of a `sift_up` function that implements an *insert* by checking a new leaf object against its parent, and so on up the tree to the root if necessary. Use of a `sift_up` function would allow each insertion to be carried out in $O(\log n)$ time, and a heap of n items to be built in $O(n \log n)$ time.

Function `build_heap` in Figure 12.12 shows a more efficient way of building a heap when an initial set of n items is given all at once. Starting with the parents of the leaves, the heap property is established in every subtree throughout the tree. Once the heap property has also been enforced at the root, the tree is a heap. The cost of this process is at most $2n$ comparisons and $O(n)$ time. Overall, heap sort operates in $O(n \log n)$ time in the worst case.

> Construction of a heap of n objects requires $O(n)$ time. Once a heap has been constructed, *get_maximum* operations require $O(1)$ time, and *delete_maximum* operations require $O(\log n)$ time.

Figure 12.14 shows some of the intermediate trees formed when the input array $\{13, 16, 14, 10, 15, 17, 18, 30, 25\}$ is sorted using heap sort. Items in grey squares are no longer active – they are still stored in the array, but are outside the active set. The notation `25->13->16` indicates that `25` was in that location at the beginning of the iteration, but was replaced by `13` as a result of a swap with its parent, and was subsequently replaced by `16` as a result of a swap with its larger child. As each item is swapped out of the root position, the small item that replaces it moves back down the tree, and the next largest item in the structure ends up replacing it at the root.

One final comment about heap sort is necessary: the implementation in Figure 12.12 uses a recursive `sift_down` function, which suggests that $O(\log n)$ additional space is required. But if the recursive function is replaced by a loop within function `sift_down`, only scalar variables are required. That is, heap sort can be implemented to sort n items in $O(1)$ additional space. In contrast to this result, quick sort always requires $O(\log n)$ of stack space – either on the stack, if it is implemented recursively as was shown in Figure 12.8, or in a declared array storing pending subproblems, if the recursion is replaced by iteration (Exercise 12.12 on page 227).

> Heap sort requires $O(n \log n)$ time in the worst case. It uses a negligible amount of additional memory.

Table 12.4 lists the number of comparisons per item required by heap sort and merge sort, using the same test framework as for Table 12.3 on page 217. Now the number of comparisons per item grows slowly as the size of the input array grows, for all of the four types in input list. As expected, heap sort requires about twice as many comparisons as merge sort.

The three sorting algorithms introduced in this chapter are appropriate in different situations. Quick sort is the preferred sorting method when good behavior on average is sufficient, and a modest amount of temporary storage may be used. It executes quickly, and should be the first method considered for general-purpose applications.

If worst-case guaranteed performance is required, because the application is a safety-critical one, then one of the other two methods needs to be used. When additional memory can be assumed, merge sort is the next option. It has extremely good

Array size / Algorithm	Initial array data			
	ascending	descending	uniform	random
$n = 1{,}000$				
Heap sort	17.6	16.0	3.0	16.9
Merge sort	4.9	5.0	5.0	8.7
$n = 10{,}000$				
Heap sort	24.4	22.7	3.0	23.5
Merge sort	6.5	6.9	6.9	12.0
$n = 100{,}000$				
Heap sort	31.1	29.3	3.0	30.2
Merge sort	8.2	8.5	8.5	15.4

Table 12.4: Comparisons per item required to sort $n = 1{,}000$, $n = 10{,}000$, and $n = 100{,}000$ items using heap sort and merge sort, and four different types of input array.

performance in terms of comparisons, but requires linear extra space. Even so, if comparisons are relatively expensive, then the extra space may well be warranted. As a third choice, heap sort is also available. It operates in situ, and takes $O(n \log n)$ worst case time, but experimentally tends to be a little slower than both quick sort and heap sort. But all of three methods execute quickly, and on a Macbook Pro all three can sort $n = 1{,}000{,}000$ integers in less than 0.25 seconds of CPU time. Computers really are fast!

Algorithm choice is dominated by the asymptotic execution cost. When algorithms have the same asymptotic cost, other practical factors affect the selection.

12.7 Other problems and algorithms

This chapter has barely scratched the surface of the topic of algorithm design and analysis. It is intended only as an introduction, to whet your appetite for the kinds of mechanism that you will study if you take further subjects in computer science or software engineering. There are a large number of other problems that we can solve by computer. For example, given a road network, and the travel times between each pair of towns that are connected by a direct road, what is the fastest way of getting from point A to point B? Or, given a set of student subject enrollments, what is the minimum number of sittings into which examinations must be assigned so that no student is scheduled to sit two different examinations in the same sitting? Or, given a set of symbols and the probabilities of occurrence, how should each symbol be assigned a code of “0” and “1” bits so that the message can always be decoded, but the expected cost of sending a message is minimized?

Some of the exercises challenge you to find algorithms, but all of them are related to the methods presented in this chapter. If you want to learn further algorithmic techniques beyond those described here, you are going to need to enroll in more computing subjects.

Exercises

12.1 Which of these functions can be described as $O(n \log n)$?

a. $3n + 5$.

b. $3n \log_{10} n + 6n + 1{,}000$.

c. $0.001n^{1.5}$.

d. $5n + n(\log_2 n)^2$.

e. $100n^2$.

f. $1.00001^{0.0001n}$.

Which of them are $O(n)$? And which of then are $O(n^2)$? Can they be ordered from slowest-growing to fastest-growing?

12.2 Trace the action of binary search in the following list of values when the keys 3, 6, 21, and 23 are searched for: $\{4, 5, 7, 10, 13, 15, 16, 18, 19, 21\}$.

12.3 Read the manual page for the `stdlib` function `bsearch`.

Then using Figure 12.1 on page 206 as a basis for your development, write a polymorphic binary search function. Array `A` will need to be passed as a type-anonymous byte address. You might also wish to alter the order of the arguments and the return type so as to match the specification of `bsearch`.

Write a calling program that tests your function by searching in a sorted array of character strings.

12.4 Consider the process of binary searching a large set of strings, for example the words in a dictionary. When both `lo` and `hi` indicate strings that start with the same character, it is pointless to continue including that first character in any subsequent string comparisons.

Implement a strings-only version of binary search that includes an additional argument that notes, at each recursive call, how many leading characters are known to be identical at `A[lo]` and `A[hi]`, and offsets the arguments to `strlen` by the amount of the match to avoid re-testing known characters.

Locate the system dictionary on your computer (possibly located in `/usr/share/dict/words` if you are using a Unix system) and test your program by searching for words in it.

12.5 Trace the action of quick sort on the list $\{28, 24, 34, 18, 22, 27, 21\}$. Use the `A[n/2]` pivot selection strategy.

12.6 When the items in the array are largely different, the partitioning process described in Figure 12.6 on page 213 performs a swap for nearly every item examined. If the ordering of the three groups in the array is altered to "less than", "greater than", "unknown", and then "equal", the number of item swaps can be reduced.

At the end of the partitioning process the "equal" group must be swapped into the middle, but if there are only a few "equal" elements, the additional cost is small.

Implement this alternative partitioning strategy. Then instrument `swap_data` and quantify the savings you have achieved.

12.7 Another partitioning strategy goes like this: start one pointer at the left, and move it right until an item is found that is not "less than or equal to" the pivot. Then move a similar pointer in from the right, until it too encounters a data item that does not belong in a "greater than or equal to" group. Exchange these two objects, and then continue scanning from the left again. When the two pointers cross, recursively sort the two array sections that they represent.

Implement and test this mechanism using the test harness assumed in Table 12.3 on page 217. Is your implementation robust?

12.8 Devise an algorithm for finding the median (middle value when they are sorted) of a set of numbers. Your algorithms should require $O(n)$ time on average, which means that you can't just sort the list and then pick out the middle value.

Hint: think of quick sort-style partitioning, and the resulting partitioned array. If the sizes of the partitions are known, where is the median?

12.9 Read the manual page for `qsort`. Implement a polymorphic quick sort that meets that specification. You will need to write a generic swap routine that exchanges two data items using a byte-by-byte swap.

Test your quick sort against the `stdlib` quick sort on the types of arrays considered in Table 12.3 on page 217. Which is the better implementation?

12.10 (*For a challenge*) Suppose that a set of strings is being sorted. Exercise 12.4 above suggests a way of handling character strings that avoids redundant tests on leading characters that are known to be irrelevant to the outcome.

Design a similar improvement to quick sort that partitions based upon a single character in each string. Hint: there will be *three* recursive calls.

12.11 Verify that the solution to the recurrence $C(1) = 0$, $C(2n) = n + 2C(n)$ is given by $C(n) = n \log_2 n$ when n is a power of two. Hint: use induction.

12.12 (*For a challenge*) Implement a non-recursive version of quick sort. Pay particular attention to the space requirements, as you will need to manipulate an explicit stack of pending array sections waiting to be dealt with.

Can you arrange your function so that the space required is guaranteed to be $O(\log n)$ when n items are being sorted?

12.13 Trace the action of merge sort on the list $\{28, 24, 34, 18, 22, 27, 21\}$.

12.14 Suppose that it is highly likely that the input to a sorting function will consist of a relatively small number k of ascending runs of objects. For example, the sequence $\{17, 19, 20, 34, 54, 18, 33, 35, 22, 28\}$ contains just three runs.

Design an algorithm based on merge sort that operates in $O(n + n \log k)$ time in the worst case when there are k ascending runs.

Hint: the value of k, and the starting points of the runs, can be located in $O(n)$ time. Then what?

12.15 The memory space required by the temporary array `T` in merge sort can be traded against the number of comparisons required in the worst case, without compromising merge sort's asymptotic $O(n \log n)$ performance. For example, if `mid` is selected as being `1+n/3`, then the two recursive calls are somewhat unbalanced, but the memory required by `T` is smaller.

Execute a modified merge sort program, and collect data showing the extent of the tradeoff. Draw a graph showing the relationship between additional memory space for `T` and the constant coefficient of $n \log n$ governing the cost of sorting random data.

12.16 Merge sort requires fewer comparisons than does heap sort or quick sort. Another important component in the actual running time of a sorting algorithm is the number of data movements, or item swaps.

Instrument the three sorting functions by adding a counter to the function `copy_data` (count three copies for a swap, and one for an assignment) and record the number of data movements per item when sorting lists of various sizes.

Which algorithm performs the fewest data movements? And if you implement the suggestion made in Exercise 12.6?

12.17 Trace the action of heap sort on the list $\{28, 24, 34, 18, 22, 27, 21\}$.

12.18 Design an algorithm for finding the kth largest of an unsorted set of n numbers that is efficient when k is small relative to n.

Give an analysis of your algorithm.

Chapter 13

Everything Else

This closing chapter is a bit of a collection of things that should at least be mentioned in a book about C, but didn't fit into any of the earlier chapters. Section 13.1 starts by briefly summarizing a number of C programming constructs that have not been used in any of the example programs.

Section 13.2 then considers the way in which numbers are stored and manipulated inside the computer. While this is not strictly a part of your C education, if you are going to have any kind of non-trivial dealings with computers, you need to know about storage representations. Section 13.2 also includes a final precedence table that includes all of the C operators.

Finally, to close both the chapter and the book, Section 13.3 introduces the C preprocessor, a useful facility that adds considerable flexibility to your program, including options for conditional compilation. A number of other C tools are also briefly summarized. For information on how to use them, you will need to explore the documentation that describes the software available on your computer system.

13.1 Some more C operations

There have been several C programming facilities discussed in this book that you have been warned about on the way through – as if they have "use at your own risk" cautions attached to them. These included the `switch` statement, the `do` statement, the `gets` function, `strcpy` and `strcat`, static variables in recursive functions, and global variables, to name just a few. There are a few more C programming facilities that are sufficiently risky that prudent programmers should avoid them. There are also several C facilities that simply haven't come up in the applications that have been used to drive the discussion. Table 13.1 lists a range of other C operators and options, and a brief summary of each. Table 13.2 similarly lists a range of additional C library functions.

To understand these options, you need to investigate them via the manual pages, and small exploratory programs – like many things in connection with computers, in the end you should just try them out for yourself in order to master their use.

> The only sure way of firmly grasping the details of some function or programming construct is to try it out in some scaffolding.

<table>
<tr><th>Operator</th><th>Purpose</th></tr>
<tr><td>unsigned, short, long, long long</td><td>Further integer types. See Section 13.2.</td></tr>
<tr><td>auto, extern, register, volatile</td><td>Additional storage classes like static and const.</td></tr>
<tr><td>continue</td><td>Used inside a loop, in the same way that break is. Terminates the current loop iteration, but not the loop itself. Use with caution.</td></tr>
<tr><td>union</td><td>A bit like a struct, except that the various options share the same section of memory. The data equivalent of an if statement. Use with extreme caution.</td></tr>
<tr><td>enum</td><td>An explicit listing of the values comprising some type.</td></tr>
<tr><td>goto</td><td>Allows execution to be jumped to another location. Don't use this one at all, and be deeply suspicious of any program that does.</td></tr>
<tr><td>?</td><td>Conditional operator, a kind of in-line if statement that selects one of two alternative values. For example, 1+(x<y)?x:y is an expression that yields a value one greater than the smaller of x and y. Terse, but can also be cryptic. Use sparingly.</td></tr>
<tr><td>,</td><td>Expression sequencing operator. Allows multiple expressions to be joined together. For example, n=0,m=k is considered to be a single expression that has two side effects. Best avoided.</td></tr>
<tr><td>bit operations</td><td>These operators, including <<, >>, ^, ~, &, and |, work on integer and unsigned values on a bit by bit basis. Used for masking and shifting operations when individual bits must be accessed. See Section 13.2.</td></tr>
<tr><td>++variable, --variable</td><td>Preincrement and predecrement operators. In these the variable is incremented before its value is used in the surrounding expression. If n=0 and A[0]=A[1]=0, the statement A[++n]=2 leaves A[0] unchanged, sets n to 1, and sets A[1] to 2. Use with caution.</td></tr>
<tr><td>%o, %x</td><td>Octal and hexadecimal input and output format conversions. There are numerous other conversions, including for dates and times; and facilities that allow matching of characters in the input stream. Explore the manual pages for printf and scanf to find out more.</td></tr>
</table>

Table 13.1: C operators and concepts that have not been discussed in previous chapters.

13.2 Integer representations and bit operations

Section 2.2 warned of the need to watch out for integer overflow, and of the way in which C is silent when overflow does occur. In that section the details of the integer arithmetic were not given, and it was simply labeled as being "little short of bizarre". The time has come to try and explain what is really happening, so that the C bit manipulation operators can be introduced.

Computers store all information using *bits*, binary digits that take one of two values, zero and one. In our normal decimal world, each digit takes one of ten dif-

Function	Purpose
memset, memcpy, memcmp	
	Clear a region of memory by assigning null bytes; or copy or compare a sequence of bytes from one location in memory to another, without regard for null bytes.
character and string searching	
	There are several functions that search strings for characters in a specified set, or for substrings. Functions are also available that break strings into tokens. Look at the manual pages for strchr, strcspn, strspn, strpbrk, strrchr, strstr, and strtok if you need this kind of function.
ftell	Returns the current byte location within a file stream, useful if a later fseek operation is to return to the same location.
fflush	Sends all buffered output for a file from memory to the output device, without closing the file.
ungetc	Pushes a character back into the front of the input stream, to be read in a subsequent operation on the file. Best avoided.
sprintf, sscanf	
	These offer the same functionality and options as fprintf and fscanf, but the first argument is a char* string pointer. For example, sprintf(str,"%6d",n) creates a character representation of integer n in the character array str. Can be useful, but are also risky.
stdarg	This is a complex facility that allows functions to have variable-length argument lists. For example, fprintf and fscanf are passed argument lists that contain any number of variables. See the manual page for stdarg for details.
system	This function allows a Unix command to be executed from within a program. It is useful, but needs to be employed carefully.

Table 13.2: Some of the C library functions and facilities that have not been discussed in previous chapters. The manual entry for each function lists the required header file.

ferent values, zero through to nine. So we understand that a representation like 345 describes the calculation $3 \times 10^2 + 4 \times 10^1 + 5 \times 10^0$, and we are familiar with operations on such numbers.

In the binary world, the underlying base of all number representations is two. So the number 1101 describes the computation $1 \times 2^3 + 1 \times 2^2 + 0 \times 2^1 + 1 \times 2^0$. When that calculation is carried out, the value thirteen results. That is, the binary representation 1101 refers to the same integer value as the decimal representation 13. Counting in binary (starting at one) thus proceeds like this: 1, 10, 11, 100, 101, 110, 111, 1000, 1001, and so on.

So far, so good. But there is an additional complication – computers use memory words of a fixed number w bits in which to store integers. For example, consider what happens when $w = 4$ is imposed. Now the counting sequence that was started above cannot proceed beyond the value 1111, which is fifteen in decimal. Adding

Bit pattern	Integer representation		
	unsigned	sign-magnitude	twos-complement
0000	0	0	0
0001	1	1	1
0010	2	2	2
0011	3	3	3
0100	4	4	4
0101	5	5	5
0110	6	6	6
0111	7	7	7
1000	8	−0	−8
1001	9	−1	−7
1010	10	−2	−6
1011	11	−3	−5
1100	12	−4	−4
1101	13	−5	−3
1110	14	−6	−2
1111	15	−7	−1

Table 13.3: Integer representation options when $w = 4$ bits are used.

one, and truncating the result back to the four bit limit, means that $1111 + 1$ yields the answer 0000. That is, when binary arithmetic is limited to $w = 4$ bits, $15 + 1$ is zero. The second column of Table 13.3 lists the complete set of $w = 4$ bit numbers that is possible in such an *unsigned* binary numbering system.

> Integer values are stored in fixed words, the width of which is determined by the architecture of the hardware, and by the design decisions embedded in the compiler.

The desire to accommodate negative as well as positive values further clouds the issue. In decimal, we just add a minus sign at the front: -345 means $-1 \times (3 \times 10^2 + 4 \times 10^1 + 5 \times 10^0)$. The same approach could be adopted for binary computer arithmetic, with the first bit of each number reserved to indicate whether or not a number is positive or negative, and the other $w - 1$ bits used to indicate the magnitude of the stored number. The third column of Table 13.3 shows the number assignment that results is such a *sign-magnitude* binary numbering system.

However, for reasons to do with the implementation of integer arithmetic using electronic circuits, most computers use a different system when negative numbers must be allowed for, called *twos-complement* numbering. Now the first bit of the w-bit binary number has a weight of $-(2^{w-1})$ rather than 2^{w-1}, and is a sign as well as contributing to the value. For example, the bit-string 1101 is expanded as $1 \times -(2^3) + 1 \times 2^2 + 0 \times 2^1 + 1 \times 2^0$, which is minus three.

The revised arrangement is shown in the final column of Table 13.3 and has several nice properties: there is no duplication of the representation for the number zero, so one more negative number can be handled; and it also means that subtraction can be handled as addition. For example, consider the difference $4 - 7$, which can also be

```
int i;
unsigned val;
val = atoi(argv[1]);
printf("\t");
for (i=8*sizeof(unsigned)-1; i>=0; i--) {
    if (val & (1<<i)) {
        printf("1");
    } else {
        printf("0");
    }
    if (i%8==0) {
        printf(" ");
    }
}
printf("\n");
```

```
mac: ./intbits 13
        00000000 00000000 00000000 00001101
mac: ./intbits 1000000
        00000000 00001111 01000010 01000000
mac: ./intbits -1
        11111111 11111111 11111111 11111111
mac: ./intbits 2147483647
        01111111 11111111 11111111 11111111
mac: ./intbits -2147483648
        10000000 00000000 00000000 00000000
```

Figure 13.1: Using bit operations to extract and print bit patterns that show internal number representations. The lower box shows several executions of the program fragment in the upper box.

thought of as $4 + (-7)$. Using the twos-complement representation, this is worked out as $0100 + 1001 = 1101$, which is the correct answer of minus three.

> Most computers use twos-complement representation for storing integer values.

Modern computers typically use a $w = 32$ bit word-size for `int` variables. Figure 13.1 shows what happens when the bit patterns corresponding to a range of input integers are printed out, as 32-bit strings broken up into eight bit bytes. To isolate the bits in a memory word, some new operations are introduced: "`&`" is a bitwise "and" operation that operates on a bit-by-bit basis over the w bits of its two arguments; and "<<" is a left shift operator that moves its left operand left by the number of bits specified by the right operand, discarding the bits that move off the left-hand (most significant) end of the word, and introducing zero bits at the right-hand (least significant) end of the word. For example, if $w = 4$, then 1101 `&` 1001 yields 1001; and $1101 << 2$ yields 0100.

Worth commenting on is the unfortunate reuse of an operator symbol for a quite different purpose: "`&`" also means "address of", and so the compiler must determine which interpretation to apply to an "`&`" operator by examining the context in which it is used. This issue is referred to as *overloading*, and can cause confusion. Similarly, in C the operator "`*`" means both multiplication and address dereferencing.

Left shift operations are equivalent to multiplying by a power of two, and the similar right shift operator ">>" has the effect of dividing by a power of two. There are also bitwise operators for the "or" of two integers, "`|`"; and for the bitwise complement of an integer, "`~`". For example, 1101 `|` 1001 yields 1101, and `~` 1101 is 0010. Finally, there is a bitwise *exclusive or* operator "`^`" that sets a bit in the result to 1 if the corresponding bits in the two operands differ: 1101 `^` 1001 gives 0100.

The use of "`&`" as shown in Figure 13.1 is sometimes known as a *masking* operation, since it selects from the first operand the bits that match places where the second operand has a 1 bit. Using these two bit operations, the program in Figure 13.1 extracts in turn each bit of the integer value `val`, and prints either a zero or a one.

Looking at the output, some of the earlier overflow behavior of integers can now be explained. The $w = 32$ binary equivalent for thirteen is easily checked, and, with a bit more work, the value for one million can also be verified. The last three values represent some of the limiting values for 32-bit integers, and fit the general pattern shown in Table 13.3. Can you see now why the program fragment on page 16 gives the results it does?

By now you will also have realized that the C type `unsigned` declares an unsigned integer variable. The right shift operator ">>" has different behavior on signed values than on unsigned values, and you need to be careful – any variables that are participating in these logical operations should be declared to be `unsigned`. Using the $w = 32$ bit word-size associated with most computer hardware, an `unsigned` variable can take on values that are between 0 and $2^{32} - 1 = 4{,}294{,}967{,}295$. It is also possible to declare `unsigned char` variables, and `long` and `short` integers. None of the byte sizes for these different integer types are tightly specified, but a `char` variable will usually have $w = 8$ bits; a `short` variable is often represented in $w = 16$ bits; and `int` and `long` integers in $w = 32$ bits. Some C systems also offer a `long long` type which might provide $w = 64$ bits. All of these integer types can also be `unsigned`. For example, an `unsigned char` variable takes only positive values, and on most hardware can hold a number between 0 and 255.

> Variables that are declared as `unsigned` types store positive values only.

The two floating point types `float` and `double` are represented in three parts: a *sign*, an integer *exponent*, and a fractional *mantissa*. Typically in a `float` one bit is used for the sign; seven or eight bits are used for the exponent, which is either a power of two or a power of 16, and stored as an integer (but typically not as a twos complement integer); and another 23 or 24 bits for the mantissa, stored as a value between zero and one either as 23 or 24 bits following an implicit binary point, or as 6 hexadecimal (base 16) digits after an implicit radix-16 point. Twenty-four binary digits corresponds to approximately seven decimal digits of accuracy. In a `double`, the sizes of the fields allocated to the exponent and mantissa are increased as part of a 64 bit two-word quantity, and the exponent is typically 11 bits and the mantissa

Number (decimal)	Number (binary)	Exponent (decimal)	Mantissa (binary)	Representation (bits)
0.5	0.1	0	.100000000000	0 000 1000 0000 0000
0.375	0.011	-1	.110000000000	0 111 1100 0000 0000
3.1415	11.001001000011···	2	.110010010000	0 010 1100 1001 0000
-0.1	-0.0001100110011···	-3	.110011001100	1 101 1100 1100 1100

Table 13.4: Floating point representation when $w_s = 1$, $w_e = 3$ and $w_m = 12$, and the exponent is a binary numbers stored using w_e-bit twos-complement representation, and the mantissa is a w_m-bit binary fraction.

another 52 bits. Compared to a `float`, the number of decimal digits of precision that can be manipulated in a `double` before rounding errors intrude more than doubles.

Variables of type `float` and `double` are stored as an integer exponent part, and a fractional mantissa part.

As an example, suppose that on some computer `float` variables are stored in 16 bits, with $w_s = 1$ bit used for a sign, a $w_e = 3$ bit binary exponent part, and a $w_m = 12$ bit fractional binary mantissa. Table 13.4 shows the bit representation for four values. Note how even a number as simple as one tenth in decimal has a non-terminating binary representation. The last column shows the 16-bit combination that would actually be stored in this hypothetical representation. The inverse value for the last entry is

$$-1 \times 2^{-3} \times (2^{-1} + 2^{-2} + 2^{-5} + 2^{-6} + 2^{-9} + 2^{-10})$$

which in decimal is calculated as

$$-0.125 \times (0.5 + 0.25 + 0.03125 + 0.015625 + 0.001953125 + 0.0009765625)$$

and equals -0.0999755859375. Can you see now where floating point rounding errors come from?

As a further twist on these floating point representations, note that in a normalized binary mantissa, the first bit after the binary point of non-zero numbers is always a 1. Hence, this bit need not be stored, and on many architectures a w_m-bit mantissa in effect stores $w_m + 1$ bits of precision.

To complete this section, Table 13.5 lists all of the C operators, and their precedence, and replaces the earlier version of the same table given on page 31. The same advice as has already been given continues to apply: if in doubt, parenthesize.

13.3 The C preprocessor

The `#define` was introduced in Chapter 2. It is one of the facilities provided by the *preprocessor*, the first pass of the C compiler. The preprocessor searches for lines that start with a "#", and removes them from the file that is passed onto the main part of the compiler. Those lines are instead taken to be directives that determine the

Operators	Operation class	Associativity
Highest precedence		
`[]`, `.`, `->`	component selection	left to right
`++`, `--`	post/pre increment/decrement	right to left
`!`, `~`, `-`, `(`*type*`)`, `&`, `*`, `sizeof`	unary operators	right to left
`*`, `/`, `%`	multiplication	left to right
`<<`, `>>`	bit shifting	left to right
`+`, `-`	addition	left to right
`<`, `>`, `<=`, `>=`	comparison	left to right
`==`, `!=`	equality	left to right
`&`	bitwise and	left to right
`^`	bitwise exclusive or	left to right
`|`	bitwise or	left to right
`&&`	and	left to right
`||`	or	left to right
`?`	conditional evaluation	right to left
`=`, `+=`, `*=`, etc	assignment	right to left
`,`	expression composition	left to right
Lowest precedence		

Table 13.5: Final precedence hierarchy for all C operators.

final form of what gets compiled. For example, the value established by a `#define` directive is replaced everywhere that identifier appears in the program, and provides symbolic constants.

There are several other facilities available in the preprocessor, some of which are illustrated by the program in Figure 13.2.

First, note that the symbolic quantity `__LINE__` (two underscore characters prior, and two more after) is available at all times, and represents the line number in the current file. Similarly, the value `__FILE__` provides as a string the name of the file currently being compiled, and can be printed out if required.

Second, note that type-less arguments can be supplied to a `#define`. For example, the macro `MUDDLE` combines two arguments to produce a result. Observe that every occurrence of an argument in a macro is parenthesized, and the macro itself too. This is the only way of ensuring that there will be no precedence clashes, as the macro arguments are handled by direct textual substitution, rather than converted to values. The expanded text is then inserted in-line at exactly the point at which the macro was used. A macro should not be confused with a function, which exists at one location in a program and is passed control when called. A macro is fully expanded at each and every place it is used, and is executed as if it had been typed at that location. Exercise 13.5 explores the ramifications of this mechanism.

Third, note the use of the `#` prefix on one of the references to the argument `x` in the `DEBUG_INT` macro. The same textual substitution is employed, except that when `x` is expanded, it is represented as a string. For example, in the expansion of `DEBUG_INT(i)`, the reference to `x` is replaced by `i`, and the reference to `#x` by `"i"`.

```
/* Show some facilities of the preprocessor.
*/
#include <stdio.h>

#define DEBUG

#define MUDDLE(x,y)   (((x)<<(y))|((y)&((y)-1)))

#ifdef DEBUG
#define DEBUG_INT(x) printf("line %3d: %s=%d\n", \
        __LINE__, #x, x)
#else
#define DEBUG_INT(x)
#endif

int
main(int argc, char *argv[]) {
    int i=2, j=3;
    i = MUDDLE(i,j);
    DEBUG_INT(i);
    j = MUDDLE(j,i);
    DEBUG_INT(j);
    return 0;
}
```

```
line  20: i=18
line  22: j=786448
```

Figure 13.2: Using the facilities offered by the preprocessor. The lower box shows an execution of the program in the upper box.

Finally, note the use that can be made of conditional compilation. The guard in a `#if` or `#ifdef` directive must be something that can be evaluated at compilation time, and so cannot make use of any program variables. But even so, this option gives great power. For example, a block of code that is to be temporarily cut from a program for some reason is much more sensibly dealt with via `#if 0` than by trying to wrap a `/*` comment around it, as the latter will not work correctly when there are already comments in the group of statements being cut out.

In the example in Figure 13.2, the `#ifdef` selects between two alternative definitions for the macro `DEBUG_INT`. When `DEBUG` is set, as it is in the example, the values of variables, and the location in the program of the corresponding output statement, are easily produced. When the program is finalized, and the diagnostic output no longer required, the `#define DEBUG` line is removed, and the program recompiled. By magic, all of the additional output is turned off. Should a fresh problem be discovered, diagnostic output can just as easily be turned on again. Indeed, most C compilers allow preprocessor values to be set from the command line, avoiding even the need to edit the file. For example, using `gcc`, this command compiles the program as if a `#define DEBUG` appeared at the beginning of it:

```
gcc -Wall -ansi -DDEBUG -o preproc preproc.c
```

The preprocessor is part of the suite of software that comes with most C systems. There is often other software provided that you should also explore if you seek to become a serious programmer: the *profiler*, which monitors executing programs and provides information and statistics relating to run-time performance, such as the number of times each function or statement was executed; the *debugger*, which allows you to pause the execution of a program and inspect the values of variables, and single-step program execution so that the cause of mysterious results can be identified; and a *source code revision control* mechanism, which logs edits made to files, and allows old versions of files to be recovered if necessary. In addition, the compilation manager `make` has already been mentioned in Section 5.2; and some C systems provide a *pretty printer*, which formats C source files according to an in-built idea of how a good program should be laid out.

13.4 What next?

Now that the major features of C have all been covered, you should feel empowered to tackle a wide range of programming tasks. The difference between the small programs that have been used as examples in this book, and the large programs that are written by software engineers, is planning and experience. Software projects are like any other large construction exercise, in that they require careful design and extensive consultation; and are built by teams of people who have undertaken similar tasks in the past. No construction engineer would ever start pouring the concrete for an office building without a detailed plan from an architect that shows the whole building to be feasible in terms of time and money; and without a reliable crew that have the experience necessary to bring the project in on time and on budget.

The same is true for software engineering. No-one should commence a large software project without a carefully thought-out design, including evidence that the techniques being used have been successfully employed previously. And as for any construction project, a successful outcome in a software engineering project depends entirely upon the professional skills and experience of the team working on it. So to enhance and refine your programming skills, you need to tackle some larger and more detailed programming tasks, and work with other people to appreciate the co-ordination skills involved in software engineering teams. What you have learned in this book is just the beginning. An analogy that might help is that programming is to computing what calculus is to mathematics: an important tool, but by no means the whole story.

To be a computing professional you need knowledge in a range of other aspects of computer science, including operating systems, networks and communications, graphics, artificial intelligence, databases, programming language implementation, and the theory of computation. To be a software engineer you also need to learn the techniques that facilitate software design and implementation on an industrial scale.

> The material covered in this book is only the beginning of your study in computer science and software engineering. There is plenty of excitement still to come.

Exercises

13.1 Suppose that a machine uses $w = 6$ bits to represent integers. Calculate the twos-complement representations for each of these values: $0, 4, 19, -1, -8$, and -31. Verify that $19 - 8 = 11$.

13.2 Using the $w_s = 1$, $w_e = 3$ and $w_m = 12$ floating point representations shown in Table 13.4 on page 235, calculate the 16-bit representations for these numbers: $2.0, -2.5, 7.875$.

13.3 Referring again to the same 16-bit floating point representation, what are the largest and smallest (in terms of absolute value) numbers that can be represented? What are their corresponding 16-bit patterns?

What about the number zero? How might it be represented?

13.4 If you are working on a Unix machine, read the on-line manual page for the command `od`, which stands for "octal dump". It can also be used to generate hexadecimal (base-16) representations for a file, and from that the bits can be readily calculated, since each hexadecimal digit corresponds to four bits.

Write a program that writes an array of integers to a file using `fwrite`, with each `int` initialized to its index, `A[i]=i`, and then with `A[i]=-i`. Use `od` to inspect the file created by your program. Can you verify that your C system is using a 32 bit twos complement representation for integers?

(*For a challenge*) Now change the type of the array to `float`, and repeat the exercise. Can you infer the representation used for `float` values on your hardware? How is zero represented?

What happens when the special `float` values `nan` and `inf` get written to the file?

13.5 Consider the following preprocessor macro:

```
#define TRIANGLE_SIDE(x,y) sqrt(x*x + y*y)
```

Suppose that `float w=3,v=4` have been declared. What is the value of `TRIANGLE_SIDE(w,v)`?

How about `TRIANGLE_SIDE(w+1,v+1)`? Hint: perform the direct textual substitution of the two argument strings, and then apply the precedence rules. How should the macro definition be altered to avoid this problem?

13.6 Find out about the debugger for your C system. (If you are using `gcc`, the debugger is called `gdb`.) Read the manual for it, and explore its features.

Index